Catching Fire

PROGRAM IN MIGRATION AND REFUGEE STUDIES
Program Advisors:
Elzbieta M. Gozdziak and Susan F. Martin,
Institute for the Study of International Migration

Catching Fire

Containing Forced Migration in a Volatile World

Edited by Nicholas Van Hear and Christopher McDowell

LEXINGTON BOOKS

A division of
ROWMAN & LITTLEFIELD PUBLISHERS, INC.
Lanham • Boulder • New York • Toronto • Oxford

LEXINGTON BOOKS

A division of Rowman & Littlefield Publishers, Inc.
A wholly owned subsidary of The Rowman & Littlefield Publishing Group, Inc.
4501 Forbes Boulevard, Suite 200
Lanham, MD 20706

PO Box 317
Oxford
OX2 9RU, UK

British Library Cataloguing in Publication Information Available

Library of Congress Cataloging-in-Publication Data

Catching fire : containing forced migration in a volatile world / edited by
Nicholas Van Hear and Christopher McDowell.
    p. cm.— (Program in migration and refugee studies)
  Includes bibliographical references and index.
  ISBN 0-7391-0923-5 (cloth : alk. paper)—ISBN 0-7391-1244-9 (pbk. : alk.
paper)
    1. Forced migration. 2. Refugees. 3. Ethnic conflict. I. Van Hear,
Nicholas. II. McDowell, Chris. III. Title. IV. Series.
HV640.C378 2005
325—dc22   2005022453

Printed in the United States of America

♾ ™ The paper used in this publication meets the minimum requirements of
American National Standard for Information Sciences—Permanence of Paper for
Printed Library Materials, ANSI/NISO Z39.48-1992.

Contents

v

Contents

Acknowledgments

This book is one of two volumes that are the outcome of the project "Complex Forced Migration Emergencies: Towards a New Humanitarian Regime." We are very grateful to the John D. and Catherine T. MacArthur Foundation for providing funding which made possible this collaborative venture involving an international research team drawn from the Institute for the Study of International Migration at Georgetown University, Washington, DC; the Refugee Studies Centre at the University of Oxford; the Project on Internal Displacement at the Brookings Institution, Washington, DC; the Centre for Development Research (now incorporated into the Danish Institute for International Studies) in Copenhagen, Denmark; the Centre for the Study of Forced Migration at the University of Dar es Salaam, Tanzania; and the Regional Centre for Strategic Studies in Colombo, Sri Lanka.

Colleagues at Georgetown University—Susan Forbes Martin, Patricia Weiss Fagen, Kari Jorgensen, Andrew Schoenholtz, and Lisa Mann-Bondat—have presented policy analysis and recommendations in the companion volume *The Uprooted: Improving Humanitarian Responses to Forced Migration* (Lexington Books, 2005), which can be read in conjunction with this volume of case studies that informed the project.

This volume is the outcome of the efforts of a great many people and has been long in the making. The authors thank all those who made it possible. For their contributions to the research and writing, the authors thank Stephen Castles, Roberta Cohen, Khoti Kamanga, R. A. Ariyaratne, Lars Buur, Helene Kyed, Cathrine Brun, Tamuna Tsivtsivadze, Juan Guataqui, Brian Jeganathan, and Renuka Senanayake. The editors would also like to thank for their support colleagues at the Refugee Studies Centre and the Centre on Migration, Policy and Society at the University of

Oxford, the Danish Institute for International Studies, Copenhagen, King's College London, and Macquarie University, Sydney.

Special thanks go to Margaret Okole at the Refugee Studies Centre for making her copyediting skills available to us in the later stages of the project, and to Sarah Cannon and Jenni Navratil for drawing the maps. We thank Serena Krombach, Rebekka Istrail, and Katie Funk at Lexington Books for keeping their patience with us.

Finally, we express our appreciation to the staff of humanitarian and development agencies and departments who gave up their time in headquarters and the field to talk to us, and above all to the refugees and displaced people who shared their experiences and inspired us with their resilience.

Acronyms

ACBAR	Agency Coordinating Body for Afghan Relief
ACH	Acción Contra el Hambre, Action against Hunger
ACFOA	Australian Council for Overseas Aid
AI	Amnesty International
APEC	Asia-Pacific Economic Cooperation
AUC	Autodefensas Unidas de Colombia, United Self-Defense Forces of Colombia
CAP	Consolidated Appeal Process
CDR	Centre for Development Research, Copenhagen, Denmark
CEDAW	Convention on the Elimination of all forms of Discrimination Against Women
CGES	Commissioner General for Essential Services
CIS	Commonwealth of Independent States
CNDD–FDD	National Council for the Defense of Democracy–Forces for the Defense of Democracy, Burundi
CNRT	National Council of Timorese Resistance
CHA	Consortium of Humanitarian Agencies
CIREFCA	Conferencia Internacional sobre Refugiados Centroamericanos, International Conference on Central American Refugees
CODHES	Consultoría para los Derechos Humanos y el Desplazamiento, Consultancy on Human Rights and Displacement
CONPES	Consejo Nacional de Política Económica y Social, National Council of Economic and Social Policy
CPDIA	Consulta Permanente para el Desplazamiento Interno en

ix

	las Americas, Permanent Consultation on Displacement in the Americas
CRS	Catholic Relief Service
CSCE	Conference on Security and Cooperation in Europe
CSFM	Centre for the Study of Forced Migration, University of Dar es Salaam, Tanzania
DFID	(UK) Department for International Development
DHA	(UN) Department of Humanitarian Affairs
DIAL	Diálogo Inter-Agencial, Inter-agency Dialogue
DIIS	Danish Institute for International Studies, Copenhagen
DRC	Democratic Republic of Congo; Danish Refugee Council
ECHO	European Community Humanitarian Office
EDF	European Development Fund
ELN	Ejército de Liberación Nacional de Colombia, Army of National Liberation
ERC	(UN) Emergency Relief Coordinator
EU	European Union
FAO	Food and Agriculture Organization
FARC	Fuerzas Armadas Revolucionarias de Colombia, Revolutionary Armed Forces of Colombia
GoI	Government of Indonesia
GAD	Grupo de Apoyo a Organizaciones de Desplazados, Support Group for IDP Organizations
GTZ	German Technical Cooperation
HAER	Humanitarian and Emergency Rehabilitation
HROAG	(UN) Human Rights Office in Abkhazia, Georgia
ICBF	Instituto Colombiano de Bienestar Familiar, Colombian Institute of Family Welfare
ICRC	International Committee of the Red Cross
IDPs	Internally Displaced Persons
IFRC	International Federation of Red Cross and Red Crescent Societies
INCORA	Instituto Colombiano de la Reforma Agraria, Land Reform Institute
INTERFET	International Force for East Timor
IOM	International Organization for Migration
IRIN-CEA	Integrated Regional Information Network, Central and East Africa
ISIM	Institute for the Study of International Migration, Georgetown University, Washington, DC
JCC	Joint Control Commission
JLC	Joint Logistics Centers
JPKF	Joint Peace-Keeping Force

JRS	Jesuit Refugee Service
LTTE	Liberation Tigers of Tamil Eelam
(M)RRR	(Ministry of) Relief, Rehabilitation and Reconciliation
MSF	Médecins sans Frontières, Doctors without Borders
NEIAP	North-East Irrigated Agriculture Project
NGOs	Non-Governmental Organizations
NRC	Norwegian Refugee Council
PAHO	Pan American Health Organization
OAS	Organization of American States
OCHA	(UN) Office for the Coordination of Humanitarian Affairs
OSCE	Organization for Security and Cooperation in Europe
PKF	Peace-Keeping Force
QIP	Quick Impact Project
RESO	Rassemblement, Echange et Solution entre Organisations non-gouvernementales (Meeting, Exchange and Solution among NGOs)
RCSS	Regional Centre for Strategic Studies, Colombo, Sri Lanka
RRTG	Relief and Rehabilitation Theme Group
RSC	Refugee Studies Centre, University of Oxford, UK
RSS	Red de Solidaridad Social, Social Solidarity Network
RUT	Registro Unico Tributario, single registration system
SCF	Save the Children Fund
SCOPP	Secretariat for the Coordination of the Peace Process
SRSG	Special Representative of the UN Secretary General
TNI	Tentara Nasional Indonesia, Indonesian Armed Forces
UAS	Unified Assistance Scheme
UMCOR	United Methodist Committee on Relief
UN	United Nations
UNAIDS	UN Program on HIV/AIDS
UNAMA	UN Assistance Mission for Afghanistan
UNAMET	UN Assistance Mission in East Timor
UNDAF	UN Development Assistance Framework
UNDCP	UN International Drug Control Program
UNDG	UN Development Group
UNDP	UN Development Program
UN-ECOSOC	UN Economic and Social Council
UNFPA	UN Population Fund
UNGA	UN General Assembly
UNHCHR	Office of the UN High Commissioner for Human Rights
UNHCR	Office of the UN High Commissioner for Refugees
UNICEF	UN Children's Fund
UNIFEM	UN Development Fund for Women

UNOCA	UN Office for the Coordination of Humanitarian and Economic Assistance Programs to Afghanistan
UNOCHA	UN Office for the Coordination of Humanitarian Affairs; UN Office for the Coordination of Humanitarian Assistance to Afghanistan
UNOMIG	UN Observer Mission in Georgia
UNOPS	UN Office of Project Services
UNSC	UN Security Council
UNSMA	UN Special Mission to Afghanistan
UNTAET	UN Transitional Administration in East Timor
UNV	UN Volunteers
USAID	United States Agency for International Development
USCR	United States Committee for Refugees
WFP	World Food Program

Maps

Note on Currency

In the text most sums of money mentioned are denominated in US dollars ($US). Where euros (€) are mentioned, for guidance the euro is roughly in parity with the US dollar.

Chapter 1

Introduction

Christopher McDowell and Nicholas Van Hear

COMPLEX FORCED MIGRATION—
FORCED MIGRATION COMPLEXES

The Great Lakes of Central Africa, the Balkans, Afghanistan, Sudan, the Horn of Africa, the Caucasus, West Africa—many recent humanitarian emergencies feature complex movements of refugees, internally displaced people, stateless people, environmental refugees, war-affected populations, and returnees. Moreover, these categories are not mutually exclusive and forced migrants may belong to more than one group, either concurrently or over time. It is widely accepted that the current "humanitarian regime" is not up to the task of dealing with these diverse categories of people who are forced to move, and who in aggregate make up what we might call "forced migration complexes."

These observations prompted the formulation of a collaborative research project whose objectives were to examine the current humanitarian regime and to make recommendations for change in order to address complex forced migration crises more effectively. The project team comprised researchers and policy analysts from the Institute for the Study of International Migration (ISIM) at Georgetown University, Washington, DC; the Refugee Studies Centre (RSC) at the University of Oxford; the Project on Internal Displacement at the Brookings Institution, Washington, DC; the Centre for Development Research (CDR, now incorporated into the Danish Institute for International Studies) in Copenhagen, Denmark; the Centre for the Study of Forced Migration (CSFM) at the University of Dar es Salaam, Tanzania; and the Regional Centre for Strategic Studies (RCSS) in Colombo, Sri Lanka. The work was supported by two grants from the John D. and Catherine T. MacArthur Foundation, for which we are extremely grateful.

Most of the research for the project was carried out in 2000–2002, updated subsequently wherever possible. Broadly, it involved two main approaches. The first approach involved wide consultation with the agencies which make up the humanitarian regime in Geneva, Brussels, New York, Washington, DC and other "headquarter" locations. This process involved interviews with a wide range of agency staff, together with participation in consultative meetings such as the UNHCR pre-Executive Committee sessions. The second approach involved undertaking studies of particular complex forced migration crises at various stages of unfolding and from different regions of the world: Burundi, Colombia, East Timor, Georgia, and Sri Lanka were scrutinized. This involved field visits to each study country by members of the collaborating group: each country study team comprised researchers from two of the collaborating institutions. In the aftermath of the military intervention in Afghanistan, that country was later added to this set of case studies. The agency consultations and the country studies were analyzed with a view to drawing out the main obstacles to effective responses to forced migration and to deriving proposals that would help the humanitarian regime address forced migration more effectively. The proposals were aired at a series of regional workshops in North America, Europe, Africa, and Asia. These proposals are laid out and analyzed in the companion volume to this book (Martin et al. 2005). This volume sets out and analyzes the case studies that were carried out in the course of the study.

The cases present the range of protracted, ongoing, frozen, suspended, part-resolved, and resolved conflicts that characterize such complex forced migration crises. Each of these requires a different kind of response: this book is concerned then with the response of the humanitarian regime to different types of conflicts and forced migration complexes. It explores the character of the forced migration complexes, and how and why responses change over time, charting what internal and external pressures are brought to bear. The implications of those changes are investigated for addressing protection and assistance needs of the displaced, for peace processes, and in relation to longer-term post-conflict development. This demands analysis of the institutional, political, and humanitarian context in which protection and assistance for forced migrants are provided and return, repatriation, and reintegration programs are conducted.

The words "catching fire" in the title of this volume capture for us the complex nature of forced migration today in several ways. Conflict and displacement have a tendency to smolder, ignite, and spread from place to place like bush fires, inflaming new emergencies and new displacements. Moreover, like bush fires until they burn out, conflict and displacement are difficult and sometimes impossible to contain until they have run their course. To stretch the metaphor further, humanitarians can be likened to fire-fighters who have the thankless task of putting out the fires of displacement or at least containing their spread. Their duties moreover now extend to preventing the sparks that ignite the fires of displacement: in other words beyond a fire-fighting to a prevention role. The question of what should be rebuilt from the ashes of conflict also arises.

RESPONSES TO THE DIVERSITY OF CONFLICT AND TO SHIFTING PATTERNS OF DISPLACEMENT

Complex forced migration emergencies generate humanitarian action largely around physical protection and assistance in the form of addressing basic needs such as health, shelter, food, and clean water. International responses to such emergencies vary from conflict to conflict, and change over time depending on a range of factors: they can take the form of UN diplomacy or coalition-type military interventions, contributions to peacekeeping or consolidated appeals, signaling various levels of responsibility and engagement by individual governments and agencies. In recent years the international humanitarian regime has generated a range of responses from, at one end of the scale, an almost unequivocal generosity and political unanimity in the case of East Timor, to one of continuing neglect in the case of Burundi or Sudan. The availability of resources and political commitment is clearly a significant factor in determining the size, scope, and effectiveness of any response. Efficiency in the use of resources and agency coordination are also critical factors. Within specific emergencies, responses are shaped and reshaped by political assessments molded by the public demand for continued involvement, historical responsibility, concerns about threats to regional or global security, or economic national self-interest in the short and longer term. In addition, perceptions about a particular conflict influence levels of commitment to a humanitarian response: areas in conflict are continually reassessed and redefined according to whether they are in transition from full conflict to intermittent violence, in a state of uneasy peace or "pre-peace," or in conditions amenable to post-conflict development. The political and institutional response to a particular crisis, and the ways it changes over time, determines assistance and protection programs for refugees and displaced people who remain within the borders of their countries but unable to return home, as well as for those who repatriate.

Since the early 1990s forced displacement has increasingly defined conflicts, and the ability to control populations has become a decisive component of military strategy. Protection and assistance activities and return and reintegration programs cannot escape this. Even when a given conflict may be resolved or in abeyance the political, social, economic, and cultural impacts of forced displacement will still be felt and humanitarian needs associated with them will remain. This book explores the diversity of conflicts and shifting patterns of displacement associated with them, the humanitarian efforts that follow, and the continuities and discontinuities in the institutional and political responses. The priorities of host governments, international agencies, and civil societies shift, as do institutional structures and funding arrangements. More widely, institutional changes reflect shifts in the discourse of protection and assistance. The case studies introduced in what follows illuminate some of these shifts in practice and discourse.

COMPLEX FORCED MIGRATION: SIX CASES

Susan Forbes Martin and Trish Hiddleston detail the dramatic humanitarian impacts of almost continuous conflict in *Burundi* since 1993, part of the wider complex of upheavals in the Great Lakes region of central Africa. Hundreds of thousands of people fled to neighboring Democratic Republic of Congo, Uganda, and Tanzania to escape fighting between mainly Hutu rebels and the military which left more than 300,000 people dead. Many more were displaced within Burundi so that at the beginning of 2004 some 281,000 people were in camps for IDPs, and 100,000 others dispersed throughout the country. A number of peace deals have been brokered over the past five years but most proved short-lived and, reflecting the insecurity which grips Burundi, population flight actually increased. In the continuing environment of uncertainty, the displaced remained skeptical about the prospects for enduring peace and for many, permanent return home was unattractive.

The prospects for sustainable return and the rebuilding of livelihoods are complicated by the effects of war, but also as a result of social and economic problems that predate the 1993 conflict, including widespread rural poverty, drought and its impacts, food shortages, poor health, and collapsed markets. The international response to the protracted crisis in Burundi, since 1972, is described as a failure of coordination, commitment, basic knowledge, awareness, and planning. The urgent humanitarian needs of the displaced, particularly women and children within Burundi, have been consistently underestimated and often overlooked by the UN, foreign governments, and successive Burundian administrations.

Any return flow of refugees will exacerbate ongoing and new tensions around access to land, land ownership, and overcrowding.

The chapter focuses on two main war-affected populations, the internally displaced (IDPs) and those refugees repatriated mainly from camps in Tanzania. It is concerned with protection of and provision of assistance to these two groups, and the shortfalls in both. In relation to IDPs, the authors distinguish between IDPs living in camps (established spontaneously), in *regroupment* camps (established by the government by force to house Hutus after 1996 ostensibly for their own protection), and those dispersed throughout the country but not in camps. They found problems that are general to all three situations and problems which are specific. *Regroupment* camps in particular, with very limited humanitarian access, were hostile and dangerous places, and the closure of the camps exacerbated the problems for their former inhabitants because post-closure programs for return and reintegration were not in place. For all three populations, Martin and Hiddleston found that security was the principal constraint on assistance and protection, affecting negatively both the quality and the amount of assistance available. They recommend that attention to security, for both aid workers and the displaced, is vital if humanitarian work is to be effective.

The authors suggest that all war-affected populations suffered as a result of incoherence in the coordination and planning among and between the UN and national and international agencies. A weakened UN in Burundi was unable to play the coordination role vital to enhance protection and assistance or to build capacity among local organizations that were well positioned to respond to local needs. These same weaknesses in the international humanitarian response to successive Burundian crises impacted negatively on programs for the return and reintegration of refugees from neighboring countries. Martin and Hiddleston found that poor security was a major obstacle to return. However, even when security improved, poor planning meant that agencies were ill-prepared to initiate return and rehabilitation programs. Resources were not forthcoming to guarantee that measures to promote a durable peace (such as demobilization, peacekeeping, addressing poverty and land issues) were in place. The authors conclude with practical recommendations about how the weaknesses identified in the humanitarian response could have been addressed. Since the chapter was written there have been substantial returns of IDPs within Burundi, but by and large the protracted Burundian refugee population remains a neglected case.

Nicholas Van Hear and Darini Rajasingham-Senanayake examine the evolving discourse, policy and practice of humanitarian intervention in *Sri Lanka*, which has experienced armed conflict for more than two decades. The authors provide a review of displacement within the island and internationally, assess its socioeconomic and political consequences, and describe and evaluate the response of the humanitarian regime, in particular to the challenge of internal displacement. The wide range of displacement circumstances is addressed and it is suggested that each situation requires specific protection and relief interventions, and that the proof of humanitarian effectiveness must be measured at the local level.

The authors argue that the institutional response to the humanitarian dimensions of the Sri Lankan conflict has been relatively well developed, with encouraging but limited progress made in, for example, consultation among war-affected populations and in linking return and reintegration initiatives with reconciliation processes. The modest successes are in part attributed to the civilian government's responsiveness to humanitarian concerns despite military obstructiveness, some internal organizational incoherence, and the fragmented nature of the overall relief provision. UNHCR, in effectively extending its competence by becoming involved in the protection and assistance of IDPs in the 1990s, was also a significant player in the response. The chapter charts the efforts at improving coordination among humanitarian agencies and describes, in particular, the Government-initiated and World Bank–backed Framework for Relief, Rehabilitation, and Reconciliation which attempted to streamline structures dealing with conflict and displacement. It also details parallel UN and bilateral initiatives to improve coordination.

The chapter considers the "view from the field," describing the experience of displacement and relief from the perspective of the displaced in Sri Lanka and providing a typology of these experiences and the entitlements or absence of entitlements associated with each category of displacement. Disparities in treatment and coverage of the displaced and war-affected people are highlighted through case studies drawn from the districts of Puttalam in the west of the island and Vavuniya in the north. Despite the same kind of uprooting, the life chances and living conditions for populations within and between these two areas are described as differing markedly. It is argued that uneven institutional coverage in different parts of war-affected areas contributed to this uneven and unequal treatment. The chapter identifies further dimensions that determine variations in the humanitarian response. These include the frequency and duration of displacement, the government's unwillingness to address displacement, and the reactive rather than proactive nature of humanitarian assistance.

The dynamics of displacement and the nature of the response are then put in the context of the post-2001 peace talks, donor meetings, and the events that subsequently interrupted peace negotiations. Issues around return, particularly the reclaiming of land and homes, and the continuing presence of military forces, are considered in relation to the fragile "pre-peace" situation that currently prevails in Sri Lanka. The authors explain how ongoing assistance to the displaced and programs for their return are at the heart of post-conflict strategies and as such have the potential to contribute to peace or in some instances actually increase the likelihood of destabilization. They describe a situation that is delicately poised and recommend that any transition to peace will not be assisted by the pursuit of a neo-liberal transformation of Sri Lankan society and economy at the expense of genuine humanitarian need and a peace process that addresses the ethnic division of the country's territory.

Against the background of more than four decades of conflict in *Colombia*, Patricia Weiss Fagen, Amelia Fernandez Juan, Finn Stepputat, and Roberto Vidal Lopez describe the growing crisis of displacement there and assess both national and international responses to that crisis since 1994. The situation in Colombia is highly complex, violence is pervasive, and security issues dominate political life. The authors describe the extent to which the response to the IDP situation is in many ways more developed than in other emergency situations. The government has shown itself open to international involvement, it is compliant with international humanitarian law (including the incorporation of the Guiding Principles on Internal Displacement into its national law), and has established structures at national, regional, and municipal levels to assure access of rights and services to its internally displaced population. As the chapter describes, international agencies, including UNHCR, UNHCHR, UNDP, ICRC, the World Bank, and many others, are present in the country, and while their programs may be relatively small, they have cooperated to develop a common strategy for addressing the needs of IDPs. At the local level, NGOs have successfully focused on collecting and disseminating information about displacement and the effects of displacement on human rights. They have represented IDPs' rights and interests before local and national authorities, and have supported threatened communities. Many other NGOs are actively engaged in relief projects of their own.

However, despite the fact that Colombia would appear to have among the most comprehensive structures for IDPs, the authors describe a forced displacement crisis that is deepening and intensifying. The major constraint on the success of any program to assist and protect IDPs is the continuing conflict and the rejection by irregular armed parties of attempts to reform their practices. Massacres, hostage taking, and massive displacement remain tactics of armed factions and the drug trade remains a significant factor in sustaining the conflicts.

Significantly, the issue of internal displacement in Colombia is not in itself a major political issue. Indeed, the 2 million IDPs, rather than being considered victims of the conflicts, are continually stigmatized as collaborators with armed groups, as criminals, as a collective threat to societal stability, and as a population that has carried the conflict with them from rural areas into the heart of Colombia's major cities. The authors link this oscillating invisibility and stigmatization of IDPs to an enormous gap between the stated purposes of government entities established to deal with IDPs and actual implementation. As a result barely one-third of the two million internally displaced receive assistance from either government or the international agencies. The authors identify the specific weaknesses and gaps in the provision of humanitarian aid. They address, among others, a lack of protection for the displaced, the insufficiency of aid, bureaucratic obstacles in the way of receiving aid, and serious funding shortfalls.

The chapter by Peter Marsden examines *Afghanistan*'s experience of more than two decades of conflict, colonization, international military intervention, and the consequences of this traumatic history in relation to forced displacement, repatriation, and humanitarian responses. The Soviet invasion of Afghanistan in 1979 saw one of the largest refugee flows on record, with six million people crossing into Pakistan and Iran, and throughout the following years Afghanistan continued to experience large-scale population displacement. The international response to this movement has been complex, influenced by political factors including the perceived stability and legitimacy of ruling Afghan parties, troubled relationships with Pakistan and Iran, and the subsequent growing pressures on both governments to repatriate Afghan refugees. With the US-led military intervention in 2001, the image of large-scale voluntary return by Afghans, backed by the United Nations, was used to add weight to arguments that the change of regime had been successful.

Marsden discusses a number of issues resulting from the conflict, some of which are unique to the Afghan situation while others resonate with case studies elsewhere in this volume. In an Afghanistan ruled by unstable and illegitimate governments, the UN and NGOs operated with a considerable degree of freedom to determine policy and plan programs. The emergence of an internationally recognized government in 2001, however, saw UN agencies and NGOs redefining the terms of their relationships with Afghan authorities. In this transition the UN's presence and its scope to influence events was reduced and further weakened as a result of poor coordination and a lack of an assumed leadership role. The situation was further complicated, the author argues, by a quite deliberate policy on the part of the US and its partners to undertake humanitarian projects in order to "win the hearts and minds" of the local population. This practice was regarded by many in the NGO community as counter-productive as it eroded the humanitarian space available to agencies and threatened to undermine the neutrality and impartiality that was considered critical to the continued delivery of protection and assistance in extremely insecure conditions.

As Marsden describes, the post-2001 security situation in Afghanistan has proven unstable and international aid flows insufficient to capitalize on early progress made in infrastructure improvements. Nonetheless, spontaneous and planned refugee return, despite deteriorating security and the lack of protection for returnees and the communities into which they return, has continued on a scale which was often unmanageable. In particular, refugee protection is described as an enormous challenge. In many cases returnees were influenced by unrealistic expectations of the economic opportunities available on return. Support structures were not available, Marsden writes, and while returning refugees have in many cases been able to build their own shelter, return land to productivity, and clear irrigation ditches, necessary large-scale infrastructure to guarantee these improvements—such as complex irrigation systems—are frequently missing. Marsden's analysis questions the efficacy of UNHCR planning and whether it could have been better prepared for the conditions in Afghanistan after the military intervention of 2001.

Matthew Karanian's chapter explores the political background to the sustained conflicts in the south Caucasus, focusing on *Georgia*. He analyzes the causes and effects of displacement on populations directly and indirectly affected by inter-ethnic conflict, and also the impacts of displacement on the development of the Georgian state as a whole. The chapter describes the humanitarian consequences of the long-standing tension and fighting between the authorities in Georgia and Abkhazia which broke out in fighting in 1992 when Georgian troops invaded Abkhazia following a vote for independence. Around 300,000 people were displaced during this period up to a ceasefire and the introduction of a peacekeeping force. The country's agricultural and tourist economies were severely damaged, and official refugee return programs proved only partially successful over the next four years. Following the kidnapping of UN staff in 1998, 1999, and 2000 and a direct fatal attack on UN observers in 2001, the international community was unable to put in place agreements to bring about stability, and the security situation rapidly deteriorated. The author describes the mass displacement the civil war created and the economic collapse which deepened impoverishment and generated acute food and medical needs. The response of the international community to these humanitarian issues is examined, as are the more proactive attempts to address underlying causes.

The chapter also describes the situation in South Ossetia, where a violent conflict with Georgia broke out in 1989–1992. Again, the fighting created widespread damage and led to the displacement of more than 60,000 people, mainly ethnic Ossetians, of whom 40,000 became refugees in the

Russian Federation. However, as in Abkhazia, UNHCR programs to promote the return of IDPs and refugees had only limited success as conditions, particularly in relation to the rebuilding of livelihoods, were not thought conducive for return.

Having described the background to the conflicts and their outcomes in terms of population displacement, the chapter then discusses the living conditions, employment, and education prospects of Georgia's internally displaced population, most of whom are women and children. A second IDP population is also identified, described here as "itinerant" or the seasonally (and repeatedly) displaced moving between their old homes and established collective centers. Finally, the situation of Chechen refugees in Georgia is addressed alongside the threat to security in Georgia posed by continued instability in Chechnya. Other related issues, including trafficking and the situation of the non-displaced population, are also analyzed in relation to the wider political and socioeconomic situation in the South Caucasus.

The chapter analyzes the humanitarian response to Georgia's complex emergency from the mid-1990s to March 2004. The Georgian government, which, the author argues, is genuinely concerned for the welfare of its citizens, has taken on a coordination role in relation to refugee and IDP programs. The wide-ranging roles and responsibilities of the international community through UNOCHA and various specialized agencies are described, as are the activities of the ICRC, various Refugee Councils, and NGOs. Coordination mechanisms are examined and finally a so-called "New Approach to IDP Assistance" is assessed, with its emphasis on development rather than emergency programming, and projects to promote self-reliance and the political and economic integration of the displaced rather than their marginalization.

By contrast with the other cases, *East Timor* presented an acute emergency that flared violently, but then was contained. The humanitarian crisis in East Timor, triggered by pro-Jakarta militia violence and assisted by the Indonesian military, followed the UN-backed independence referendum in 1999 and led to almost two-thirds of the territory's population of 750,000 people being displaced. This sudden mass displacement of such a large proportion of the territory's population was only the latest in a series of forced migration crises in East Timor. From 1976, the Indonesian military undertook a massive program of forced resettlement for political and strategic reasons. The processes and repercussions of past and more recent forced migration and involuntary resettlement have shaped current political and social dynamics in East Timor. The crisis reviewed here resulted in almost 80 percent of the housing stock being destroyed in a scorched earth retreat by pro-Jakarta militia intent on denying the newly independent nation access to vital infrastructure, and inflicting as much damage as possible to the economy. The chapter considers the challenge posed by this mass upheaval and dispersal of so many people in such a short space of time for the international community as it assumed sovereignty over the territory and embarked on an ambitious state-creation exercise.

Christopher McDowell tracks the build-up of an international intervention force, the relatively successful coordination and priority setting that marked the early stages of the humanitarian/military response, and the gaps which appeared in that response over the following three years until East Timor's independence in 2002. A major set of humanitarian challenges for the UN Transitional Administration in East Timor (UNTAET) was related to the forcible, coerced, and—for a small number— "voluntary" movement of more than 240,000 people across the East Timor border into makeshift camps in West Timor set up by militia gangs, and the eventual return of those refugees. The flight of refugees across the border was complex in motivation and composition. Many were "hostages" taken as pawns in the militia's continuing political objectives to destabilize East Timor and to maintain a power base. Other refugees in the West Timor camps were long-time East Timorese residents dependent on the Indonesian state for pensions and salaries, who feared for their future in an independent country.

The presence of the camps remained a major unresolved humanitarian issue for the UN in East Timor for the duration of their administration. Access to the camps was extremely limited, the West Timor authorities were generally uncooperative, and following the murder of three UN workers in September 2000, the UN and its agencies were unable to provide assistance or protection to the refugees. McDowell describes the various attempts made to encourage the refugees to return to East Timor, and explains how the urgency to secure return heightened as the deadline for independence neared in 2002. The repatriation program that ensued was underfunded, security issues on return were not addressed, and "development" initiatives for sustainable reintegration were not in place.

McDowell nevertheless finds that the response was generally well-coordinated, relatively well-funded through the Consolidated Inter-Agency Appeals Process in which the NGOs were heavily involved, and that staff were strongly committed to the East Timorese people. There were no major outbreaks of violence following the militia retreat, and no serious episodes of disease or malnutrition. The reconstruction task was enormous, and apart from the church network local capacity was weak in important areas. "Timorization" and the UN's stated determination to include the East Timor people in the nation's rebuilding suggested a new approach to post-conflict assistance, but in practice this was not realized and the people remained distant from the international bureaucrats who largely managed the process. There were very few programs aimed specifically at the displaced, but rather an overall humanitarian program addressing immediate and basic needs. McDowell argues that while the initial response to the emergency crisis was relatively successful, the determination to move East Timor, as an emerging nation, beyond a crisis state to nation-building in preparation for hand-over and elections, withdrew too early the focus on needs directly related to the initial emergency. The needs of returning refugees and internally displaced people in the territory were not addressed in a comprehensive manner.

COMPLEX FORCED MIGRATION IN COMPARATIVE PERSPECTIVE AND IN CONTEXT

As these summaries indicate, the case studies in the chapters that follow represent a range of types of conflict and diverse dynamics of displacement, each at various stages of unfolding or resolution. All of these crises feature complex mixes of refugees, internally displaced people, returnees, and other uprooted and war-affected people. These different categories often exist side by side in a given emergency, and can be extremely volatile: people sometimes change statuses rapidly, so that an IDP may become a refugee, then a returnee, and then an internally displaced person again. The uprooted exhibit different capacities and degrees of resilience in the face of insecurity. The types of governments involved are also diverse, ranging from weak or failing to more competent states, and exhibiting different capacities and willingness to deliver public goods. The involvement of international actors likewise ranges, from neglect or minimal engagement in the case of Burundi, through varying degrees of engagement with state authorities in the case of Colombia, Sri Lanka, and Georgia, to substantial international intervention—humanitarian and/or military—in the case of East Timor and Afghanistan. Finally, in addition to the complexities generated by the various forms of population displacement and the responses to them, the conflict-ridden societies covered in this book are themselves transformed in the process of conflict and its aftermath, prompting the questions of what kind of society should emerge in the wake of conflict and displacement, who should determine the shape of it, and how it should be molded.

The chapters in this volume attempt to capture the volatility of complex forced migration and the humanitarian and development challenges associated with them. There is of course a wider context within which such volatile movements and challenges are set. The complex movements of people resulting from conflicts and the international response to them are shaped by the interests of the world's dominant powers, which pursue changing and sometimes conflicting geo-political strategies including the management of international migration. Such strategies are not well thought out, are not consistent, and powerful interests sometimes conflict over them, but such strategies have consequences for forced migrants, for fragile states, for attempts to resolve conflicts, and for efforts to rebuild post-conflict societies. In recent years there have been significant shifts in such strategies and in their policy manifestations, notably in the fields of security, migration management, and development, as well as in humanitarian action. Some of these changes were in train during the period when the research was under way for the chapters in this book: indeed the crises we examined helped to shape some of the policy shifts. The concluding chapter attempts to set the experiences of the displaced in the context of these shifts in policy and in the wider geo-political order.

Chapter 2

Burundi: A Case of Humanitarian Neglect

Susan Forbes Martin and Trish Hiddleston

Conflict in Burundi has lasted over thirty years, the most recent crisis developing in 1993. During this period, more than 300,000 Burundians lost their lives. Many fled abroad and many more were displaced, some temporarily and some more long-term (USAID 2003a). By 2003 some 750,000 Burundian refugees were living in Tanzania—most of these since 1972—in refugee camps, villages and communities along the border with Burundi (UNSC 2003). Another 281,000 internally displaced persons (IDPs) resided in camps in Burundi, while approximately 100,000 other men, women, adolescents and children were otherwise dispersed in the country (Norwegian Refugee Council 2003: 36). The number of refugees and IDPs combined thus amounted to more than 17 percent of the total Burundian population (UNSC 2003). Damage to the infrastructure inside the country due to the conflict has been devastating and the conditions and quality of life have deteriorated severely because of the crisis (Minist-ère de la Planification 1999: 10, and chapter 2).

In 1998 negotiations for peace were initiated. The Arusha Peace and Reconciliation Agreement for Burundi (subsequently Peace Agreement) was signed by most, but significantly not all, of the parties to the conflict on August 28, 2000. No ceasefire was agreed upon. The agreement remained fragile and liable to collapse. In fact, fighting intensified following the signing of the Peace Agreement, primarily between extremist Hutu rebel factions and the Burundian armed forces. Refugee flows to

15

Tanzania, which had been decreasing steadily between January and July 2000, consequently increased. Civilians continued to be caught in the middle and the numbers of deaths continued to rise. Both rebel forces and extremists within the Burundi military also were implicated in attacks against civilians and humanitarian aid organizations. Regional instability and conflict further complicated prospects for peace in Burundi.

The deterioration in the security situation inside the country, and the inability to forecast when peace would be established and what would happen in the meantime, made operating conditions for humanitarian aid agencies particularly difficult. Inevitably, therefore, the quality and level of planning and humanitarian assistance that could be provided were adversely affected. Of particular concern was the often-desperate situation of the large internally displaced population, which generally did not improve after the signing of the Arusha Peace Agreement in 2000. Should lasting peace come, and repatriation become feasible, the needs of returnees from Tanzania and within Burundi will require significant new attention.

Political developments since the 2000 Peace Agreement produced guarded optimism that Burundi should return to peace in the near future. A power-sharing government was established in November 2001, when Pierre Buyoya was sworn in as the country's ethnic Tutsi president for an 18-month period. In line with the provisions of the Peace Agreement, President Buyoya handed over power in May 2003 to Domitien Ndayizeye, the former vice president and a member of the ethnic Hutu opposition. The generally smooth and bloodless character of the political transition demonstrated progress toward creating a more representative national government. Another key achievement was the ceasefire agreement signed in October 2003 between the Burundian government and the National Council for the Defense of Democracy–Forces for the Defense of Democracy (CNDD-FDD), previously the largest Hutu rebel faction to remain outside the peace process. Brokered by South African President Thabo Mbeki, this agreement included important provisions to end the fighting and establish a more inclusive, power-sharing government (*New York Times*, October 8, 2003). Together, these events suggested Burundi gradually was making progress to halt the violence and resolve the political tensions that have plagued the country for so many years. However, the second largest rebel faction, the Forces Nationales de Libération (FNL), still refused to negotiate. The FNL announced in November 2003 that it would continue to fight and warned of renewed violence in the capital, Bujumbura (Reuters, November 4, 2003).

This chapter reports on the findings of a site visit to Burundi and Dar es Salaam, Tanzania, in October 2000, as well as a subsequent review of developments in both countries. It is based on two interconnected activities: a delegation of the Women's Commission for Refugee Women and Children and a pilot site visit for a project on the evolving humanitarian regime for complex forced migration. The chapter draws heavily on the Women's Commission delegation report. The situation has been updated to January 2004 and reflects the most current information at that time. It is worth noting that, despite important political developments since the site visit in 2000, little overall improvement has occurred in terms of the humanitarian situation of IDPs in Burundi or Burundian refugees in Tanzania.

INTERNALLY DISPLACED PERSONS

Protection and assistance to the various groups of internally displaced persons (IDPs), including specifically women and children who form the majority of IDPs, has been among the most urgent needs in Burundi. Protection requires access and security, as noted above, neither of which can be guaranteed everywhere or all of the time. It also requires basic knowledge about the IDP population and this is severely lacking in Burundi.

Categories of Displacement

Broadly, three categories of IDPs, with some movement between the categories, are referred to in Burundi: the *displaced* in IDP camps, the *regrouped* in regroupment or former regroupment camps and the *dispersed* who do not live in camps but rather live in the forests and marshes or have sought refuge with relatives or friends. The terminology employed can lead to confusion. For instance, references to IDPs or displaced persons can sometimes refer only to those in IDP camps.

IDP Camps and Sites

IDPs living in camps or sites for displaced persons are the most visibly displaced. IDP camps generally came into being in response to reprisals against Tutsi following the murder of President Ndadaye in 1993. Tutsi civilians assembled around military bases where they could be afforded greater protection. As the homes of many were subsequently destroyed, they now have no house to return to even if their security could be guaranteed. Some of the IDP camp inhabitants are now well established and might be unlikely to move to their place of origin, even if security could be guaranteed and their homes recovered or rebuilt if need be. The majority are assumed to be keen to return home if they could be guaranteed

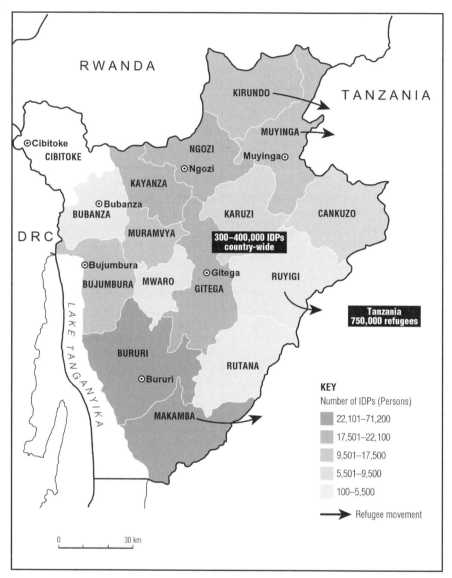

Map 2.1.   Burundi: Protracted Displacement, circa 2003
Source: UNHCR; USCR.

protection, were able to reconstruct their homes and had access to land and a livelihood. ''You can see it from the infrastructure [in the camps]. They use plastic sheeting and locally made roofing. There is less investment and involvement. They hope they can go home when conditions allow,'' the UNDP Resident Representative told the Women's Commission in 2000. That assumption needs to be investigated further, however, to ascertain just what it would take for them to return home.

Figures for the number of men and number of women in the camps currently are not available, although the Women's Commission was told in 2000 that there are more women than men in the camps. About 40 percent of households in the camps are probably headed by women.

IDP camps generally were established spontaneously. Inhabitants of IDP camps are free to come and go as they please. Regroupment camps, in contrast, were established by force. Movement in and out of the camp may be controlled and/or restricted. There are also qualitative differences in the way the camp populations have been treated and in the conditions inside the camps. Treatment and conditions inside the IDP camps were generally better than the regroupment camps although poor conditions and suffering have been features of both.

Regroupment Camps

Regroupment has been a tool of the Burundian government since 1996 when about 300,000 persons, mainly Hutu, were forced into camps, ostensibly for their protection. Most of these camps closed in 1998, but the last quarter of 1999 saw the creation again of regroupment camps, officially termed "protection sites." Approximately 350,000 people, mostly rural Hutu, were forced into about fifty designated camps mostly in or near the capital on security grounds. As many as three-quarters of all residents of Bujumbura Rural province were living in such camps at the end of 1999 (USCR 2000: 69). Conditions inside the camps were for the most part appalling and some of the camps were inaccessible to humanitarian agencies (Refugees International 2000a, 2000b; Human Rights Watch 2000; Amnesty International 1999). Women and children in particular were vulnerable when food was short. They often were sidelined at food distributions, sometimes despite the efforts of distribution agencies. There also were reports of the rape and sexual abuse of women and young girls in the camps (Human Rights Watch 2000: 18–20).

There was almost universal condemnation of the camps, as well as extensive calls for their closure. Most were dismantled in the third quarter of 2000 following pressure from Nelson Mandela, the international community and local organizations. The final pressure came from the rebel groups, who made closure of the camps a precondition for joining the peace negotiations (Human Rights Watch 2000: 30, 33–34).

The camp closures occurred within a very short period and with no preparation for the safe return of the regrouped. Some camps were closed very quickly, either because the authorities wanted them emptied as fast as possible, but more often because as soon as the camp population was allowed to leave they did, despite the risks and conditions they then faced (Human Rights Watch 2000). Asked why people would return home despite known security risks and with no guarantee of protection, one young man simply replied with a smile, "Home Sweet Home . . ." Asked the same question, another woman replied, "Liberty has no price."

When the regrouped population left the camps, many faced serious risks without assistance or protection from either the government or the humanitarian and protection agencies. Fighting continued and even intensified in many areas to which the regrouped returned. While the international community rightly demanded the closure of the camps, neither they nor the government made adequate preparations for this contingency. Communication, coordination and cooperation at all levels were gravely lacking.

The current location of most of the formerly regrouped population remains unclear. Many appear to have gone home, but others are believed to be living in or near former regroupment camps. Still others are likely to have moved to Bujumbura or other parts of the country. No statistics are available on the relative size of each group.

While all regroupment camps reportedly were dismantled in Bujumbura Rural province, others persisted in the southern and eastern sectors of the country until late 2000. Some of the inhabitants (often women and children) were unwilling or unable to return home (for security reasons or because their homes had been destroyed), but the authorities did not allow some other groups to return (IRIN-CEA February 8, 2000, September 18, 2000; Human Rights Watch 2000: 31). Most observers nevertheless agree that the majority of the Burundian regroupment camps have been closed. During 2000, the number of displaced persons living in such camps declined dramatically, from 800,000 to 325,000 individuals (UNICEF 2001). Since then, international pressure largely has prevented the Burundian government from using regroupment as a policy to provide security or assert control over rebel-held territory. Renewed concerns arose in April 2002 when UNICEF reported that Burundian armed forces had regrouped over 32,000 people in Ruyigi province in eastern Burundi. Authorities then excluded humanitarian workers from the camps, citing the lack of security. This left the displaced without access to proper assistance and many suffered from malnutrition and disease (Norwegian Refugee Council 2003: 50–51). The Ruyigi camps eventually were dismantled in mid-2002.

For those who have been able to return home from regroupment camps, life has been far from secure. The homes and livestock of many have been looted or destroyed in whole or in part. Many fields were not cultivated during the period of regroupment, adding to current food shortages, exacerbated by recent droughts. In some areas the water system has been destroyed (Human Rights Watch 2000: 31–32). Insecurity due to rebels or military activity remains a real threat both for those previously regrouped and those wishing to assist them. Reports are common of formerly regrouped who returned home only to be forced to flee from their homes to escape attacks from one or the other side of the conflict. But without a more accurate impression of the situation of these people, their needs cannot be assessed and met and they cannot be adequately protected.

Dispersed Persons

The least visibly displaced, and the group about which the least is known, are those persons who are dispersed in the countryside or urban areas with no permanent home. Some are former camp residents and remain in or near dismantled IDP or regroupment camps because they are either unable or unwilling to return home. Others have been forced out of their homes or repeatedly have fled their homes owing to military or rebel threats. Some may be able to stay in their homes on and off, while others are constantly on the move, finding shelter wherever they can and for however long is necessary. Some may be sheltering with friends or family on a short- or long-term basis. Again, largely because of insecurity, the size, demographic breakdown, condition and particular needs of this category of displaced persons are unknown. This group is likely to be the most vulnerable group among the displaced, but is also the least likely to receive assistance. While they are not living at home, they may have no access to their fields to cultivate and may not be registered to receive food assistance. The children of this group are obviously the least likely to go to school.

Included within this category of IDPs are a sizable number of street children and unaccompanied minors. UNICEF estimates that there are 25,000 orphans as a result of the war, including 5,000 child-headed households, 7,000 separated children, 240,000 orphans as a result of HIV/AIDS (UNICEF 2003a) and 2,000 street children (UNICEF 2001). The numbers of street children and unaccompanied minors have increased since the crisis in Burundi began in 1993 and the numbers appeared to rise even more after regroupment began. Whereas the number of street children was estimated at 3,000 in February 2000, it had risen to around 5,000 children by May 2000 (Norwegian Refugee Council n.d.).

Some agencies, local and international, are addressing the particular needs of these children. For children who have become separated from their families as a cause of the war, there are various agencies involved in tracing efforts. If the child's direct family cannot be found, sometimes a member of their extended family can and will take them in. Children also are fostered informally, sometimes by people who knew the child before and sometimes by people who did not. Fostering is not without problems, as a member of an NGO who works with such children explained: "Unfortunately orphans (placed in homes) are often exploited. We have follow-up visits after they are placed with relatives, foster parents, and if they are being exploited we tell the authorities and try to educate the family. There's not much more we can do."

Another category of children separated from their families and in need of assistance is child soldiers. Secretary-General Annan estimated in his November 2002 report on children and armed conflict that up to 14,000 children in Burundi served as child soldiers. Both government and Hutu rebel forces are known to have engaged in the recruitment and use of child soldiers. The Burundian government since has disavowed this practice, and it has signed a Memorandum of Understanding with UNICEF to begin demobilizing children from the ranks of its armed forces (UNICEF 2003b). Similar commitments are needed by the rebel forces to secure protection for the rights of these children. In addition, the government of Burundi has requested international assistance to demobilize child soldiers. It specifically asked UNICEF to conduct a census of child soldiers throughout the country and to prepare a demobilization plan, which was being developed in 2002 (UNSC 2002). Education, job training and psychosocial counseling programs further are required, to promote the reintegration of these children into society once peace is achieved.

CONSTRAINTS ON EFFECTIVE ASSISTANCE AND PROTECTION TO IDPs

Many factors constrain effective delivery of humanitarian assistance and the protection of the internally displaced. These include security problems, organizational weaknesses at the international, national and non-governmental levels, lack of information about the target population, problems with the way in which emergency assistance is defined, and lack of awareness of principles and techniques for protecting internally displaced persons.

Security

Security is the principal constraint on assistance and protection to war-affected populations, including internally displaced persons. As the peace process progressed, instead of decreasing, the fighting in fact increased. During the site visit in 2000, preplanned visits to project sites outside Bujumbura had to be delayed, some rescheduled and others cancelled, sometimes at very short notice, while security clearance was obtained or denied. It was virtually impossible for agencies operating out of Bujumbura to leave the city before 9 a.m. and most agencies required that their staff be back inside the city boundaries as early as 2 or 3 p.m. The rationale was that some roads closed at 4 p.m., after which no vehicles were permitted to travel on them. Security concerns further dictated that vehicles should be back within the city limits in reasonable time before nightfall. This in practice meant returning well beforehand, so that in case there was a breakdown en route, there would be adequate time to send a recovery vehicle to collect the team.

Restrictions on travel persist. Raids by rebel groups continue in the hills surrounding Bujumbura and the security situation is highly unpredictable. In general, though, the operating environment has improved since the Burundian government and the CNDD-FDD rebels signed the ceasefire agreement in October 2003. This has allowed humanitarian agencies to increase their access to outlying and rural communities.

During the delegation's visit in 2000 an Italian priest was ambushed and killed by soldiers. Shortly after, an Italian nun was killed by armed men. Some observers have suggested that these killings were intended to create panic and instability and others have argued that international aid staff may be targeted (JRS 2000a). International staff also are vulnerable to death threats, which are taken very seriously. During the visit, two international staff, one the country representative of an international aid agency, had to leave the country at very short notice as a result of death threats.

During the site visit, fighting broke out in Bujumbura's Kamenge zone, killing about 20 civilians and causing many others to flee. Fighting also intensified in the northern outskirts of Bujumbura at Tenga-Kivoga, a few kilometers from Bujumbura (AFP October 9, 2000, October 11, 2000; IRIN-CEA, September 30–October 6, 2000). The sound of heavy artillery involved in that fighting could be heard from time to time in the city. The sound of gunfire is not unusual in Bujumbura, especially at night. Following the delegation's departure in mid-October 2000, fighting between government troops and rebel forces intensified in the east of the country leading to an increase in the numbers of refugees, both Hutu and Tutsi, fleeing to Tanzania and an increase in the numbers of displaced inside the country. Reports attributed some of this displacement to attacks by armed groups from Tanzania (IRIN-CEA, October 7–13, 14–20, 21–27, 2000; UNHCR 2000b; JRS 2000a, 2000c). Similar incidents have recurred.

These are some of the daily realities for all agencies working in Burundi. One can only applaud the courage, dedication and commitment of staff in local, national and international organizations and individuals working under these conditions. However, this situation inevitably affects the quality and amount of humanitarian assistance that can be provided.

Humanitarian workers can easily become demoralized in these circumstances. Many humanitarian organizations and agencies are stretched to, or beyond, their capacity. Many, like the UN, may have to employ inexperienced albeit well-meaning staff.

In addition, the inability to predict whether peace will be established in the short term, or when it will come about, and what will happen in the meantime, makes forward planning and programming extremely difficult. A number of different possible scenarios must be planned for. The result is that plans may not be taken very seriously, or may not be made at all.

Security is perhaps the biggest challenge to the international community's capacity to provide humanitarian relief, not only in Burundi but throughout the world. It has been the focus of the UN Secretary-General's attention in reports to the Security Council and the General Assembly. While recognizing that the ultimate responsibility for security rests with the host government in which the humanitarian operation takes place, the UN has put into place measures to increase the safety of its personnel. According to the October 2000 Secretary-General's report on security,

> the response by the organizations of the United Nations system to threats to the safety of personnel has been divided into five phases, as follows:
> (a) In phase one, which is precautionary, travel to the area requires prior clearance by the designated official;
> (b) In phase two, all personnel and their dependants are restricted to their homes unless otherwise instructed. All movement is severely restricted and has to be specifically authorized by the designated official;
> (c) In phase three, the following measures may be taken: concentration of personnel and their dependants at sites that are deemed safe; relocation to other parts of the country; relocation of dependants and non-essential personnel outside the country;
> (d) In phase four, programs are suspended and personnel not directly concerned with emergency or humanitarian relief operations or security matters are relocated;
> (e) In phase five, all personnel are evacuated except those required for Security Council-mandated activities related to the maintenance of international peace and security (UN Secretary-General 2000).

Burundi was declared to be phase four following attacks on UN personnel (see below), but the country generally has been listed at a phase three level. In July 2003, a week-long military assault on Bujumbura by Hutu rebels, the largest offensive in three years, again prompted the United Nations to increase the security level to phase four and to evacuate a large number of staff from the country. Most returned on July 25, once rebel attacks had subsided, allowing the UN to reduce the security level to phase three (USAID 2003b).

The United Nations has focused on increased training and assessment of security risks as its principal response to security problems. More comprehensive approaches, such as the development of a UN military or police force capacity to protect aid personnel, have been discussed but with little agreement or action. Various field operations have successfully negotiated safe access, as described by the Secretary-General:

> In a number of countries, arrangements have been made between the Government, warring parties and international humanitarian organizations which lay down ground rules defining the arrangements for secure access by humanitarian organizations to the victims of the conflict. These arrangements are based on a recognition by all parties of the importance of observing humanitarian principles. Such operational arrangements have proved, in several countries, to be indispensable for the work of humanitarian organizations and have had a positive impact on the safety and security of humanitarian personnel (USAID 2003a).

Such arrangements have not been successfully negotiated throughout the crisis in Burundi, however, at least in part owing to the weak field presence of the United Nations, as discussed below.

Organizational Weaknesses

A further impediment to effective humanitarian assistance to IDPs and other war-affected populations has been the weakness of the United Nations in Burundi. This is due to a number of factors including the security problems described above, demoralization, and staffing difficulties.

The UN significantly pulled back its presence, withdrawing all nonessential international staff following the murder of two UN officials and seven Burundians who were carrying out a humanitarian mission in the southeastern province of Rutana in October 1999. The killings shocked the humanitarian community, especially the UN, and their impact can still be felt. Following this attack, coordination among UN agencies and between the UN and national and international organizations deteriorated. The need to improve the situation and to restore stronger collaboration and coordination was recognized by agencies working in Burundi (UNHCR 2000a: 10, parts VI and VII).

The UN in Burundi experienced high turnover in key positions and it could be difficult for both the UN and international organizations to find staff, let alone experienced staff, willing to work in the country under the prevailing conditions. Burundi is one of the most difficult places in which to undertake humanitarian and protection work. While the unfulfilled needs are immense, the security limitations are enormously restrictive. The disparity between what can be done in safety and what urgently needs to be done is highly frustrating for all involved (RESO 2000).[1]

All these factors contributed to the weakness of the UN in Burundi at the time of the site visit. In the light of continuing peace negotiations, the delicate ongoing situation and the urgent material needs of the Burundian population, especially IDPs, the UN needs to strengthen greatly its capacities in Burundi.

The weakness of the UN presence in Burundi was particularly pertinent in relation to IDPs. As one international head of agency told the study team, "the UN is still floundering" in relation to IDPs. He said that he had money available for the reintegration of IDPs and refugees but could not release it without concrete information. Speaking of refugees, although the same points apply to IDPs, he said: "A plan is okay but insufficient. We need more. We need to know where the people are going to go. We have asked for socio-economic details of these people. It is all very well picking someone up at the border and taking him home but then what? He may be a farmer and need land. He may be a teacher and not want to be a farmer. And we have none of that information. They blithely say they can set up training centers; sure they can but they should be doing that now." In relation to IDPs, this detailed information was lacking and no plan existed.

Theoretically, there should be a multi-sectoral, collaborative approach to IDP issues. What appeared to be the case in Burundi is that most agencies recognized that insufficient assistance and protection was being provided to IDPs but none was willing to step forward to insist that more be done. The collaborative approach can work, and has worked in the past in Burundi, when there is a strong, competent Humanitarian Coordinator and a strong, competent leader in OCHA. But given the history of the UN presence in Burundi (the killings of the UN personnel in Rutana, the staff demoralization and high staff turnover, including that of the Humanitarian Coordinator), and the lack of a strong leader in OCHA at the time of the site visit, another approach was urgently needed.

To enhance protection and assistance of IDPs, particularly given the fragility of the peace process, there was a need to designate institutional responsibility for coordination of IDP assistance and protection. In particular, there was a need to improve access to and security of internally displaced persons, including through strong representations to the Burundian government and rebel forces to protect civilian populations, displaced and otherwise, affected by the conflict. There was further need for better coordination and cooperation between UN agencies and local and international organizations with regard to IDPs.

While OCHA would be the obvious agency to fulfill such a role, its weak capacity and absence of a leader made this agency a less obvious choice. UNHCR appeared unwilling to take on greater responsibility for the internally displaced, although it recognized that the reintegration of refugees (see below) and IDPs was linked inextricably and both groups would face many of the same needs and risks. Differentiation between the two groups could cause additional tensions. UNHCR appreciated that it would deal with IDP needs in the areas where it would be operational in the event of a repatriation, and that it would make sense to implement some of its plans, such as peace-building and reconstruction of infrastructure, ahead of a return.

But UNHCR also told the study team it would not get involved with IDPs in areas where the agency would not otherwise be operational, namely those regions where there would be few returnees. UNHCR has considered the issue of IDPs and has stated that it will only become engaged with IDPs if certain conditions are met. This is in line with the UNHCR's official policy toward IDPs. These conditions are that UNHCR:

1. receive a specific request or authorization from the UN Secretary-General or other competent principal organ of the UN;
2. obtain the consent of the concerned state or other parties involved in an ongoing conflict;
3. have access to the affected population and adequate security for UNHCR and its partners;
4. have clear lines of responsibility and accountability; and
5. most importantly, possess adequate resources and capacity to conduct the necessary activities (UNHCR 1994).

An important step toward addressing the needs of the internally displaced was a visit to Burundi made by the Senior Inter-Agency Network on Internal Displacement in late October 2000. The Inter-Agency Network confirmed the institutional problems discussed here. Its March 2001 report to the UN Secretary-General specifically faulted the UN and NGOs for failing to provide adequate protection to IDPs in Burundi. It argued that coordination problems among UN agencies and other international organizations, compounded by inadequate funding from the donor community, led to serious gaps when addressing the needs of internally displaced persons. To address these concerns, the Inter-Agency Network proposed three basic recommendations:

1. create a unit specifically dedicated to IDP issues within OCHA, to serve as the UN focal point on internal displacement, and to conduct systematic country reviews and develop inter-agency policy;

2. strengthen the leadership role of the Humanitarian Coordinator/ Resident Coordinator (HC/RC) with regard to IDPs and deploy IDP field advisors at the country level to support the work of the HC/ RC;

3. encourage the government of Burundi to establish a formal, inter-departmental mechanism for dealing with operational issues relating to IDPs and to act as a counterpart for international humanitarian actors (OCHA 2000).

Following the recommendations made by the Inter-Agency Network, a Unit for Internal Displacement was created within OCHA in January 2002. It has completed site visits to nine countries experiencing internal displacement crises (OCHA 2003a) and has worked as a liaison between UN agencies and international organizations (Robinson 2003: 44). In the case of Burundi, OCHA has deployed a Head of Unit on internal displacement to the country to finalize an inter-agency IDP plan. The UN Humanitarian Coordinator in Burundi also has succeeded in establishing a Framework for Consultation and Protection of Internally Displaced Persons in conjunction with the Burundian government. The result is a committee jointly headed by the Burundian Minister of Human Rights and the UN Humanitarian Coordinator, which oversees issues related to IDPs and works to secure implementation of the UN Guiding Principles on Internal Displacement (OCHA 2001: UNHCHR website n.d.).

In addition to the need to strengthen the presence of the UN—and international NGOs—there also was need to develop stronger working relationships, to the extent possible, with local NGOs, including women's and children's associations. National institutions also may have a greater ability to reach internally displaced persons in less secure areas as well as better knowledge and understanding of their needs. Various actors in Burundi expressed their impression that the government's plan for IDPs was not sufficiently developed and needed to be considered in greater detail. Greater contact with local authorities and local NGOs could lead to more accurate and faster information on IDP movements, their condition and general security. The more frequently and the earlier such contact is established, the sooner it can be determined as reliable or not and further strengthened.

Some such local organizations are well established and known, and some international NGOs and UN agencies already have established partnerships with local NGOs. Examples are literacy programs, HIV/AIDS education, peace-building and conflict resolution programs. Other groups are less well known or developed, and may lack experience, sophistication, strength and funding. It will require a conscious effort on the part of international partners to identify and reach these less formal groups.

The greater involvement of Burundian organizations and individuals may further contribute to reintegration and reconciliation as Burundians see fellow Burundians coming to their assistance. By working with local NGOs, international organizations can encourage such NGOs to have a gender focus where they otherwise may not have considered gender issues. Identifying such organizations now, and forging such alliances sooner rather than later, will result in beneficial capacity building for Burundian civil society institutions and individuals.

This will not only benefit the development of Burundi, but also enable international NGOs to establish working relationships now, which can be built on in the time of any greater need or crisis, such as repatriation. Such capacity will be particularly needed if peace comes, repatriation occurs and international humanitarian organizations reduce their programs. In due course, should peace be established and hold, international organizations will be able to withdraw earlier in the knowledge that local institutions have the capacity to continue their work as appropriate. The impact of closer collaboration may be difficult to monitor, but strengthening the capacity of civil society will provide a better basis for a more durable peace.

Support to civil society groups needs to be done in a flexible manner. This may not always mean financial support, as financial input at times may harm the original aims or effectiveness of the initiative. Any injection of financial support should be careful to avoid taking ownership of the program away from those who initiated it. Some local initiatives may not require any financial input; others may require more substantial amounts. But all parties would most likely benefit from more and better partnerships, contact and collaboration. In any event, the international requirements for financial accountability might have to be flexible and be reassessed so that international organizations can work with more and less formal groups. Support and collaboration should go beyond the well-known, well-established organizations. In some cases, requiring local NGOs to establish accounting mechanisms that meet international stereotypical expectations or requirements will so delay their ability to provide aid as to be counter-productive.

Lack of Information about the Needs of the Internally Displaced

At the time of the site visit, there was little if any systematic collection of data about the internally displaced population. The UN agreed in October 2000 to undertake a comprehensive, inter-agency survey of IDPs, but the first thorough survey of internally displaced persons did not occur until 2002.

Any comprehensive survey of IDPs should meet two principal aims:

1. to identify the immediate situation and needs of the various categories of IDPs, in camps and otherwise dispersed, including specifically women and children, in order to develop and implement plans for improving their current protection and assistance. The survey should be comprehensive and the data should be broken down by age and sex; and
2. to help the UN and other agencies plan and provide for the return, integration in place or resettlement of IDPs in the event of peace and in advance of any significant movements of people, from inside or outside the country, and take the necessary preliminary steps toward that end. Information should be sought on the future intentions or wishes of IDPs, and what IDPs say it would take for them to return home.

The 2000 UN survey was to be carried out all over the country, beginning first with the camp populations and only then addressing the situation and needs of the dispersed population. However, security concerns prevented the survey from covering large areas of the country.

Between August 2002 and June 2003, the United Nations Population Fund (UNFPA) conducted a separate demographic and reproductive health survey in Burundi, which simultaneously compiled data on IDPs. The survey was funded by the European Union and supported by various institutions in the Burundian government. This report currently is the most thorough census of the internally displaced in existence. It identified 281,000 IDPs in permanent resettlement sites, in addition to 100,000 IDPs temporarily displaced in any given month. These figures conflicted with data from a March 2003 survey completed by OCHA, which reported a total of 525,000 IDPs in the country, including some 387,000 IDPs registered at permanent sites (Norwegian Refugee Council 2003: 35). However, OCHA later accepted the UNFPA results as valid. The UNFPA data currently serve as the baseline to determine humanitarian assistance needs in Burundi (OCHA 2003b).

In addition, a network of thirty-seven international NGOs—the Rassemblement, Echange et Solution entre Organisations non-gouvernementales (RESO)—has worked to compile data gathered from their individual member NGOs' activities on the ground regarding the numbers and situations of displaced persons (Norwegian Refugee Council n.d.). The UN should make full use of such information and share any additional information they gather from their own surveys with the NGO community.

The relevant government ministry, the Ministry of Reintegration and Resettlement of Displaced and Repatriated Persons, also should be involved and kept fully informed.

Where security restrictions prevent the gathering of first-hand data, efforts should be made to obtain best estimates from secondary sources such as local and international NGOs, local authorities, church representatives, local health centers, and schools. Very often local authorities have very detailed and accurate data on their local population. Although it is recognized that there may be a tendency in some cases to deliberately distort the data, efforts should be made to access that information.

Definition of Emergency Assistance

While insecurity is undeniably a major impediment to assistance and protection, and organizations will continue to be unable to reach everyone in need of aid all of the time, there are nevertheless secure pockets where aid can be provided. The UN and international NGOs must be flexible in their assistance programs to adapt not only to increasing security threats but also to periods or areas where the threat is decreasing. International agencies and NGOs should press the government to provide them with secure access and security to the IDP population.

One country representative of an international NGO said that because major needs in the country were insufficiently funded, less pressing needs get pushed back. They know they are there and are not ignoring the issue, but inevitably they cannot address all problems. In this specific case he was referring to the problem of street children.

On the other hand, the EU delegate told the delegation in 2000 that the EU had allocated €48 million (almost US$48 million) for reconstruction projects for the interior of the country. Once infrastructure has been renovated, the economy of the people living in the interior of the country can be addressed in preparation for the return of the refugees and internally displaced. "There is a lot of money available to Burundi," he said. "It has about $200 million worth of aid money either in place or in the pipeline. But it is hard to mobilize it. We need access, consistent access, to the countryside to do so. At the moment we are waiting for the next stage of the peace process to start. If the Implementation Monitoring Committee [set up in Bujumbura in terms of the Arusha Peace Agreement at the end of November 2000] is successful, I imagine that things will stabilize and we will expand our activities." Donor pledges for Burundi continue to be substantial, particularly from the European Union. EU officials announced in July 2003 that €285 million in European Development Fund aid currently was available to Burundi. Target sectors for 2003 included: rural development, infrastructure, institutional capacity building, and macro-economic support (European Union 2003). Over the medium term, these goals were to be pursued through the 2003–2007 Country Strategy Paper and National Indicative Program, which earmarked €172 million in assistance to Burundi (European Union n.d.). However, the EU was not likely to implement these programs fully until security could be achieved nationwide.

While donors may be reluctant to support development projects until there is more convincing evidence of an end to the hostilities, there is still much more that can be done immediately in terms of humanitarian assistance. Donors therefore should define emergency aid in the widest possible sense. It is essential that programs in reproductive health and for victims of sexual violence be recognized as fully consistent with emergency standards, and also that NGOs (local and international) implement more programs in those fields and donors support them as necessary.

Emergency humanitarian assistance should include the following, in addition to the programs generally offered.

- Reproductive health services, urgently needed because of the very high infant mortality rate (114 per 1,000 live births; UNICEF 2003c), urban and rural maternal mortality rate (13 per 1,000 live births), and prevalence of sexually transmitted diseases (STDs) and HIV/AIDS (around 20 percent of the population; see below) (UNAIDS 2000, 2002). Reproductive health services are now included in the Sphere minimal standards for disaster relief, adding to the justification that they should be intensified and multiplied at this stage.
- Increased and better coordinated education on the prevention of STDs and HIV/AIDS is required. Projects targeting youth, males and females, should be encouraged.
- Programs to help women victims of violence address the traumas of rape and other violence against them and programs dealing with prevention of sexual violence.
- Psychosocial programs for children. The development of new programs in this area by some international NGOs is very welcome.
- Education programs, particularly rehabilitating schools, supplying books, training teachers and—very important for IDPs—helping particularly vulnerable families pay school fees for their children or abolishing fees altogether at primary school level (as well as helping to obtain uniforms and books). Such programs will help reduce poverty in the longer term and increase access to education for all children, the poor and girls in particular. They also will contribute to breaking the cycle of violence by providing pupils with realistic alternatives. Education is discussed in greater detail below.
- Micro-credit and other income generating programs to help women-

headed households and others to be self-supporting through productive work. Normal requirements for loans may have to be waived or adapted to meet the particular circumstances of women heads of households and displaced women. As one displaced woman told the Women's Commission: "If you get aid it is just for a day. But if you get credit you can improve your situation. But with women no guarantee, no property, can be given so they get no credit [from credit agencies]. They have no salary, no land they can give as a guarantee. The interest is also too high. Lots of women can't carry out their projects as a result." The women said they needed interest-free credit or low interest with generous repayment schedules.

The displaced population—in camps or otherwise dispersed—are often forgotten when it comes to such programs. In 1999, the US Committee for Refugees asserted that "International donors, dismayed by continued bloodshed in Burundi, provided virtually no new funding for 'children in distress' programs or for 'peace training' in displacement camps" (USCR 2000: 70).

Lack of Training on Protection

At the time of the site visit, it was apparent that international and national humanitarian staff had little awareness or training with regard to protection standards for internally displaced persons. Few staff members were familiar, for example, with the Guiding Principles on Internal Displacement, although many upon learning about them said they would be useful in advocacy with the government.

At the time of the site visit, the delegation recommended that the UN should disseminate widely the Guiding Principles on Internal Displacement in both French and English and should translate them into Kirundi, the national language of Burundi. It also recommended that OCHA should disseminate the Brookings Institution/OCHA Handbook on Applying the Guiding Principles and the OCHA Field Practice Manual that describes specific projects that support protection, also in French and English. Finally, the delegation recommended that on an urgent basis, the UN should institute training programs for UN agency staff, international NGOs, the national government, local NGOs and others on their application. The dissemination of these documents and the training sessions should be repeated at regular intervals to reach the maximum number of relevant staff, especially given staff turnover in relevant agencies. Follow-up training also should be given regularly. The Guiding Principles should be used in advocating increased access and security for IDPs.

The UN further was recommended to disseminate widely the Guidelines on Protection of Refugee Women, Guidelines on Sexual Violence, and Guidelines on Refugee Children, and provide training for staff in ways to adapt these guidelines to the situation of internally displaced women and children (for the full text of these guidelines, see the UNHCR website at www.unhcr.ch). These Guidelines, similarly, should be distributed in French and English, translated into Kirundi, and explained to relevant staff at regular intervals.

Success at circulating the above documents has been mixed. On the positive side, UNICEF translated the Guiding Principles into Kirundi in late 2001. The Framework for the Protection of IDPs in Burundi then organized a series of training sessions to distribute and explain the Guiding Principles, beginning in January 2002, and make them available to officials in military, government and administrative positions (Norwegian Refugee Council n.d., section national and international responses, sub-section guiding principles on internal displacement). Minimal progress, however, has been made in disseminating the Handbook on Applying the Guiding Principles, the OCHA Field Practice Manual, or the UN Guidelines on protection of refugee women and children. UNHCR did take the initiative to draft a manual that provides information on women's and children's rights, according to national and international law, titled *Rights of Children and Women: Awareness Training for Adult Refugees*. The draft has been tested in several two-day-long workshops with Burundian, Congolese and Rwandan refugees in Tanzania. Programs such as these represent an initial step toward the empowerment of displaced women and children, but much remains to be done to improve their overall level of protection (UNHCR 2001).

REPATRIATION AND REINTEGRATION

In September 2003, UNHCR reported that 95 percent of Burundi's 500,000 refugees resided in Tanzania (UNHCR 2003a). In March 2003, however, OCHA reported more than 800,000 Burundian refugees scattered throughout the region. (See NRC n.d., section population profile and figures, sub-section global figures). The majority of these lived in twelve refugee camps along Tanzania's western border (UNHCR 2003b). An estimated 51 percent are female, and 56 percent are children (UNHCR 2003c). Most are ethnic Hutu who fled between 1993 and 1996, after violence erupted following the murder of President Ndadaye, although there has been a continuous albeit less dramatic flight in each of the intervening years, mainly to Tanzania. More than half of all Burundian refugees in recent years have originated from four provinces and by far the majority are from provinces bordering Tanzania. These provinces are Muyinga and Kirundo in the north, Ruyigi in the east, and Makamba in the south. Most new refugees in 1999 fled from Makamba, Gitega and Kirundo provinces. (See USCR 2000: 68; UNHCR 2000a: §32.)

In addition to those refugees living in camps, an estimated 170,000–200,000 Burundians (mostly Hutu) live in Tanzanian settlements, some since 1972 (UNHCR 2000b). Some of these were born in Tanzania, have lived all their lives there, and may speak little or no Kirundi. It is unlikely that substantial numbers of this group will return in the initial stages of repatriation (UNHCR 2000a: §59). A further 300,000 Burundians are estimated by the Tanzanian government to be spontaneously settled in Tanzanian villages along the border with Burundi (UN Country Team in Burundi 2000: 10). UNHCR places the figure closer to 470,000. There is no available information on their exact location or their profile (USAID 2003b).

More than 200,000 refugees returned to Burundi between 1996 and 1999, but many of these fled again when they found the situation in Burundi not conducive enough to retain them (UNHCR 2000a: §§32–33). In 1999, there were 64,200 spontaneous new refugees from Burundi, mostly to Tanzania, and 12,200 repatriations (UNHCR 1999).[2] Arrivals from Burundi had been decreasing steadily, UNHCR reported, between the beginning of 2000 and July 2000, when increased insecurity led to the influx of 7,800 arrivals in Tanzania in August alone. (Over 200,000 refugees returned since 1996, although some of these fled again. See UNHCR 2000a: §§32–33.) Following the signature of the Arusha Peace Agreement, an additional 78,524 refugees repatriated from Tanzania to Burundi between 2001 and 2002 (UNHCR 2003d). UNHCR reported at the end of 2003 that another 81,201 refugees had returned to Burundi during the course of the year, and 44,964 of these were spontaneous returnees (OCHA 2004).

Representatives of UNHCR and the Tanzanian government assured the delegation in October 2000 that they were refraining from encouraging or assisting repatriation for the time being (UNHCR 2000a: §§89–90). In March 2002, UNHCR and the government of Tanzania launched an official repatriation program, using the Kobero border crossing to return nearly 50,000 refugees to the more peaceful northern sections of Burundi. A second official entry point was opened in September 2003 at Gahumo. However, UNHCR resisted pressure from the governments of Burundi and Tanzania to facilitate repatriation through two additional border crossings in southern Burundi until security could be guaranteed in that area (UNHCR 2003e).

In some respects, however, there is disparity between statement and actions. On July 19, 2000, the World Food Program (WFP) cut its biweekly food rations for refugees in the Tanzanian camps of Kigoma and

Kagera by 40 percent due to a severe shortage following a supply problem. The underlying reason appears to have been a dispute between the EU and WFP but the exact reason remains unclear. WFP and the Tanzanian government made a plea for an immediate response from donors (the funding shortfall for Tanzania stood at US$7.7 million for the rest of the year). Subsequently, some food rations were restored, leading to an 80 percent total cut. Refugee rations were cut again in 2003, to 50 percent of the daily recommended minimum, as a result of supply problems. Although rations were restored to 72 percent by mid-April, many refugees left the camps to return to Burundi. They cited decreased food rations and restrictions on economic activity in and around the Tanzanian camps as reasons for their return (OCHA 2003c).

Some refugees indicated their impression that the cuts were related to an imminent forced or encouraged repatriation. Burundian refugees in Tanzania expressed fear of forced repatriation following the signing of the Peace Agreement. Many reportedly did not have faith in the agreement, claiming it is unrealistic, and was signed in haste, at least in part, because of external pressure (JRS 2000b). The cut in food rations was readily perceived as a first step in "encouraging" the refugees to return home. Although UNHCR stated it did not have evidence that Tanzania was engaging in *refoulement*, concerns persisted that decreased food rations and recent restrictions on freedom of movement around the camps amounted to indirect pressure on the refugees to return home (UNHCR 2003f).

Planning for Repatriation

In July 2000, UNHCR completed a comprehensive operations plan for the repatriation and reintegration of refugees, the Strategic Framework for the Repatriation and Reintegration in Burundi, in response to the renewed impetus in the peace process.

Additional planning to ensure a safe and orderly repatriation process was particularly crucial in light of later developments in Burundi and Tanzania. Progress in peace negotiations with rebel groups during 2003 encouraged international support for a timely return. In addition, in April 2002 the governments of Burundi and Tanzania and UNHCR signed the Tripartite Agreement on the Voluntary Repatriation of Burundian Refugees in Tanzania (UNHCR 2002). Since then, pressure has mounted within the Tanzanian government to see the refugees return home. Donor fatigue has become commonplace now that certain Burundian refugees have spent more than thirty years in the camps. Planning for return, however, should be done carefully to avoid any impression of a forced repatriation. It also should specifically involve consultations with refugee women and include them as decision-makers. At present, most planning is conducted between UNHCR and Burundian and Tanzanian government officials, as the members of the Tripartite Commission charged with overseeing repatriation, but these discussions should be broadened to include key sectors of civil society. Finally, donors should support continued planning to ensure sufficient resources exist to carry out the necessary assessments and take the preliminary steps needed to prepare for an eventual return.

Within Burundi, planning should involve a more systematic, in-depth assessment of the needs of locations to which returnees will go. Such evaluations should begin in the eight provinces UNHCR currently has designated as safe for return (UNHCR 2003b). Advance rehabilitation of infrastructure is another key preparatory measure. UNHCR already has agreed to provide building materials for the construction of houses and to assist in the rehabilitation of schools, water systems and public health facilities (UNHCR 2000c).

For repatriation to be successful, complete demographic, socio-economic and other information about the refugees in camps, as well as those in settlements, is needed to help prepare for return. To date, information only exists as to the number of refugees who voluntarily wish to repatriate. Approximately 70,000 refugees have registered with UNHCR to repatriate to Burundi, but over half of these originate from provinces still affected by war (Norwegian Refugee Council n.d., section patterns of return and resettlement, sub-section general). A survey of the 1972 caseload was completed at the time of the site visits; it appeared that refugees would return home only if issues pertaining to land ownership were resolved (see below). Monitoring of conditions of return and land ownership issues, however, has been severely limited. Only four UNHCR staff members are charged with investigating these issues. As a result, only the most basic spot-checks have been conducted in Burundi on land-related issues (Norwegian Refugee Council 2003: 101).

To prepare for increased repatriation in the future, important developments occurred during 2003. Specific activities in Burundi included: construction of 64 reception centers in provinces targeted for repatriation; provision of legal assistance to receiving communities and returnees in Kirundo, Muyinga, Ruyigi and Bururi provinces; and creation of a support program for women through the Ministry for Social Action in Muyinga Province. UNHCR, UNDP and the World Bank also established an Inter-Agency Reintegration Unit, in order to ensure coordinated planning and programming in regions to which IDPs, refugees and ex-combatants were returning (OCHA 2003d).

There are capacities within the refugee population in Tanzania that are particularly needed in Burundi (e.g., reproductive health workers, teachers). Ensuring that their credentials will be recognized on return is a challenge. Recertification will go some way to providing work and an income for qualified returnees, as well as encourage them to feel an integral part of the Burundi from which they fled. Reintegration and reconciliation in the longer, as well as the shorter, term will be encouraged as a result. This will help ensure that these essential skills, which are in short supply in Burundi, are not lost or wasted.

In some cases, the refugee population has fared better than their counterparts in certain regions of Burundi. Education and health are areas where attention should be paid to improving the situation for the whole population in Burundi to match provision in the camps.

- Education: Ninety percent of school-age children are reported to be in school in the Tanzanian camps—well above the numbers in Burundi—with again a lower proportion of girls. All follow the Burundi curriculum. To date the Ministry of Education in Burundi has been uncooperative in integrating children from the camps into the Burundian system. Not only will this discourage refugees from returning, but it reinforces the divisions between those inside the country and in power and those outside the country and not in power, thus endangering prospects for peace. Cooperation between the Education Ministry and refugee camp schools should begin at the earliest opportunity. In addition, education in the Tanzanian camps is free while payment of the required school fees in Burundi is beyond the capacity of many families (International Alert 2000: 30). Education is discussed in greater detail below.
- Health care and reproductive health services are apparently better in the camps and are poor inside Burundi where much of the infrastructure has been damaged and trained health workers are in short supply.

Cross-Border Coordination

At the time of the site visit, when repatriation discussions were just beginning, the need for cross-border consultation and coordination was apparent. It continued to be needed as the potential for large-scale repatriation increased. Particularly needed was consultation between displaced populations and those who remained in their home communities. The Committee of Women for Peace was facilitating visits of internally displaced women to their place of origin to meet up with former neighbors who are still there, in order to dispel misimpressions and reduce fear in preparation for a possible later return. The benefits of bringing women together and dispelling misconceptions have been discussed above. In due course, it is possible that women's organizations in Burundi could facilitate these kinds of visits by women in the Tanzanian refugee camps in advance of a future return. To the extent that a neutral site is needed in which to bring together Burundian women from inside Burundi and the refugee camps, the Tanzanian and other governments should help make such arrangements.

It is essential that Burundian refugees have access to as much accurate, unbiased news and information from Burundi as possible. Likewise they should be fully informed about the peace process, as should Burundians inside the country. Their reported distrust of the process mentioned earlier is evidence of why this is necessary. The peace and reconciliation broadcasting that Studio Ijambo transmitted in Burundi should have been made available to all Burundians in the Tanzanian camps, as well. Since the time of the site visit in 2000, access to impartial radio news in the camps has increased. Radio Isanganiro, an independent radio station, was launched in 2002 by the journalists who work at Studio Ijambo. Radio Isanganiro broadcasts much of Studio Ijambo's output and reaches large sectors of Burundi, western Tanzania and Rwanda (Search for Common Ground 2003). Studio Ijambo also distributes its programming through Radio Kwizera, run by the Jesuit Refugee Service from Tanzania, which covers refugee camps along the entire Burundi-Tanzania border. Because of political sensitivities, Tanzanian officials have been concerned in the past about Tanzanian stations collaborating with Bujumbura-based media. Efforts to resolve this source of contention should be supported.

Reintegration and Securing the Peace

When peace is established in Burundi, it will likely remain fragile for some time to come, particularly while regional conflict continues. It can be expected that most of the refugees and displaced persons will return home, with the exception possibly of those who were especially damaged during the crisis and those who have been displaced or exiled for very many years. Burundi will require ongoing political and material help from the international community to reintegrate refugees and displaced persons and to build a durable peace. The damage to the social fabric and infrastructure of the country must not be underestimated.

Refugees International argues that "the relationship between peace and reconstruction is such that the two processes must occur simultaneously so that neither process is unraveled by the lack of the other. . . . A meaningful investment in public works programs will not only contribute to the necessary reconstruction of infrastructure, but will also reduce violence by promoting reconciliation, boosting morale, and stimulating economic activity" (Refugees International 2000c). Rehabilitation of infrastructure, shelter, health clinics and hospitals, schools, etc. is an imperative. Much of the country has been destroyed and massive rehabilitation and reconstruction will be needed. The international community must stand ready to provide this essential support without lengthy delays.

Even with considerable support it will take many years to reconstruct the infrastructure and social fabric necessary for a durable peace. The international community must be prepared to commit the necessary, significant resources to do so over an extended period of time.

The government of Burundi and local organizations will need international assistance in the following areas.

- Protection and security. If peace is to be durable, the people of Burundi must feel secure from both rebel and governmental abuses. The Office of the High Commissioner for Human Rights–Burundi should be strengthened, with support from the international community, and a staff member designated to monitor and promote women's rights.
- Peacekeeping. If ceasefire agreements are to be respected, an international peacekeeping force should be endowed with the capacity to monitor effectively the ceasefire and ensure demobilization of former combatants. The African Union so far has deployed some 3,100 peacekeeping troops to Burundi as part of the African Mission in Burundi (AMIB) (OCHA 2003e). AMIB possesses a one-year mandate to monitor and verify implementation of ceasefire agreements, facilitate delivery of humanitarian assistance, and assist in disarmament, demobilization and reintegration programs (African Unification Front 2003). Greater diplomatic pressure and financial resources are needed, in particular, to move forward the demobilization process. Only one cantonment camp has opened to date and minimal numbers of former rebel fighters have reported for cantonment (OCHA 2003f).
- Demobilization of soldiers, with particular attention to children and youth. "Children follow the soldiers because they want to get something to eat," one international worker commented. While the political process determines the nature of the demobilization, the government of Burundi and the international community should begin planning for reintegration of demobilized soldiers and combatants. In particular, soldiers will need skills training and access to legitimate income-generation activities to avoid a return to violence, as will youth if they are to avoid entering a life of violence. Attention also should be given to the families of former combatants.
- Addressing poverty. Underlying much of the conflict is income disparity and extreme poverty. As the UNHCR Representative

explained in 2000 to the delegation, "All of our focus is on ethnic issues. There comes a time when the economic situation affects reintegration. It is the whole point of a durable solution." If Burundi is to achieve peace and stability, attention must be given to building up its economy and providing equal economic opportunities for all Burundians. Micro-credit and other income-generating programs to enable women to be self-sufficient should be supported, recognizing that women may find it impossible to put up commercially required guarantees or meet standard repayment terms. Access to education for all Burundian children, girls included, is another critical issue in addressing poverty. At present, fees are too high for many children, and the vestiges of discriminatory policies that favor Tutsi students must be removed.

- Land issues. Two interlinked problems are the need to provide land to returnees and women's rights to land. Many displaced persons inside Burundi and refugees in exile have lost land and homes. These will need to be restored to them and their homes reconstructed if they are to be able to return. In some cases, the availability of land will be a precondition for return. Many of those who left in 1972, sometimes referred to as the *"sans addresses"* or *"sans terre"*—those without addresses or without land—and those who have been internally displaced for a lengthy period may genuinely have nowhere to return to because their land has been taken over or their property destroyed. Specific attention should be given to addressing their needs for land. Access to land has been identified as possibly the determining factor in whether the 1972 refugees return to Burundi or not. A UNHCR survey was carried out among the 1972 refugees to assess their feelings toward land. It found that 84 percent claimed they wanted to return home and would accept land or compensation in lieu of land. However, UNHCR's finding is not reliable given that only original heads of households were interviewed, not their now adult children.

- Justice. The justice system must continue to be strengthened to provide equal access for and protection of Burundian men and women from all ethnic groups, regions and backgrounds. Issues relating to the questions of justice and impunity must be discussed and debated more openly if the peace settlement is to reflect what Burundian men and women want and if it is to be accepted not only by political leaders and politicians, but also by the mass of the population. The various alternatives are complicated and some highly politicized. Most Burundians have suffered in one way or another as a result of the violence. There is no easy solution to the issue, but shying away from discussing the problems will not contribute to the best solution nor enable the population to come to terms with the outcome. It is inevitable at this stage, especially without more open discussion and debate at all levels of society, that whatever solution or solutions are opted for, they will be seen by one group or another as an unacceptable compromise. The Burundian government should encourage debate on these issues and the international community should support such initiatives in whatever form—through radio, small group meetings, rest breaks while women are working in the fields, schools, and other fora.

Even after a peace settlement is reached, projects to promote peace and reconciliation will continue to be needed. There is no instant, easy solution to the various, complex problems Burundi faces and all those involved must appreciate that sustained intervention and support will be necessary. It is not clear, however, whether the international community, writ large, or the United Nations, in particular, have the capacity or the resources to respond to these pressing needs.

CONCLUSION

Burundi has been a case study in humanitarian failure, but with peace and reconciliation could come progress. It has been a failure largely because of the unwillingness of any of the principal actors to address seriously the humanitarian needs of the civilian population. Many actors are responsible for this lack of attention. The UN significantly pulled back its presence, withdrawing all non-essential international staff following the murder of two UN officials and seven Burundians carrying out a humanitarian mission in October 1999. Following this attack, coordination among UN agencies and between the UN and national and international NGOs deteriorated. The UN mostly stayed in urban areas, restricting the movement of its staff because of continued security threats. The UN recognized the seriousness of the situation; a high-level mission went to Burundi in December 2000 to assess the needs of the internally displaced.

The government of Burundi also bears great responsibility for the inattention given to internal refugees. In particular, it failed to provide adequate security for civilians and aid workers alike. By not sufficiently reining in extremist military groups, and by forcibly relocating civilians without regard to their security, the government compounded the harm to its own citizens. At the same time, the rebels who refused to sign a peace agreement bore major responsibility as they continued to raid villages, killing residents and forcing others to flee, and attacked aid workers.

A number of steps could be taken pending the consolidation of real peace. First, the UN must continue to strengthen its own capacities in Burundi. The intermittent presence in Burundi of strong humanitarian actors has had serious ramifications for assistance and protection, particularly to displaced populations.

Second, support for the peace process must continue with full recognition that it is fragile and incomplete. In particular, the international community should continue to provide financial support for projects aimed at peace and reconciliation. There are many small but effective programs. More are needed, especially those that fully utilize the resources that women bring to the peace process.

Third, the UN, donors and international NGOs should take all steps necessary to reach the largest number of displaced persons with assistance programs. While insecurity is undeniably a major impediment, the international aid community should work with local associations and institutions that may have greater ability to reach internally displaced persons in less secure areas.

Fourth, aid packages in the type of emergencies experienced by Burundi should address more completely the needs of internal refugees, particularly the majority who are women and their dependent children. In addition to food, shelter, sanitation and basic health services, there is a strong need for reproductive health services. This is made urgent by the very high urban and rural maternal and infant mortality rates, as well as the prevalence of HIV/AIDS. Micro-credit and other programs would enable women-headed households to be self-supporting through productive work. Also needed are programs to help women victims of violence address the traumas of rape and other violence against them, as well as psychosocial programs for children who have grown up with constant warfare. And, for the future, education programs—particularly rehabilitating schools, supplying books, training teachers and, very important for internally displaced persons, helping the most vulnerable groups pay school fees for their children—will help reduce the cycle of violence by providing youngsters with viable alternatives and by increasing access to education for all children, including girls.

Burundi has been one of the most difficult places in which to undertake humanitarian work. The disparity between what can safely be done and what urgently needs to be done is highly frustrating. The dedication and commitment of the humanitarian aid staff working in Burundi cannot be overstated. It is time for the international community to give them the opportunity to make a difference for the hundreds of thousands of refugees and internally displaced persons whose lives depend on it.

For a brief update on developments in Burundi since this chapter was completed, see the editors' postscript, page 223.

SOURCES

The authors conducted interviews in Bujumbura and Bubanza, Burundi with representatives of the principal United Nations organizations, international and national relief agencies, human rights organizations, Burundian government agencies, donor governments and groups working toward peace and reconciliation during field visits in October 2000. Susan Martin conducted interviews in Dar es Salaam with Tanzanian government officials and UNHCR in October 2000. Trish Hiddleston was the principal author of the Women's Commission report, *Out of Sight, Out of Mind: Conflict and Displacement in Burundi*, from which parts of this chapter are drawn. A complete list of interviews can be found on page 36 of the report. The information was updated via e-mail correspondence with key informants and review of written sources. Our thanks go to Alexander Hartman, our research assistant, for his help in updating the information on the continually unfolding situation in Burundi.

NOTES

1. Following the killing of the UN staff members in October 1999 in Rutana, the RESO (a group of 37 international NGOs working in Burundi) had contact with various parties concerned in the conflict. A seminar was arranged by the Centre for Humanitarian Dialogue in Geneva in February 2000 that brought representatives of the Burundian military, the rebel forces and the humanitarian community together. It focused on and requested that the parties involved apply the principles of international and humanitarian law to the civil population and to those involved in humanitarian action in the field. The RESO is convinced that this initiative had a positive impact during the period following the meeting (March and April 2000) although it may have been limited in time. See press release by the RESO, *Call for Support of Ceasefire Efforts*, Bujumbura, September 18, 2000.

2. Table 2.2, Indicative Refugee Population and Major Changes by Origin, found on UNHCR website, www.unhcr.org, under Refugees and Others of Concern to UNHCR, 1999 Statistical Overview. See also table 2.3, Prima Facie Refugee Arrivals by Origin and Country/Territory of Asylum, 1998 and 1999, and table 2.4, Repatriation of Refugees by Origin and Country/Territory of Asylum, 1997–1999.

Chapter 3

From Complex Displacement to Fragile Peace in Sri Lanka

Nicholas Van Hear and Darini Rajasingham-Senanayake

The armed conflict in Sri Lanka and consequent displacement both within the island and abroad form a paradigmatic case for the international humanitarian regime. First, and most obviously, the country and its conflict have contributed substantially to the global crisis of displacement, and the related expansion of the international humanitarian industry in the post–Cold War period. Second, the case of Sri Lanka encapsulates the changing role of UNHCR globally, as it moves beyond protection and relief for refugees to growing involvement with internally displaced people. Third, Sri Lanka is one of the countries where the debate about how to integrate a development focus into emergency relief has been posed most sharply, not least because of the great fluidity of the security situation: areas that have been the subject of rehabilitation interventions have rapidly reverted to needing relief as the conflict has ebbed and flowed. Fourth, as the country moved toward an uneasy peace in 2001–2002, dealing with protracted displacement in conditions of "post-conflict, pre-peace" became the issue.

This chapter looks at the evolving discourse, policy and practice of humanitarian intervention in a country which has experienced armed conflict for two decades. It first briefly indicates the complex and shifting historical and geographical patterns of displacement in Sri Lanka. The chapter then reviews the institutional landscape of humanitarian action in the country, focusing on coordination structures within and among government bodies, UN agencies, and local and international non-governmental organizations. It suggests that coordination structures are generally quite well developed, and points to some encouraging consultation initiatives. The chapter then shifts to the view from the welfare center, resettlement or relocation site to explore the effectiveness of the humanitarian regime at the local level. While there have been some modest improvements in living conditions as a result of initiatives since the later 1990s, there were still great disparities in protection and relief of displaced and war-affected people. The chapter explores why this should be the case, and suggests the need for integrated and flexible policy appropriate to local contexts of displacement; this requires drawing on local knowledge for improved understanding of the dynamics and diversity of displacement in the country. This analysis covers developments in the context of protracted conflict and displacement up to about 2001. A final section reflects on how conditions have changed since the fragile peace process got under way in 2002.

THE DIVERSITY OF DISPLACEMENT

Sri Lanka has experienced complex forms of migration within and outside the country over the last three decades (Fuglerud 1999; Rotberg 1999). A complex combination of ethnic, nationalist, socio-economic and religious tensions contributed to the armed conflict which took off in the early 1980s between the Sri Lankan military and the separatist Liberation Tigers of Tamil Eelam (LTTE). A large outflow of asylum-seekers, mainly Tamils, has taken place, largely from the north and east of the island where the conflict has been waged; there have been intense periods of fighting in 1983–1987, in 1990–1994 and from 1995 until 2001. Much of this refugee movement was initially to Tamil Nadu in southern India, but many Sri Lankan Tamils have sought asylum farther afield, adding to the diaspora of Sri Lankan migrants who left for work, education or to take up professional positions abroad in Europe, North America and elsewhere. During interludes or lulls in the fighting, notably in the late 1980s and early 1990s, large-scale repatriations from Tamil Nadu have taken place; but the resumption of fighting rendered these return movements short-lived. In 2000 there were around 110,000 Sri Lankan Tamil refugees in southern India, of whom about 60,000 lived in camps, and some 200,000–300,000 in Europe and North America, who joined other Sri Lankan migrants. In addition to movements outside the island, there has been large-scale displacement within the country. Depending on the intensity of the conflict, between 500,000 and one million people have been displaced within Sri Lanka at any one time in recent years (USCR

2001). Some individuals and households have been displaced many times, and members of a single household may be dispersed in different parts of the country or in different countries abroad. The conflict has thus produced a complex range of forcibly displaced and war-affected populations that poses difficult challenges to the regime charged with providing protection and assistance.

A full review of displacement, its consequences and the response of the humanitarian regime would have to take account of those who have sought safety in India and farther afield, since those abroad both shape and are an integral part of Sri Lanka's "forced migration complex." This chapter limits its focus to the situation within the country. That situation is extremely complex and diverse, with a wide range of local and regional contexts of internal displacement arising from two decades of armed conflict. A few examples follow.

- The 1983 pogrom that is usually taken as marking the start of the conflict entailed the internal and external displacement of minority Tamils from the south, principally the capital city of Colombo and the central hill country. Members of the small local Sinhalese minority in Jaffna were also displaced south in retaliatory attacks.
- In 1990 Muslim and Sinhalese minorities were displaced by the LTTE from the northern Jaffna peninsula and Mannar district. Some 75,000 Muslims ended up on the west coast of the island in Puttalam district.
- Large numbers have been displaced since what is termed the third Eelam War started in 1995. One of the major displacements was the entire population of Jaffna when the Sri Lankan military recaptured the northern city.
- Substantial numbers of people have been caught in the crossfire between the combatants in the north and east, some of whom have been repeatedly displaced along the "border areas" of the conflict.
- In the east, attacks on Muslims and Sinhalese villages have led to the creation of monoethnic enclaves, with Muslims moving to Muslim majority areas and Sinhalese moving to Sinhalese majority areas. Tamil civilians who have been subject to harassment, intimidation and retaliatory attacks by the military have also fled their homes.

As these examples indicate, the circumstances of displacement vary greatly. Currently, there are several relatively stable displaced communities, such as those in Puttalam district, who have been displaced for fifteen years; in some districts, such as Polonnaruwa and Anuradhapura, resettlement or relocation is almost complete. Elsewhere, such as in Jaffna, Vavuniya, Mannar, Trincomalee and Mullaitivu districts, people come and go depending on the security situation, military operations, and the

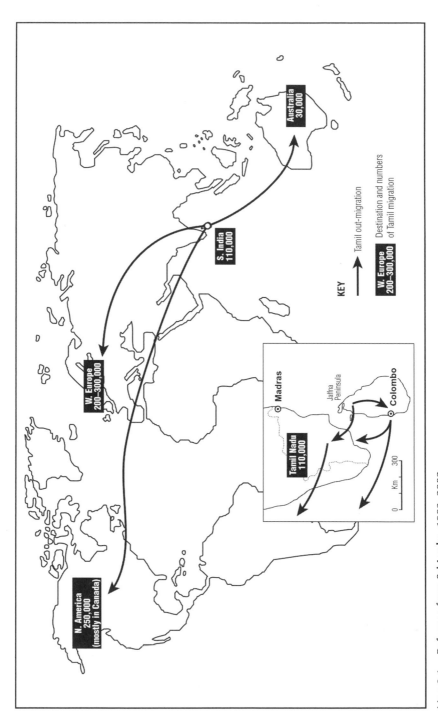

Map 3.1. Refugees from Sri Lanka, 1983–2002

Source: UNHCR; USCR.

KEY

Tamil out-migration

W. Europe
200–300,000
Destination and numbers
of Tamil migration

Australia
30,000

S. India
110,000

W. Europe
200–300,000

N. America
250,000
(mostly in Canada)

Madras

Jaffna
Peninsula

Colombo

Tamil Nadu
110,000

0   Km   300

conditions of shelter. The shifting patterns of displacement require the development of context-specific protection and relief interventions. Patterns of displacement and the responses to them vary according to:

- the duration of displacement: long- or short-term displacement shapes which relief-development interventions are feasible;
- the security situation in the region of displacement: whether the displaced find themselves within or outside conflict areas shapes the protection challenge;
- residence of the displaced: residence in or outside camps or with relatives shapes both protection and relief-development measures;
- the conditions of resettlement or relocation, which again shape relief-development interventions.

This diversity of displacement and the challenges it poses are explored further below. The following section briefly reviews the large body of institutions that has become engaged in addressing displacement and other consequences of the conflict in Sri Lanka.

THE INSTITUTIONAL LANDSCAPE

As in other countries where there are protracted conflicts and widespread displacement, a wide range of institutions has emerged to address the consequences of the upheavals. Coordination of these institutions, or at least an awareness of the need for it, has been quite well developed in the context of conflict in Sri Lanka. A number of initiatives have been launched in recent years, with varying degrees of success. Modest efforts at consulting parties involved in the conflict, including the displaced and war-affected themselves, have been quite encouraging. Some agencies have also attempted to decentralize their activities in an attempt better to address needs on the ground. The following section reviews some of these developments among the various agencies involved.

As well as being a party to the conflict, the *government of Sri Lanka* has been by far the most significant actor in the provision of assistance to the displaced and other war-affected people. In 2000, the government was said to have provided food and other assistance to about 690,000 displaced and war-affected people; there were thought to be up to 800,000 displaced people in all. The main form of assistance has been a food ration, but there has also been a commitment to rehabilitate infrastructure in government-held areas and to provide amenities such as drinking water, schooling and health facilities to displaced and war-affected

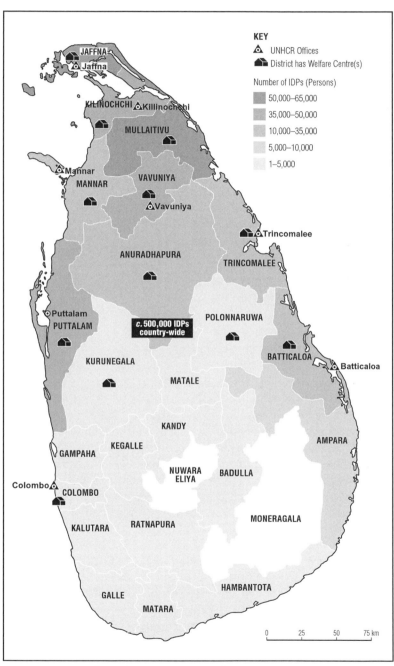

KEY

⊿ UNHCR Offices

🏠 District has Welfare Centre(s)

Number of IDPs (Persons)

■ 50,000–65,000

■ 35,000–50,000

■ 10,000–35,000

■ 5,000–10,000

□ 1–5,000

JAFFNA
⊿ Jaffna

KILINOCHCHI ⊿ Kilinochchi

MULLAITIVU

⊿ Mannar
MANNAR

VAVUNIYA
⊿ Vavuniya

⊿ Trincomalee
TRINCOMALEE

ANURADHAPURA

⊙ Puttalam
PUTTALAM

c. 500,000 IDPs country-wide

POLONNARUWA

BATTICALOA
⊿ Batticaloa

KURUNEGALA

MATALE

KANDY

KEGALLE

AMPARA

GAMPAHA

NUWARA
ELIYA

BADULLA

Colombo ⊿
COLOMBO

KALUTARA

RATNAPURA

MONERAGALA

GALLE

MATARA

HAMBANTOTA

0   25   50   75 km

Map 3.2.   Internal Displacement in Sri Lanka, circa 2003

Source: UNHCR.

people wherever they resided, including areas held or controlled by the LTTE (WFP 2000). Arguably, the government's concern to support the displaced in the areas controlled by the LTTE was related to its interest in preserving minimal sovereignty in such territory. By maintaining a skeletal staff and essential services in such areas, and supplying basic food rations, the government could maintain its claim of sovereignty over these areas.

While the civilian government has been fairly responsive to humanitarian concerns and appears receptive to initiatives and recommendations made by humanitarian agencies, the military often stymied them. Moreover, policy formulation, decision-making and implementation in the arena of displacement were dispersed among many government departments. As a thoughtful report by a well-placed and experienced government official showed, "there are more than ten institutions involved in human disaster management and most of them act independently of each other resulting in fragmentation of the institutional framework and non integration of projects" (Lankaneson 2000: 3). Thus there have been two ministries for handling rehabilitation and reconstruction, one for the north and the other for the rest of the island (respectively the Ministry of Rehabilitation, Reconstruction and Development of the Northern Region and the Ministry of Port Development, Rehabilitation and Reconstruction); two bodies handled the distribution of relief (the Commissioner General of Essential Services (CGES) and the Department of Social Services); and security questions were likewise divided among the Ministry of Defense and other bodies. This fragmentation explained some of the inconsistencies in coverage and treatment of displaced people in Sri Lanka, which are explored further below.

A wide range of UN organizations, other multilateral and bilateral agencies, and local and international nongovernmental organizations are engaged in interventions relating to the conflict in Sri Lanka. The involvement of *UNHCR* dates from 1987 when at the request of the Sri Lankan government the organization became engaged in the repatriation of refugees from south India (UNHCR 2000). The resumption of fighting in 1990 disrupted the return program, but it resumed intermittently from 1992, only to cease again when hostilities broke out again in 1995. Meanwhile UNHCR became involved in the protection and assistance of internally displaced people, together with communities that hosted IDPs, on the grounds that it did not make sense to distinguish between such people and returnees. This involvement was formalized in 1993, and included UNHCR's experiment with Open Relief Centers in the northwest (Clarance 1991). However, the organization's remit was limited to those districts in which there were significant populations of returnees from abroad, namely the north and northeast. This had consequences which are explored further below.

The *World Food Program* has been active in Sri Lanka since 1992. It has not been operational in the conflict areas, but supplied food to residents of government-run camps known as "welfare centers" who did not receive rations through the government body, the Commissioner General for Essential Services (CGES). In 2000 the WFP reviewed its operations in Sri Lanka (WFP 2000), and the consequences of this review are considered below. Other organizations within the UN system engaged in the conflict-related work include the *UNDP,* which has been involved in rehabilitation activities when conditions allowed, and *UNICEF,* which has been active on the question of child soldiers and other issues involving the protection and welfare of children.

Outside the UN system, the *International Committee of the Red Cross* has been active in conflict areas since 1989, providing protection and assistance to the civilian population under fire, tracing lost or separated family members, acting as an intermediary and other humanitarian activities (ICRC 2000). *Bilateral donors,* such as the British, German and Dutch governments, have been active in conflict-related work through their respective development agencies, such as the UK's Department for International Development (UK DFID 1999) and German Technical Cooperation (GTZ), or through various nongovernmental organizations. From the later 1990s, the *European Union* and the *World Bank* were relatively new players with plans for rehabilitation programs in or near the conflict areas.

The non-governmental sector in Sri Lanka is well established and vibrant. *International non-governmental organizations* significant in conflict-related areas included Oxfam, CARE, Save the Children, the Scandinavian NGO FORUT and the Dutch NGO Refugee Care (ZOA). These and other such organizations both implemented their own projects and worked with partners drawn from the burgeoning *local nongovernmental and community-based sector*: prominent NGOs included Sarvodaya and the Sewa Lanka Foundation. As in other countries in conflict, there were complex relations of contracting and subcontracting among the main donors, the government, multilateral agencies, and international and local NGOs.

Government Coordination Initiatives

In recognition of the fragmented nature of relief provision, there have been various government attempts to improve coordination in recent years. The Presidential Task Force on Human Disaster Management, set up in 1998, drew up an "Action Plan" as a basis for developing a national program to address displacement. In addition to the structures based in the capital, there were coordinating mechanisms at the Provincial and

District levels, but these were largely defunct or inactive in the areas that matter: the north and east.

Further measures to improve coordination began to take shape late in 1999. In December of that year, the Framework for Relief, Rehabilitation and Reconciliation was initiated as part of an effort to improve coordination among ministries and agencies. The initiative started life as an effort to tackle poverty coherently, as part of preparation for a meeting of international donors in Paris. Partly at the prompting of some donors, consideration of the conflict was included in the undertaking. What became known as the "Triple R Framework" covered four areas: assistance and modes of operation; coordination mechanisms; prioritization; and community capacity for reconciliation. A steering committee was set up to oversee the process, comprising the principal ministries concerned with RRR activities, UN agencies, non-governmental organizations, and donors. The committee was chaired by the External Resources Department of the Ministry of Planning, a key gatekeeper between donors and government. Assisted by the World Bank, UNDP, UNHCR, the Dutch government and other international agencies, a team of local and international experts was set up to elicit the views of stakeholders on how the government, civil society and donors could work together in promoting peace and reconstruction (Government of Sri Lanka 2000). The objectives were to ensure basic needs of people affected by the conflict, to rebuild productive lives where feasible, and to facilitate reconciliation and partnership across ethnic lines (Government of Sri Lanka 2002). This initiative was indicative of the broad approach adopted by the international donor community and the government—an approach linking relief with sustainable development.

A progress report on the framework was tabled at the Paris Donor Group meeting in December 2000 (Government of Sri Lanka 2000). It recognized the issue of institutional fragmentation and that better institutional coordination was crucial to improve effectiveness of relief, reconstruction and reconciliation efforts. Recommendations included the establishment of a national consultative committee to assess regularly the overall humanitarian situation, and the creation of a single institution to handle relief, rehabilitation and reconstruction in Sri Lanka. As elsewhere, implementation of these recommendations was difficult, given the culture of mistrust and the absence of political will among rival parties. The RRR framework was much criticized for a variety of reasons, and its pursuit led to some bad feeling among agencies, but it did at least represent recognition that action was needed to streamline unwieldy structures dealing with conflict and displacement, particularly within the government. Moreover, as explored below, the framework process brought together various parties involved in the conflict, including the displaced and war-affected, which was in itself an encouraging development.

Agency Coordination

As in other countries beset by conflict, the UN Resident Coordinator (RC) is responsible for the coordination of the international response to the needs of displaced people. Various coordination bodies covering UN agencies have been set up in recent years. In 2000, the Relief and Rehabilitation Theme Group (RRTG) was the principal forum for UN agency cooperation and coordination in the capital. The group comprised the heads of the UN agencies directly concerned with the conflict in Sri Lanka and was chaired by the RC, supported by the Humanitarian Advisor to the RC. The RRTG was charged with maintaining an adequate level of emergency preparedness, and with promoting collaborative programming in the areas of relief, rehabilitation and recovery; it helped with information-sharing and made joint assessments of the humanitarian situation in Sri Lanka (UNOCHA 2000). A UN Inter-Agency Working Group on Relief and Rehabilitation, drawn from agencies which are members of the Relief and Rehabilitation Theme Group, was responsible for implementing decisions made by agency heads. The working group appeared to operate as an intermediary mechanism between Colombo and the field, gathering operational and program-level input coming from the field, and communicating deliberations of the RRTG to the field. In addition to these structures, UN agencies established a focal point system in areas where more than one agency was operational. The UN focal point was designated by the RC in consultation with other UN agencies and played representation, information and coordination roles (UNOCHA 2000).

Displacement, relief and rehabilitation also figured in broader UN coordination structures. One prominent example derives from the "common country assessments" initiated as part of UN reform in the later 1990s; these sought to draw up a UN Development Assistance Framework (UNDAF) for each country of concern. The UNDAF for Sri Lanka explicitly linked conflict with poverty and manifested the shift to viewing the evolving humanitarian crisis as part of a wider development challenge that needed to be addressed from a long-term perspective. Finalized at the end of 2000, the document identified three focus areas: "provision of humanitarian assistance to conflict-affected areas and support for efforts that contribute to establish social harmony; reduction of poverty; and governance reform aimed at people centered development" (UN 2000). The importance of the humanitarian sector was evident in the large budgetary allocations to UNHCR and WFP, the latter receiving the largest allocation of any UN agency.

UN agencies also participated in a number of bodies that attempted to encompass the wider relief and assistance/humanitarian community. At the suggestion of representatives of EU member states in Sri Lanka, a Donor Working Group on Relief and Rehabilitation was established at the end of 1999, facilitated by the UN; the Humanitarian Advisor to the UN Resident Coordinator was the facilitator of the group (UNOCHA 2000).

UN agencies and non-governmental organizations involved in assistance to the displaced also met regularly under the auspices of the Colombo-based Consortium of Humanitarian Agencies (CHA). The CHA is an umbrella group that has been operating in its current form since late 1996, bringing together some 30 Sri Lankan and international non-governmental organizations, with a further 15 observers, mainly bilateral donors, some UN agencies (the UN Humanitarian Advisor, UNHCR and UNICEF) and the ICRC (CHA 1999). The CHA provided a forum for member agencies to develop common positions, to take collective action, to facilitate inter-agency initiatives and coordination, and to meet other agencies working in conflict areas. The consortium initiated sectoral, geographical or issue-based task forces for members and non-members, and provides an information service and exchange. It also liaised with international organizations on behalf of members. There were also fora associated with the CHA at the district level, in the north (Jaffna, Vavuniya and Mannar) and east (Amparai, Batticaloa and Trincomalee) and a skeletal body in Puttalam district in the west. The CHA functioned as a forum for information-sharing, but also to some extent for the allocation of projects, particularly at the district level.

As a leading player in the humanitarian field, UNHCR also played an important coordination role across various sectors. Recognizing that key planning processes took place at the district level, UNHCR helped to establish District Review Boards in each district where UNHCR was present. Chaired by the Government Agent, the government official responsible for each district, the board oversaw implementation of UNHCR's Quick-Impact Project Programs, UNICEF's small-scale projects, and the projects of non-governmental organizations with various sources of funding. UNHCR also established return committees in some districts with representatives of government, NGOs and other stakeholders to promote the return of the displaced or their relocation to new areas of settlement, where this was possible (UNOCHA 2000).

In addition to attempts to bring together various parties concerned with relief and assistance in and around the conflict areas, there were a number of bilateral arrangements between agencies. One such was the agreement between UNHCR and World Bank covering the North-East

Irrigated Agriculture Project (NEIAP), a five-year $32 million scheme to assist war-affected households in the northeast (UNHCR 2000). This was a manifestation in Sri Lanka of the "Brookings Process," which envisaged closer cooperation among agencies, like the World Bank and UNHCR, whose concerns have not traditionally been seen as coinciding (Crisp 2001).

As the principal international agencies engaged in operations related to the conflict, UNHCR, WFP, UNICEF and ICRC have attempted to coordinate their activities (UNHCR 2000), although this has not always been as successful as it might have been. While UNHCR and UNICEF had offices in some districts, WFP did not have a field presence. As the organizations themselves conceded, links between WFP and the other two UN agencies were sometimes poor at the district level, a serious shortcoming given the importance of WFP in provisioning welfare centers and other settlements for the displaced with food (WFP 2000). Coordination and relations between UNHCR and ICRC were also at times strained, particularly in Jaffna during the upsurge in conflict during 2000, when ICRC saw UNHCR as acting beyond its mandate in conflict areas. The whole nature of coordination was also found to be seriously wanting in the agencies' response or lack of emergency preparedness in the face of the emergency brought about by an LTTE offensive on Vavuniya in November 1999, when much of the town's population fled as the LTTE advanced.

Consultation and Decentralization Initiatives

In addition to initiatives much needed to improve coordination, there have been a number of recent efforts to consult parties affected by the war at the ground level. Although again not without flaws, these initiatives represented an encouraging trend. Two such initiatives are reviewed briefly here, the consultation associated with the Triple R Framework, and the "Listening" projects initiated by Oxfam and SCF.

The groundwork for pursuing the RRR Framework involved a consultation exercise which, after some resistance, eventually became extensive, involving the "uncleared" areas as well as those under the control of the government. The consultation took two forms: workshops held at the district level, facilitated by the CHA; and workshops at the sectoral level conducted by the National Peace Council. More than 50 workshops and consultations were held in 13 conflict-affected districts in 1999–2000, and district representatives met in the capital to discuss findings and recommendations. Twelve sectoral or thematic workshops were held with displaced Muslims, religious leaders, women's groups, trade unions, business leaders, ex-combatants, the media and others. Additional workshops were held with Indian or Estate Tamils, and on the issues of children and youth (Government of Sri Lanka 2002).

The consultation process had many shortcomings: among them were the omission of some arms of government from the consultation (notably the crucial Ministry of Defense, and district-level administrations); an at times mechanical approach to consultation; and lack of forethought as to how to use the findings. But it does appear to have been a useful exercise, attempting to reflect concerns on the ground and to communicate them to the centers of power and decision-making. It brought together parties who previously had interacted little or not at all, and furnished information that was incorporated into some relief and assistance planning. The consultations fed into the National Framework for Relief, Rehabilitation and Reconciliation, and proposed a raft of policy recommendations on the rights and entitlements of the displaced (including the adoption of the Guiding Principles on Internal Displacement), on the application of international humanitarian law, on maximizing rehabilitation and development, on reconciliation and peace-building, on decentralization, uniform standards, transparency and accountability, on the movement of people and goods, and on the transition to peace and recovery (Government of Sri Lanka 2002).

Another extensive consultative project was carried out by Oxfam and SCF (UK) (Oxfam and SCF 1998; Harris 2000). Called "Listening to the displaced," three surveys were conducted between 1996 and 1998. The project's scope, methodology and specific areas of inquiry evolved over time, but there were four basic objectives, focusing on the opinions and perspectives of those people directly affected by the conflict: "to assess changes in the concerns, needs and capacities of people affected by conflict; to evaluate humanitarian and development inputs from a constituency perspective; to identify issues on which international NGOs could provide improved support to their constituents; and to enable the voices of conflict-affected people to be heard by humanitarian agencies and key parties to the conflict" (Harris 2000: 20). Nearly 2,500 people from 25 displaced communities in the Vanni region (Kilinochchi and Mullaitivu districts) and more than 800 returnees to Jaffna participated in the Listening program in 1998.

A further encouraging development was a trend toward decentralization among some agencies, notably UNHCR and Oxfam which took steps to move responsibility for decision-making out of Colombo and into the conflict-affected areas. UNHCR created the post of "Coordinator for Operations" located in the conflict areas rather than in Colombo, and Oxfam restructured its operational side so that there are two program coordinators for the north and east with greater autonomy from Colombo. A notable exception to this trend was the government, whose decision-making structures remained resolutely centralized, despite the conscientious efforts of some officials at the district level (notably Trinco-malee and Vavuniya).

Despite some serious shortcomings then, there were some encouraging signs of improvements in coordination, consultation and to some extent decentralization among agencies concerned with conflict in Sri Lanka. Given these modest advances, the questions then arose, first, why the general condition of displaced and war-affected people improved little, if at all, and second, why there were such glaring disparities in the treat-ment and coverage of displaced and war-affected people. This chapter continues by pursuing these questions at the crucial local level, where agency interventions were actually felt.

THE VIEW FROM THE FIELD

The proof of the effectiveness of the humanitarian regime is at the local level. As was noted above, there has been much variation in patterns of displacement, depending on the security situation, and on the social, eco-nomic and political circumstances in the locations where the displaced found themselves.

Typically, the following stages were encountered in the process of dis-placement (WFP 2000). After arrival or interception at a checkpoint or road block, displaced people were moved to a transit center for security checking. This could take two or three months, during which time the displaced were often housed in poor and overcrowded conditions. In the transit camps they were provided with cooked rations by the government CGES, often using local suppliers. After security clearance, the displaced might be moved to a camp or so-called "welfare center," or they might be accommodated by friends and relatives. In the welfare centers they were re-registered for food rations, usually supplied by the CGES, or sometimes by the WFP. There was commonly a delay of a month or two until rations were received. Conditions in welfare centers varied greatly according to location. Camps sited on government land usually had bet-ter access to water and sanitation than those on private land. Conditions in camps in towns were generally worse than those located in rural areas where there was less pressure on space; however, location in towns might mean that employment opportunities, schooling and other amenities and services were better.

Depending on where they were from and their circumstances, the dis-placed might eventually be resettled or relocated (WFP 2000). In official parlance, *resettlement* meant the return of displaced people to their own homes. By *relocation* was meant settlement of displaced people on state or private land in the administrative district in which they had been displaced. Once resettled or relocated there might again be a delay until they received their assistance. In the areas under government control, people being resettled or relocated were eligible for assistance in the form of phased grants under what was known as the Unified Assistance Scheme (UAS): this was meant to help the displaced build temporary and then permanent accommodation, to help set up productive enterprises, to provide compensation for death or injury, and so on. However, such assistance was only meant for those who relocated in their districts of origin (although there appeared to be exceptions to this stipulation). Displaced people might nevertheless enter private arrangements to buy or lease land for settlement or cultivation, without government assistance.

The outcome of the combination of these various factors, circumstances and entitlements was a range of experiences of displacement. The following could be distinguished (Danish Refugee Council 2000):

- *refugees* still in exile;
- *returnees,* mainly from Tamil Nadu in India, living in transit or welfare camps, or with friends or relatives;
- *internally displaced people* in transit camps or welfare centers, or living with friends or relatives; these might be locally displaced within their own districts or displaced over greater distances;
- *resettled* people: those who had returned to their homes;
- *relocated* people: those who had found or been found new homes, usually in their own districts.

Each of these categories could be further divided according to whether they were in areas held or controlled by the government or by the LTTE (which determined access to assistance); according to the distance and duration of displacement; according to the number of times they had been displaced; according to conditions (such as changed ethnic composition) in the area from which they had been displaced, and therefore the possibility or likelihood of return; and according to the time elapsed since they had been displaced, resettled or relocated (DRC 2000).

The categories "displaced" or "internally displaced people" therefore covered a great range of experience that profoundly influenced the form and provision of assistance. If the regime with its improved structures of coordination was to be effective, it had to take account of this diversity of displacement. But there were glaring disparities in the treatment and coverage of displaced and war-affected people.

From the perspective of the displaced, relief and assistance interventions could appear haphazard, overlapping and sometimes contradictory, involving a great number of humanitarian agencies. The diversity of displacement histories in Sri Lanka was compounded by the diversity of regional coverage of the humanitarian organizations that were involved. The living conditions and life chances of displaced people therefore varied greatly according to the geographical area in which they found themselves, according to the reach of the humanitarian regime, and according to the duration of displacement. These dimensions are considered in the following sections.

Geographical Variation

In this section, the contrast is explored between two districts in which there were large populations of displaced, Puttalam and Vavuniya.

Puttalam district is on the western side of the island, and is some way from the conflict zone. The district accommodates long-settled populations of Muslims expelled from the north of the country by the LTTE in 1990. Around 2000 they lived in more than 100 settlements of various kinds. Most were well-established camps or settlements, with housing built mainly of mud and thatch. Many of the displaced had taken up the relocation package offered by the government (presumably before new regulations about relocating within one's own administrative district were introduced), and some had bought land, individually or in groups, and had built more substantial homes. Movement in and out of the camps was unrestricted, and there were some limited employment opportunities. There was a well-established ration system, using food provided by the government and the World Food Program. Life in these circumstances was far from ideal—many were settled on saline land, means of livelihood were very limited, and there were tensions between the displaced and local populations, for example—but the conditions of the displaced were rather better than those of people in other parts of the country. This was likely to change, however, with a policy shift in respect of the provision of rations, which is returned to below.

Vavuniya is close to the conflict zone, the most northerly substantial town (besides Jaffna) held by the government forces. It was subject to periodic attacks by the LTTE, sometimes involving evacuation of much of the town's population. People displaced as the conflict ebbed and flowed in the Vanni region to the north were housed in 14 camps in and around Vavuniya. Most of these were so-called "welfare centers" established and run by the government; they were set up as temporary holding centers, but people had been living in them for several years. Living conditions were very poor: the camps were overcrowded and rations were often of low standard. Movement was heavily controlled, and some of the camps were effectively detention centers for people the authorities deemed to be potential security threats. Two other camps were set up by UNHCR for returnees from south India; in these, conditions were generally better than in the welfare centers. These camps were later taken over and run by the government and housed internally displaced people as well as returnees. In addition to poor living conditions, there were protection problems, particularly in the welfare centers where paramilitary groups operated; young men in particular were prone to "disappear" from the camps, and there was a general atmosphere of insecurity.

Living conditions and life chances were therefore quite different among displaced people in Puttalam and those in Vavuniya. The question then arises as to whether consistency of treatment could reasonably be expected in such different circumstances: one an area of relative peace, the other close to a war zone. However, it should be noted that there were also wide variations in treatment of the displaced within each of these areas. In Puttalam, for example, great differences were reported in access to the government's Unified Assistance Scheme. There were also great variations in the living conditions of the displaced in Vavuniya district. For example, the contrast could hardly have been greater between the living conditions of people displaced in an upsurge in hostilities in November 1999, who were relocated in well laid out and relatively well resourced settlements on one hand, and the grim, sickly, dispiriting welfare centers like Veppankulam which had housed displaced people for several years, on the other. Yet the inhabitants of both places had undergone the same kind of uprooting.

Institutional Variation

There was also substantial variation in living conditions of the displaced according to whether and which institutions operate in the areas where the displaced were resident. Here the impacts of two international organizations are considered, the World Food Program and UNHCR.

As a result of a review of WFP assistance to displaced people worldwide, in which Sri Lanka featured as a case study, the organization resolved to change its practice on the provision of rations (WFP 2000). In Sri Lanka, as elsewhere, it decided to concentrate its provision on vulnerable, recently displaced people in the areas bordering the conflict, such as in Mannar, Vavuniya, Trincomalee and Jaffna, and to phase out its activities in places such as Puttalam district with long-term, fairly stable populations of displaced. The rationale for this was that WFP interventions were intended as relief to help the displaced to become self-supporting, rather than to provide assistance over the long term. The logic of this shift was probably broadly justified and consistent with the WFP's mandate, but the consequences for the displaced in Puttalam did not appear to have been thoroughly thought through, beyond provision of a "safety net" involving vocational training and other (unspecified) interventions to boost the livelihoods of the displaced. On the other hand, there were benefits for the displaced in Vavuniya, for example, in that the WFP made provision of its rations there conditional on improvements in living conditions in the welfare centers, on restrictions on movement being relaxed so that employment opportunities could be better sought, and on IDPs remaining within welfare centers for a limited period (perhaps up to two years) before being resettled or relocated. Such modest improvements for the displaced were welcome, but they were contingent on fairly arbitrary considerations, such as the impact or influence of an organization in a particular area.

A similar story of variable coverage can be told of UNHCR. The history of UNHCR's involvement in Sri Lanka, coupled with the organization's ambivalence toward involvement with IDPs in general, contributed to uneven coverage of vulnerable people who were in need of protection and assistance; this was a shortcoming noted by UNHCR staff themselves. As was outlined above, the organization's engagement in Sri Lanka dated from the late 1980s when it became involved in the repatriation of refugees from India. With the resumption of the conflict, repatriation largely came to a halt, and many returnees who had received assistance from UNHCR became internally displaced; consequently, with the endorsement of the UN Secretary-General, UNHCR extended its protection and assistance to the internally displaced. Understandably, its operations focused on the areas in which its former caseload, repatriates from India, were largely located, so that there were branch offices in Mannar, Vavuniya, Jaffna, Mullaitivu and Trincomalee in the north. UNHCR did valuable work both in areas controlled by the government and those held by the LTTE, and continues to do so. However one important area—Batticaloa and the east—fell outside this remit determined by historical circumstances, because the pattern of displacement in the district was different here: not many had fled to India from this area, and consequently there were few returnees. Consequently UNHCR did not have a history of involvement in this district, which nevertheless featured a high degree of displacement. Nor did the WFP have much involvement in the eastern districts. Other agencies such as ICRC and Oxfam were involved in the east, but the absence of this area from coverage by two major UN players in the humanitarian regime was further evidence of profound geographical and institutional unevenness in the treatment of the displaced.

The Frequency and Duration of Displacement

The frequency and duration of displacement were further dimensions determining variation in treatment. The needs for protection and assistance of those in flight or recently displaced were obviously different from those displaced people who had secured some degree of stable settlement, however unsatisfactory that may have been. There were also obvious differences in needs between those who had suffered one time, or occasional displacement, and those who had experienced repeated uprootings as the conflict ebbed and flowed. There were differences too between those displaced over short and longer distances. All of these variations needed to be taken into account in the design of effective and comprehensive protection and assistance.

In Sri Lanka, as in other countries suffering conflict and displacement, such comprehensiveness was not achieved. Perhaps it is not reasonable to expect it to be so. It is understandable that much humanitarian effort was targeted at people in or near conflict zones who had recently been displaced. But the needs of the longer term displaced should not have been eclipsed by such focus. Perhaps the most important consideration was that humanitarian action, or its absence, should not sow the seeds for future conflict.

One common consequence of repeated displacement was the loss of identity papers by the displaced. This could present serious problems of personal security and of access to public services. People who had lost identity papers during flight were subject to arrest and harassment by security personnel and other officials. Lack of documentation was a particular problem for those repeatedly uprooted who needed to re-register for rations and other services: lack of papers could also make admission of children to school highly problematic. In Trincomalee district UNHCR helped to enhance protection and mobility of displaced people by intervening with the government over the issue of identity cards, birth certificates and other documents lost during flight. This work was much appreciated, and could have been extended to all areas where there were displaced populations.

For obvious reasons, the situation of those subject to repeated displacement also presented great difficulties in the design of projects to promote sustainable livelihoods. Micro-projects in or near conflict areas were liable to suffer destruction or looting of equipment and produce, such as agricultural implements and crops, boats and fishing tackle. Loans taken out to set up new ventures could become an additional burden for those repeatedly displaced if these enterprises failed. Limited access to markets because of restrictions on movement was another constraint on the creation of sustainable livelihoods. Taxation of economic activities by paramilitary groups presented a further hazard. Difficult though it might have been, design of interventions to enhance livelihoods obviously needed to take account of these risks: one prerequisite was greater appreciation of the local resource base, market conditions and security situation.

Those displaced for long periods but whose residence was relatively stable encountered other kinds of problems. The case of the displaced Muslims in Puttalam was again instructive in this regard (Brun 2003). October 2000 marked the tenth anniversary of the expulsion of the Muslims from the north and northeast by the LTTE. While initially the "refugees," as they were known locally, received sympathy and assistance from host populations, ten years later some in the host community felt that they had overstayed their welcome and tensions had developed. Some landlords, who had allowed the displaced the use of their land in the first years after displacement, now wanted their land back. Host fatigue was accompanied by agency fatigue, as some agencies moved to higher profile areas like the Vanni and the Jaffna peninsula. As was mentioned with respect to the discussion above of WFP policy changes, this shift was ostensibly justified by the better (though far from ideal) living conditions of the Puttalam displaced, compared with those in other areas, such as the Vanni or the east. The Puttalam displaced had also accumulated greater "social capital" and were better organized than other groups. However, long-term displacement generated its own problems. Ten years after their uprooting there were concerns that under existing property law these IDPs could stand to lose their claims to their land and houses in Jaffna, Mannar and other places from which they had been displaced. While the legal issue was debatable, it was a source of real anxiety among the displaced in Puttalam and elsewhere. Many of their properties had been taken over by Tamils who had also been displaced for long periods—the LTTE had a policy of settling the displaced. Likewise, after recapturing parts of Jaffna, the government resettled Tamils displaced from the south and from the areas near military camps in the peninsula where shelling and bombing was often severe: they were often placed in the houses of departed Muslims, Sinhalese and Tamils. In sum, the houses left behind by Muslim (and Sinhalese) refugees, if they had not been destroyed by bombing and shelling, now accommodated other displaced people. If and when peace returned, the danger was then that return of the displaced from places like Puttalam might generate yet another chain reaction of displacement and/or conflict as disputes erupted as to who had the right to occupy land and housing.

Long-term displacement also raised the issue of distinguishing between those who did and did not wish to return. In the first decade of the war, the government and agencies assumed that most if not all the displaced would return to their homes, and there was little assistance to build sustainable livelihoods in the areas where the displaced found themselves. The situation changed as the war has dragged on and displacement became protracted. Moreover, many displaced people in camps in the areas bordering the conflict did not wish to return home because of fear for their personal security, because of traumatic experiences, or because there was nothing to return to; such people were being kept dependent on relief rather than being assisted to build new lives, livelihoods and communities. Ironically, the very humanitarian relief meant to assist people who fled from their homes many years ago kept them in a state of limbo. The resulting frustration made youth in particular prey to recruitment by militant groups.

As was noted above, displaced people could be "resettled" in their place of origin or "relocated" in another setting. However, since 2000, government assistance was usually only provided for those who "relocated" within their own district. The government recognized that people who had been displaced for many years should be allowed to stay in the places they had made home, but also that this would have implications for local demography and politics: local people might object to returnees or newcomers, and such influxes could change ethnic make-up and the demography of voting. This often reduced the government's incentive to address the issue of long-term displacement, while recognizing the long-term tensions that could result. A further complicating factor was that, ultimately, military considerations took precedence.

Coordination and Inconsistency

Such was broadly the picture around 2000–2001: improved coordination at the national level among government, international, and non-governmental agencies seemed to co-exist with wide disparities in the experience and conditions of the displaced on the ground. Some of the explanations for this were common to many countries in which there are complex patterns of displacement. As elsewhere, most agencies' interventions touched only a minority of displaced and war-affected people tangibly, and then only fleetingly. Some variation in efficiency within and among agencies was attributable to the rivalries that are found in any such arena, as well as to institutional and mandate ambiguities, perhaps magnified in the extremely politicized and militarized Sri Lankan context. Further, as we have seen, some of the variation of coverage could be attributed to historical and contingent circumstances; if there had been a tabula rasa, organizations might have done things differently. Perhaps it is unreasonable to expect too much from coordination—which is in danger of being perceived as a panacea—given the complex and intractable nature of the conflict. All the same, the conditions for and constraints on action could not be used as a reason for discharging humanitarian organizations from their responsibilities for protecting and assisting those caught up in the conflict.

After 20 years of conflict and displacement, and despite some encouraging initiatives, means of confronting the long-term implications of displacement in the conflict zones were still lacking. This was partly due to the government's unwillingness and inability to address displacement, given possible political ramifications. But it was also the result of the reactive nature of humanitarian intervention and relief, and of the high turnover of personnel which undermined institutional memory within humanitarian agencies. The more proactive approach that the international relief-development debate indicated, seen in the RRR Framework and UNDAF initiative in Sri Lanka, was a shift in the right direction. The new approach recognized the complexity of the conflict and its link to poverty and governance issues in the country. But the recognition that humanitarian intervention could be more effective with a development focus was yet to be manifested in practice.

PROTRACTED DISPLACEMENT IN CONDITIONS OF "POST-CONFLICT, PRE-PEACE"

Events late in 2001 led to cautious optimism among observers and Sri Lankan citizens about the possibilities for peace. In that year, five key developments or conditions seem to have persuaded the parties to the conflict to seek peace.

First, overall stalemate and exhaustion prevailed on the military front: neither side could win. Second, there was the devastating bombing of Sri Lanka's international airport by the LTTE in July 2001, and the destruction of much of the country's civilian air fleet. Third, there was the recording of serious economic contraction for the first time since independence: Sri Lanka had until then recorded substantial growth despite (or perhaps because of) the war. These three developments seem to have jerked the government and the business classes out of a stance of rhetorically mouthing the desire for peace toward active pursuit of it. Affecting the LTTE side of the conflict was the fallout of September 11, 2001, and the anti-terrorism measures that followed. In fact, LTTE activities among the Tamil diaspora were already being clamped down upon by Western governments, seen notably in the closure of the organization's international offices in London and Paris. September 11 accentuated this process. Finally, there was the election at the end of 2001 of a new government with a fresh resolve to pursue peace.

The upshot of this combination of conditions was two unilateral ceasefires by the government and LTTE, followed by a bilateral ceasefire in February 2002, facilitated by Norwegian mediators. Six rounds of peace talks were held between November 2002 and March 2003, and rapid progress appeared to be made. The LTTE said that it would no longer seek a separate nation-state, though with a hint that secession would take place if the autonomy won was not sufficient. The government proposed a federal system of governance, though the extent of autonomy for the Tamil territory was not specified. Among many other difficult issues, neither party addressed the ways in which minorities could be incorporated into the system of governance.

The peace process ground to a halt when the LTTE pulled out of the round of talks scheduled for April 2003, highlighting its dissatisfaction with the level of its participation in the proposed interim administration of the North and East. A related concern was to regain control of Jaffna, from which the LTTE was ousted in late 1995 and early 1996, and in particular to rid the peninsula of the Sri Lankan armed forces. Tensions had come to a head over the army's refusal to withdraw from what it designated as "High Security Zones" without some LTTE disarmament. The army's occupation of such zones prevented the return to their homes of substantial numbers of displaced people, who were in turn occupying the homes of other displaced people and blocking their return. More widely the LTTE was concerned that the benefits of peace to its constituency of supporters was not sufficient.

The LTTE did not participate in the major donors' conference held in Tokyo early in June 2003, at which $4.5 billion was pledged by multilateral and bilateral donors over a four year period (2003–2006), subject to further progress in the peace process. The pledges were also predicated on the implementation of the government's policy document "Regaining Sri Lanka," Sri Lanka's Poverty Reduction Strategy, and Needs Assessments of the North and East prepared by the World Bank, the Asian Development Bank, the UN, the government and the LTTE (Government of Sri Lanka/SCOPP 2003). The government's "Regaining Sri Lanka" document was cast in a neo-liberal mold, advocating "sound macro-economic policy," "private sector led growth," and aiming to "effectively connect poor regions to rapidly growing domestic and international markets" (Government of Sri Lanka/SCOPP 2003, Government of Sri Lanka 2003).

While peace negotiations at the diplomatic level appeared to be progressing reasonably well before grinding to a halt in April 2003, matters were much less settled at the ground level. Many people, displaced and refugees, adopted a "wait and see" attitude before they committed themselves to permanent return. Property issues boiled up as returnees tried to reclaim land and houses which were occupied by other displaced people who had nowhere to go, because their own land or houses were damaged or destroyed, heavily mined, or occupied by the army. There were demonstrations in Jaffna by displaced people who wished to return to their homes which were in areas still occupied by the military.

At the same time, many people of all ethnic backgrounds, including many Tamils, were wary of having to live under an LTTE administration, just as many were suspicious of the military, of government plans and of the ploys of politicians—particularly the manipulation of ethnic demography for electoral ends and the garnering of resources from national and international allocations for reconstruction. Critics of the peace process, again including many Tamils, also seriously questioned the LTTE's monopoly of representation of the Tamil case in the peace process. They rightly argued that this did not bode well for future democracy.

Against this uncertain background, a number of institutional changes were implemented, some of which were set in motion before the change of government. Notably a "crash relocation program" was begun, which relieved some of the pressure in some of the worst of the welfare centers. The government also eased many of the restrictions on the movement of people and goods in the north and east, which helped to make life for people in these areas easier, if by no means normal.

After the change of government, the Ministry of Rehabilitation, Resettlement and Refugees (MRRR) was set up, consolidating efforts that were previously divided among separate ministries for the North and East—although there did continue to be a separate ministry for the development in the East, whose responsibilities included rehabilitation, reconstruction and resettlement of displaced people, and a ministry assisting rehabilitation in the Vanni. In conjunction with UNHCR, a Policy, Planning and Coordination Unit was set up within the MRRR to focus on issues affecting IDPs and refugees returning from abroad (Bush 2002). An evaluation of UNHCR's program for internally displaced people in Sri Lanka (UNHCR 2002) noted among other things the uneven geographical coverage referred to above, and recommended that efforts should be made to extend UNHCR's protection and assistance efforts to the east: the agency subsequently did so.

With UNHCR support, in April 2002 the MRRR set in motion an island-wide registration of IDPs, to provide details of their post-displacement history, socioeconomic condition, health status and future plans for return or relocation. Some 220,000–230,000 displaced families were registered under the survey, meaning that the total number of people displaced was of the order of 850,000. The survey suggested that just under two thirds wished to return to their homes, about a quarter wanted to stay where they were, and a tenth wanted to move to another place or were undecided.

The results of the survey were supplemented by a second form of registration more routinely done through local government structures for the purposes of distributing rations. A family had to register with the local authority to receive rations and other entitlements, such as the government's resettlement or relocation package (the UAS), a modest amount of money granted to build temporary shelter and help to re-establish livelihood. The MRRR and UNHCR collated figures from these registrations to track return movements. From these data, it appeared that some 240,000 individuals had returned to their districts of origin (though not necessarily their homes) since the peace process had gotten under way. These figures did not capture the substantial number of people who had maintained registration (and receipt of rations) in their place of displacement, but had returned to their places of origin to see if they could reclaim their houses and land, and re-establish a life there. Despite these shortcomings, the overall improvements in the quality of data about displacement helped to enhance the provision of assistance toward the objective of durable solutions for the displaced.

Like the population at large, the humanitarian agencies were guardedly optimistic at the progress of the peace process. There appeared to be a new sense of purpose among agencies, notably UNHCR, which intensified its interventions on the issue of internal displacement, providing material assistance and monitoring the voluntary or otherwise nature of returns. The agency extended its coverage, notably in the east which had been neglected in terms of protection and assistance, but was arguably the most volatile region. UNHCR was also to be key in the monitoring of the assistance package (the Unified Assistance Scheme) offered to returnees through the government, partly funded by $30 million pledged by the World Bank, Asian Development Bank and Dutch government.

By contrast to the large-scale movements of internally displaced people toward home, the return of refugees from the state of Tamil Nadu in India was minimal. There were still 66,000 Sri Lankan refugees living in camps in Tamil Nadu run by the Indian authorities, and roughly the same number living outside the camps. UNHCR felt unable to encourage repatriation, given the conditions in areas of potential return, not least the prevalence of mines and unexploded ordnance (UN IDP Working Group 2002). Nevertheless some preliminary discussions with the Indian authorities were held with a view to making preparations for eventual return of refugees currently in Tamil Nadu.

CONCLUSION

The fragile peace in Sri Lanka presented a new set of opportunities and challenges. The opportunities were principally the reconstruction of normal life in the north and east; the possibility of return for those who have been displaced from their homes, within Sri Lanka or outside; and more widely a "peace dividend" for the whole country.

However, the challenges were many. Two are highlighted here. The first related directly to return, for as was noted above, return could generate social instability, tension and friction. The return of Tamils, Muslims and Sinhalese to their districts of origin could well upset the ethnic composition that obtained in those districts during the conflict, with potentially destabilizing political impact. Returnees' attempts to reclaim land and other property—essential for the reconstruction of their livelihoods— could generate tensions where, as was often the case, that land and property had been occupied or taken over by others. Such issues were particularly acute in Jaffna and Mannar districts; in the latter there was the further complication of the prospect of the return of tens of thousands of refugees in India, also seeking to reclaim their land. This could make for a heady cocktail of locally displaced people, internally displaced people returning from other districts, and returning refugees from India—all looking to occupy or recover land for housing and cultivation. One means by which such tensions might be ameliorated, if not eliminated, would be better information exchange among the various communities of displaced people, and particularly across ethnic divides. Displaced people appeared to have little information, knowledge and understanding of the situation of the displaced in other areas, often believing that others were getting more relief and humanitarian assistance. Similarly, poorer segments of the host population often felt that the displaced received more assistance than they deserved, and that they adversely affected the local economy by driving down wages or driving up local rents and prices. Dissemination of reliable and credible information among displaced people and their host communities is itself a means of peace building, and may help to stem, if not reverse, the decomposition of mixed communities into ethnic enclaves.

The second challenge was organizational and to some extent conceptual. While there was still great room for improvement, the organizational structures of the humanitarian regime, including the government, have functioned fairly well in Sri Lanka. If these organizational structures were backed by donor funding, lasting peace in the coming years could be secured. In the short term, however, the emergence of the peace process led to the proliferation of task forces, working groups and subcommittees within the relief and aid system. Coordination almost became an end in itself. The relief and reconstruction system became even more complicated after joint bodies involving the government and the LTTE were formed on many different issues. In common with many "post-conflict" societies, "post-conflict, pre-peace" Sri Lanka has seen a proliferation of organizations and policies with the prefix "re-" in their description: "rehabilitation," "resettlement," "recovery," "reconstruction," "re-awakening." As Hammond (1999: 230–34) and others have pointed out, the use of "re-" words implies a return to the status quo ante, when in fact what is going on is construction of a new society and political economy. In fact, another kind of "re-" process is under way: the "re-casting" of the society and economy, with international and local components of capital seeking to shape it for their purposes. (See chapter 8 of this volume.)

This hints that the real challenges lie not in technocratic organizational change, still less in more "coordination," but in the local, regional and international political economy. As they have done elsewhere in post-conflict societies (Moore 2000), the World Bank and other international financial institutions may attempt to co-opt the humanitarian industry to shape post-conflict Sri Lanka in a neo-liberal mold. Donor assistance for immediate reconstruction needs has already been made conditional on such molding—through reform of the legal system and of property rights, for example. The leverage IFIs and donors will have as a result of Sri Lanka's burgeoning debt (largely military) in coming years will also be substantial. While some such "adjustment" may be warranted, humanitarians will need to be wary of co-optation and be ready to contest the excesses of such leverage if the transition to peace is to be consolidated.

For a brief update on developments in Sri Lanka since this chapter was completed, see the editors' postscript, page 224.

SOURCES

Organizations consulted included: UNHCR (in Colombo, Trincomalee and Vavuniya); the World Food Program; the UN Resident Representative (UNDP); the UN humanitarian advisor to the UN Resident Coordinator; the International Committee of the Red Cross (ICRC); the World Bank's Post-Conflict Unit in Colombo; the British High Commission/Department for International Development; German Technical Cooperation (GTZ); Oxfam; Save the Children Fund; the Dutch non-governmental organization Refugee Care (ZOA) (in Trincomalee); the Danish Refugee Council (in Anuradhapura); the Consortium of Humanitarian Agencies (in Colombo, Trincomalee and Puttalam); and local non-governmental organizations the Trincomalee District Development Association, the Community Trust Fund (in Puttalam), Population Services Lanka (in Trincomalee and Vavuniya), and the War Trauma and Psychosocial Support Program (in Vavuniya). Also consulted were various government officials in Colombo (including the External Resources Department, Ministry of Finance), district and divisional secretaries, ground-level local government officers in various locations, various military officers in the conflict areas, and refugee camp officers and camp committees in various locations. Displaced and war-affected people were consulted in and outside camps and settlements in Batticaloa, Polonnaruwa, Trincomalee, Vavuniya and Puttalam districts. We thank Brian Jeganathan and Renuka Senanayake for their research assistance in Sri Lanka.

Chapter 4

Protracted Displacement in Colombia: National and International Responses

*Patricia Weiss Fagen, Amelia Fernandez Juan,
Finn Stepputat, and Roberto Vidal Lopez*

For over forty years Colombia has experienced conflict, and the rural population has suffered displacement. However, the identification of internally displaced persons (IDPs) as a category of national concern dates only from the early 1990s, as the conflict significantly expanded the areas from which people have been forced to flee.[1] The early zones of conflict and displacement were primarily what are termed "frontier zones," or "zones of colonization," that is, they were remote areas of relatively new agricultural land. Today rural residents are forcibly displaced from the most productive regions of the country, as well as from communities strategically located on the Pacific coast and the Atlantic/Caribbean areas, where armed adversaries compete for control of land and resources. While earlier displacements during the 1980s and early 1990s took place gradually and attracted relatively little attention in Colombia or internationally, the massive and expanding displacements of the later 1990s constitute a recognized humanitarian crisis. The theme of displacement is no longer a subject solely of concern to religious, academic and human rights entities. Both national and international policy makers are beginning to see the phenomenon as a key barometer of the deepening and destructive conflict.

73

Just how many Colombians have been forcibly displaced is much debated. Colombian academics writing at the close of 2001 and combining various sources estimated some 1.7 million (Facultad de Ciencias Juridicas 2001). The population of Colombia is about 41 million. The most recent estimates range from approximately one million since 1994 (RSS: March 31, 2003) to between two and three million, as estimated by various national and international non-governmental sources. The fact that agencies tracking displacement fail to agree is not a reflection of the demographic professionalism of the various researchers. It is due to the differing bases on which the calculations are being made. The state, the Church, non-government organizations (NGOs) and the international agencies[2] have different definitions of who is an internally displaced person. These definitions vary according to whether only those whose flight is due to violence are counted, whether only those formally registered with the government are counted, how long ago the migration took place and whether the IDPs choose to identify themselves. Since the government counts only registered IDPs, and only IDPs who can establish that they are fleeing violence can register, government numbers are always the lowest.

There is agreement from all sources that displacement accelerated dramatically in the mid-1990s. Between 1995 and 1996, the numbers nearly doubled (US Committee for Refugees figures, based largely on CODHES), and saw another alarming increase in displacement between 2000 and 2002. More than half of the IDPs recorded between 1995 and 2002 were displaced during these years. Between 2000 and 2003, the number of municipalities recording displacement doubled from 480 to 955, or 85 percent of the municipalities in Colombia (CODHES April 28, 2003). During 2003, displacement numbers significantly declined for several reasons, including strengthened security imposed by President Alvaro Uribe. Demographic figures show that 48 percent of those displaced were children under 18 years old, while just under half of the adults are women. The Afro-Colombians represent close to a third of the IDP population, and their representation in the population overall is 11 percent. Indigenous Colombians are 5–7 percent of the IDP population, but only 2 percent of the total population (data from CODHES, RSS, UNHCR, Norwegian Refugee Council and the Inter-Agency Network on Internal Displacement).

THE CONFLICT IN COLOMBIA:
ARMED FACTIONS AND DISPLACEMENT

The conflict has proved resistant to resolution despite repeated attempts at negotiation. The irregular armed parties have also rejected attempts to

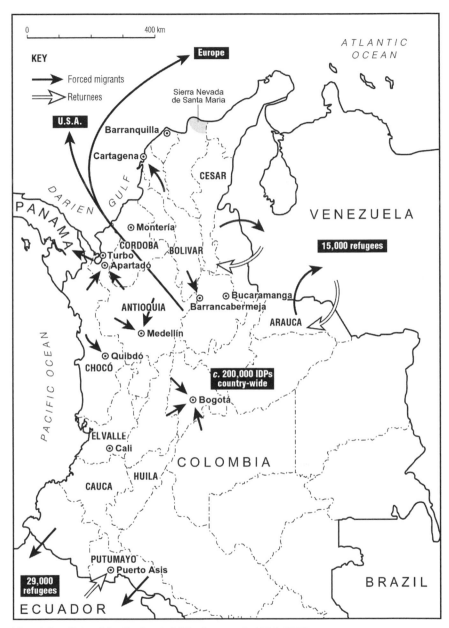

Map 4.1. Colombia: Protracted Displacement, 1994–2003

Source: UNHCR; USCR.

"humanize" their practices that include massacres, hostage taking, and massive displacement. Because they have established bases of support as well as ample funding from narcotics dealers and from kidnapping and other criminal activities, they are not especially vulnerable to public opinion. The drug trade, from which all parties have benefited financially, remains a significant factor in sustaining the conflict. The guerrillas, self-defense units, paramilitary forces, and certainly the drug dealers have amassed considerable wealth and power beyond the reach of the formal state.

The conflict—conflicts more accurately—reflect the complicated political alignments in contemporary Colombia, and all the armed groups cause displacement.

(1) Two guerrilla groups, today known as the Revolutionary Armed Forces of Colombia (FARC: Fuerzas Armadas Revolucionarias de Colombia) and the Army of National Liberation (ELN: Ejército de Liberación Nacional de Colombia), were established in the 1950s and 1960s respectively, both as leftist Marxists. Initially the FARC sought to defend peasants against the encroachments of the elite, and the ELN defended primarily oil field workers. Both pushed the government toward agrarian reform and economic and political change for the benefit of the poor and marginal sectors of the population. However, they since have evolved into military groups engaged in criminal activity and using force to gain territory and political power, often against the very peasant or trade union populations in whose name they have fought. The Colombian government has alternately sought to negotiate peace or to eliminate the guerrilla groups.

In line with the former strategy, a government-negotiated ceasefire brought the FARC into the political process as the Patriotic Union party, and its leaders won 15 seats in Congress in the 1986 elections. When right-wing forces assassinated the party's elected officials and leaders, however, the ceasefire was brought to a close. Memories within the FARC are still sharp, and militate against opting for another surrender of arms for politics. The ELN is negotiating at present through the good offices of the Cuban government.

(2) Some sources trace the present combination of self-defense forces and paramilitary units to a law in 1968 which authorized the creation of private armies. Landowners whose interests were threatened by guerrilla activity or peasant protests organized their own civilian self-defense groups. The irregular forces fighting today, however, derive as much or more from the private armies created by the drug cartels in the 1980s to confront the guerrilla forces threatening their land. The national army, around the same time, organized anti-guerrilla paramilitary forces. The two forces united and grew from decentralized armed mercenaries into

what are collectively known as the United Self-Defense Forces of Colombia (AUC: Autodefensas Unidas de Colombia), and also referred to as *paramilitaries*. They formed a centrally commanded, large, brutal and powerful counter-insurgency force. Though no longer legal and its command less centralized, these forces have had a significantly stronger presence in the conflict areas than the national army. As some units began to demobilize in 2003, violence in a few areas abated. The paramilitary/ AUC units have been far more effective than the regular army in dislodging guerrillas, but have devoted their major efforts to attacking, massacring, and forcibly displacing peasants whom they designate to be subversives (see OAS 1999: ch. 10; UNHCHR 2001a: 12). Government and non-government sources agree that the paramilitary/AUC forces have been responsible for the majority of displacements. Virtually every independent source maintains that the national army is well aware of and backs what the paramilitary units do. The latter have acted in the interests of land holders and the land-holding drug traffickers, to seize land and resources in strategic areas.

(3) Following the break-up of the major drug cartels and the US-backed anti-drug campaigns in Peru and Bolivia in the early 1990s, coca cultivation in Colombia increased and drug traffickers expanded their presence in the sparsely populated areas of Colombia's south and east, where the FARC had been dominant. The paramilitary forces entered to confront the guerrillas and to compete for land and drug money. The FARC, still present, has taxed the producers and become rich. It has also furnished armed guards for coca producers. During the 1990s, the terms "narco-guerrilla" and "narco-paramilitary" entered daily parlance. The drug traffickers seek land of their own, both to grow coca and in order to invest their profits. Accordingly, they have acquired huge tracts of agricultural and cattle grazing lands by following the pattern of the landholders and cattle ranchers and removing the peasants from their smallholdings. Few of the peasants have titles to the land their families have long occupied. This has made the task of uprooting them easier and the prospect of their return less likely.

(4) The state security sectors have proven themselves to be alternately weak and complicit, though President Uribe has been increasing the size and resources of the official military. To this day, few Colombians perform military service and those who do virtually all come from the poorest and least educated sectors. During the 1960s and 1970s, when the violence was concentrated in the zones where the state was weak and where landed elites had always dominated political and economic life, the Colombian national army intervened little. Instead, both the government and army exacerbated the violence by encouraging the establishment of private armies. The army's ability to fight the guerrillas effectively is still much

debated, as is its willingness to rein in the paramilitary forces it initially created to do this job. The links between the army and the paramilitary groups, although denied, seem largely intact; and the record of military interventions to avert paramilitary-induced displacement is practically nil. Nor has the national army acted to prevent guerrilla-induced displacements, because until quite recently the army maintained a policy of not confronting the guerrilla forces in communities under the latter's control.

In brief, during the 1980s and early 1990s, the paramilitary forces confronted the civilian population primarily in the areas where sympathy for the guerrillas was known to be high. The guerrillas, in fact, were protecting peasants in "areas of colonization," that is, in places where the latter had settled on unoccupied land, formally claimed—but not used—by large owners and to which they had no titles. The paramilitary/AUC forces displaced them in the name of preserving private property for the formal owners and in order to eliminate support for guerrillas. After 1994, as noted, drug traffickers expanded operations in Colombia and the guerrillas spread beyond their earlier bases in the poorer departments of the country. The consolidated paramilitary and AUC forces amassed wealth and power, and successfully contested guerrilla control in the latter's previous strongholds. As the armed groups compete in their quests for land, all concerned have profited—save the peasants who continue to be killed and forcibly displaced, and the Colombian state. Violence and displacement today encompass regions of commercial agriculture, large agricultural and cattle ranching holdings, and are on the rise in oil producing sites.

While displacement follows as conflict expands, relatively few among the present population of displaced persons have left simply to flee armed clashes. The majority of the displaced since 1995 attribute their flight to fear, threats, massacres, direct attacks on themselves, and extreme pressures to enter the ranks of the armed parties.

Nor is forced displacement solely the result of violence. The area around Putumayo was wrested from guerrilla influence by the paramilitaries, and is a major site of coca fumigation, supported by US funds. With the initiation of fumigation in 2000, there were predictions of significant increases both in internal displacement and cross-border flight. Until 2002, despite insufficient support to crop substitution programs, sporadic conflict and human rights violations, fewer people than anticipated left the region. Calculating the numbers has been difficult because fumigation migrants could not register with the government's Network of Social Solidarity (RSS) until the end of 2002. They are not considered victims of violence, and therefore were barred by RSS rules from receiving official assistance during its first years of operation. Since October 2002, thanks to a legal ruling in their favor, fumigation migrants have been eligible for registration by the RSS. In reality, the fumigation zones have seen increasing levels of violence since the breakdown of the peace talks in early 2002, and massive displacement has been occurring for combined reasons. Among those most affected by the recent displacements have been indigenous groups.

THE DISPLACED

Everywhere and Invisible

Although the massive displacement of approximately two million people is the most visible outcome of the ongoing conflict, the state has done little to prevent it from occurring. The displaced persons themselves are all but "invisible" in terms of their perceived importance in national policies and geopolitics. Insofar as they are visible, it is in being perceived as collective blights on society. The displaced are blamed for crime, for environmental degradation, and for lowering the living standards of the local populations in the places where they settle. Regardless of how they characterize themselves, they are assumed to have links with one of the armed groups. In Colombia the government is criticized for its failure to adequately address displacement, but it is fair to say the problem has not become an issue of national debate because of humanitarian concern so much as because the IDPs are seen to exacerbate local problems and demand services the state cannot provide.

As displacement has grown to massive proportions, the demography of the nation has been profoundly changed. Over the past several years Colombia has experienced:

- a land concentration in the rural areas that has occurred as a result of the continuing forced flight of peasants and increasing land holdings by drug traffickers and large landowners;
- a doubling or tripling of population in what were once small or medium-sized municipalities; and
- growing expanses of shantytowns in the major urban areas composed of the families of the displaced and other migrants.

These urban influxes severely tax health, education, sanitation services, transportation, electricity and water. They are associated with increased crime and social tensions and, along with other factors, have brought the conflict, once confined to the rural areas, into the heart of Colombia's major cities. Virtually no department in the country remains untouched by the effects of forced migration, having generated displacement, received displaced families, or both. The resulting losses in economic productivity, rural self-sufficiency, and social cohesion are impossible to measure. The human suffering is incalculable.

Patterns of Migration

In the early 1990s poor rural Colombians moved on a continuing basis but in small numbers to towns and cities in search of better socioeconomic opportunities and social services. Most remained in their region of origin, but gradually more individuals and families found their way to the larger cities. This typical form of rural–urban migration was transformed by the end of the decade, and by 2001, some 70 percent of the internal movement was directed at major urban centers. At the same time, political violence rather than poverty became the principal cause of internal migration.

The expanding Colombian conflict and the patterns of displacement coincide. A horizontal axis covers the area from the northwest, the region of Apartadó in Antioquia, to Arauca in the northeast. A second region of large displacement, linked to the first, encompasses almost the entire border area with Venezuela. A third line of conflict beginning in northeast Arauca goes to and through the department of Putumayo. A fourth block of conflict activity takes in parts of departments in the southwest. The small and medium towns and municipal capitals in and around these regions serve both as bases for guerrilla/paramilitary/military actions and as reception points for the persons fleeing the effects of these actions. Only those areas on the Andean slopes to the west and on the Atlantic coast, with stable populations of small and middle-sized holdings, have been able to escape the worst of the conflict.

The concentration of land for illicit products has emerged since 1999 as an additional cause of displacement in new areas of expulsion, such as eastern Antioquia, Sierra Nevada in Santa Marta, the Montes de María range, the north of el Valle and the south of Cauca, central Chocó, the wider Urabá, and Magdalena Medio. In addition to rural–rural and urban–urban displacements, which are more difficult to detect than the rural–urban displacements, a new kind of dynamic has evolved alongside displacement: Increasingly populations have seen themselves being confined to certain areas from where they cannot escape and where they have been deprived of their freedom of movement, and of their access to information, health, livelihoods and even to humanitarian aid.

Since 2002 there has been a significant increase in cross-border movements as well as internal displacement. There are no accurate counts of people crossing into the neighboring countries of Ecuador, Venezuela and Panama, because only a minority register as refugees, but the impacts are visible and add to regional instability.[3] In the case of Ecuador and Venezuela, both civilians and combatants frequently move back and forth. The consequent spillover of conflict into the border areas has complicated the refugees' situation by making humanitarian responses more difficult and raising levels of hostility toward the refugees themselves.

The Venezuelan border area has been the scene of expanding conflict among guerrillas, paramilitaries and drug traffickers, and is now more conflictive as a result of the Colombian and US military efforts to protect the pipeline in Arauco. While Colombians who can afford the airfare have been migrating to Venezuela for decades, now poor peasants are also attempting to cross the difficult and dangerous border to get there. Panamanian authorities until recently kept all but a few from crossing that border. However, UNHCR is now concerned about the rising number of attempts to cross into Panama and its increasingly conflictive border area, while Ecuador is also receiving an increasing number of Colombians.

The largest migration of Colombians is directed toward the industrialized countries, especially to the US and Spain. As of December 2002, the Colombian Ministry of Foreign Affairs estimated over 240,000 Colombians in Spain, of whom 114,000 were registered, and over two million in the US, of whom 540,000 were legally registered.[4] Additionally, by various estimates, the number of Colombians in the UK has reached between 75,000 and 150,000 with some 600–800 official arrivals per year.

The typical pattern of displacement–migration begins either with threats or attacks made against residents of a rural community, or an armed confrontation. The press, human rights reports, and international missions have confirmed dozens—if not hundreds—of such peasant dislocations. An especially large but in other ways typical example is the multiple displacements to Quibdó in the Department of Chocó. Chocó, on the Pacific coast, is one of the poorest departments of Colombia, and has been especially hard hit during the past few years. Its inhabitants are largely Indigenous and Afro-Colombians, ethnic groups that under Colombian law are entitled to self-government. From 1996, the community worked with government officials to gain titles to their properties. Throughout the process, paramilitary groups subjected the indigenous leaders to threats and assassinations. In May 2001, almost immediately after the Land Reform Institute, INCORA (Instituto Colombiano de la Reforma Agraria), finally turned over titles to the land on which two of the communities were located, the new title-holders were brutally expelled by the paramilitary forces. Within a short time, three other communities underwent the same experience, and some 1,422 families from five communities fled to Quibdó. There, they were interviewed by a humanitarian mission organized by the Diocese of Quibdó. The government, along with national and international NGOs including ICRC and Colombian Red Cross, responded with emergency assistance, and put pressure on all sides to permit the IDPs to return. Many did so but, finding their livelihoods to have been destroyed and their personal security to be once again precarious, most returned to Quibdó or went elsewhere (Diocese of Quibdó 2001).

The guerrillas, for their part, increasingly attack peasant families believed to have had dealings with the paramilitary forces and forcibly recruit youth, especially in indigenous communities. They demand active support from the peasant population, and expel those who deny such support (personal interviews with some of those displaced). The FARC has directly targeted civilians where they have sought refuge and, in addition, has been increasingly attacking urban areas. The most dramatic incident occurred in May 2002 in Bojayá, Department of Chocó, where 119 civilians were massacred (*El Tiempo* May 15, 2002). The FARC also struck civilian residences in Bogotá in 2002, although intending to bomb government infrastructure. In 2003, the FARC increasingly launched its attacks in heavily populated major urban centers.

Displaced persons follow well-established paths. The appearance of armed parties and direct threats usually cause an initial flight, which is likely to be to a nearby community to stay with relatives or friends. If the threat is withdrawn or the armed confrontations move on, people may return within a short time, albeit with a strong likelihood that they will be displaced again. (Most of the recorded returns appear to be recently displaced families.) When families find they cannot return, they go to a small or medium-sized municipality in the same district, e.g., Quibdó. The small municipalities, which are ill-prepared to absorb the growing stream of forced migrants and have suffered greatly from conflict, badly need international and national assistance. At the present time, most IDPs are already concentrated in the larger urban areas, which are scarcely better prepared to accommodate their needs. Peasant families have to establish new lives with no preparation for urban culture, residing on illegally held property, lacking most essential services, unable to access health care or education for their children and without economic options.

In addition to these rural–urban movements, humanitarian agencies that try to track displaced persons have increasingly documented continuing movements from one rural town to another, and from city to city, and within urban areas. The continuing movement from place to place is due both to unfulfilled hopes for economic opportunities, and to insecurity; the combined effect of violence and declining prices for Colombian exports has resulted in a general economic deterioration. The insecurity with which the IDPs continue to live is well documented. Interviews with IDPs in and near Barranquilla, Bogotá, and Medellín, confirmed a large number of written accounts attesting to the presence of armed bands in virtually all the sites to which migrants flee, and to a pattern of assassinations against those allegedly collaborating with the enemy (see UNHCHR

2001a: 145; GAD, August 2001: 17; International Crisis Group 2003: 4; CODHES 2003: 3). Most of these assassinations have been carried out by the paramilitary forces with assistance from bands of young delinquents who are paid to identify the targets.

THE COLOMBIAN GOVERNMENT'S RESPONSE TO INTERNAL DISPLACEMENT

International and Regional Precedents to Addressing Displacement in Colombia

Colombians were being forcibly displaced at least two decades before international recognition of IDPs as a vulnerable category of persons in need of protection and assistance. The international attention to displacement, when it did come about, significantly helped to mobilize action on behalf of IDPs among Colombian human rights lawyers and political leaders. The conflicts in Central America during the 1980s gave rise to new regional formulations regarding state responsibilities toward refugees and IDPs. The Cartagena Declaration of 1984 (hosted by Colombia) broadened the definition of refugees and expressed a regional concern for the phenomenon of internal displacement. The resulting International Conference on Central American Refugees, CIREFCA (Conferencia Internacional sobre Refugiados Centroamericanos), launched a Plan of Action that called for combined attention to refugees, internally displaced and returning populations. The international funding for programs that supported the CIREFCA Plan of Action was essential, especially for helping the internally displaced, who far outnumbered the other two categories and were not formally within international agency mandates.

Following CIREFCA, regional attention to IDPs beyond Central America led to the creation of the Permanent Consultation on Displacement in the Americas (CPDIA: Consulta Permanente para el Desplazamiento Interno en las Americas), under the Institute for Human Rights in Costa Rica. Colombia and Peru were the countries of greatest concern. Following its visit to Colombia in the early 1990s, the CPDIA recommended several measures that the Colombian government should take to assist and protect IDPs.

At the international level, the work of Francis Deng brought the problem of internally displaced persons to the center of human rights concerns. After being named UN Special Representative on Internally Displaced Persons in 1992, Deng visited Colombia in 1994 at the invitation of a large group of NGOs and the government. At that time the first serious studies of internal displacement were being produced, most influential of which was the work of the Episcopal Conference of the Catholic Church (Cervellin and Uribe 1994).

Development of Mechanisms for Responding to the Crisis of Displacement

Prior to the Ernesto Samper presidency, 1994–1998, few benefits were available to help the internally displaced. Samper, however, made this issue part of a broader policy emphasizing social responsibility. The Development Plan for 1995–1999, "The Social Leap," included the creation of a National System for Attention to the Internally Displaced Population. However, there were narrow limits placed on conditions for emergency response, and the initiatives lacked budgetary support.

Legislation in 1997 established the basis for a new National Plan for Integral Attention to Displaced Persons and a special fund. The Network of Social Solidarity (RSS), created in 1994 for programs that addressed poverty and helped the most vulnerable sectors, was given broad responsibilities for helping displaced persons. The government established the first official registry of "Persons Forcibly Displaced by Violence."

The legislation gave juridical basis to subsequent national action on behalf of internal displacement. The law anticipated many of the measures in the Guiding Principles on Internal Displacement, promulgated the following year by the UN Special Representative, Francis Deng, which provide a broader definition of an IDP and, contrary to Law 387, ask governments to provide for the safety of returnees to dangerous areas. It was expected, as in the case of CIREFCA, that the international community would provide financial assistance and expertise. The same year, 1997, the government of Colombia issued an invitation to UNHCR to establish an office in Bogotá for IDP protection, which it did in 1998. Thereafter UNHCR officially determined the persons in the government RSS registry to be of concern.

In January 1999, the government of Andres Pastrana adopted a further National Plan for Integral Attention to the Population Displaced by Violence (CONPES 1999). The plan was coordinated by the RSS, which was assigned a broad range of tasks, based on rights affirmed in the basic law on displacement and the subsequent international Guiding Principles on Displacement. Thus, since 1999, the Colombian government has had in place a system that operates on the state, departmental and local levels to meet the challenges of displacement in all its phases. Comprehensive legislation has specified the rights of the displaced and the responsibilities of government entities at all levels. The RSS is mandated to oversee local, departmental and national governmental responses to displacement. Between 1995 and 2000, the government devoted around $60 million to displacement-related activities. In 2001 it spent some $63 million and in 2002, the budget for assistance to the displaced population had risen to $70 million, though expenditure declined in 2003.

Although Colombia has in place the most comprehensive structures in the world for IDPs, a closer look uncovers a system that has been grossly underfinanced and understaffed, in which responsibilities are vaguely defined and officials are rarely if ever held accountable. Virtually every national and international analysis has identified an enormous gap in the Colombian mechanisms on displacement between stated purposes and implementation. By one credible estimate, only one third of the approximately two million internally displaced receive assistance from either the government or international humanitarian agencies (UNICEF 2002). Weaknesses and gaps can be seen in the following areas.

- *Prevention.* The support for early warning systems has been rendered ineffective because the security forces are rarely prepared to intervene to prevent threatened displacements. Knowing that the likelihood of response is small, the potential victims are all the more fearful of reprisals for speaking out in the first place. Seminars on humanitarian law and conflict resolution and human rights accompaniment have produced only isolated successes in preventing displacements from occurring. Despite the fact that human rights protection mechanisms have been constitutionally incorporated into the mandates of all state agencies, the state is incapable of protecting its citizens from violence and displacement even when the state itself is aware of and condemns the violations.
- *Emergency Assistance.* The emergency assistance made available through government and non-government sources falls far short of meeting the humanitarian challenges posed by so large a number of uprooted people. Although the system has been improving over time, it is still common for assistance to reach beneficiaries months after their displacement. The most important weaknesses in Colombia's emergency assistance program are, first, that it is unavailable to large numbers of the internally displaced who, for reasons related to security, timing, difficult access and other causes, are not registered; second, that three months of assistance is far too short.
- *Stabilization.* Internally displaced persons, for the most part, have lost whatever health and education benefits they had in their communities of origin. In their new places of residence, there are numerous bureaucratic obstacles to recovering these services even though they are mandated by law. This problem has been addressed in the 1999, 2001 and 2002 planning documents (CONPES), each time with more specific instructions for including services to IDPs in ministerial bud-

gets. The most recent policy and planning documents address a number of existing loopholes, but the improvements will take time to take effect.

- *Durable Solutions.* Neither international nor national programs have been able to contribute in a meaningful way to creating durable solutions for the victims of displacement. Resettlement projects have been few in number and rarely successful. The Uribe government generated a "Pilot Plan for Returns" as part of the Citizen Security package and related to the attempt of the government to extend the territorial control and defend national sovereignty. More than 7,000 households have returned under government auspices—mostly in collective returns—but little is known yet as to the conditions of material, physical and legal security or respect for the dignity of the returnees as well as the communities of return. However, previous returns have suffered from the fact that no entity has guaranteed the security of returning groups, while there has been no regular monitoring of conditions in places of return, and very few programs are in place to facilitate economic reintegration.

The system overall has been weakened by the tension between its centralized management (in Bogotá) and decentralized operations at the municipal and departmental levels.

For the present, the system does not work as intended and the respective parts of the system do not fulfill the roles and responsibilities they have been assigned. The obstacles are largely institutional and financial, but the problems are exacerbated by a lack of political will among the key policy actors and, obviously, the failure to win concessions from the armed groups toward "humanizing" their methods of warfare.

The institutional and financial issues are closely related. The rights guaranteed to internally displaced persons depend on the ability of hospitals to afford medical attention, schools to accept significantly more students, urban services to be extended to encompass areas previously marginal to the cities involved, and so on. A key problem lies in the bottlenecks and tensions in Colombia's system of resource allocation generally and particularly in relation to the displaced population.

The fact that the national ministries and corporations have policy mandates to provide funding for IDPs, and that the law and the National Planning Department have affirmed the IDPs' rights to services, does not mean that IDPs actually will receive services. The national government determines the overall budget, which is allocated to departments, and from departments to municipalities, on the bases of availability and population. Delivery of social services in Colombia has been decentralized, so each department or municipality pays for services from these previously budgeted resources. A departmental or municipal budget may be increased if the population grows, but the additional resources can be allocated only if the municipal and departmental entities include the new population in the planning figures they submit. In fact, local planners rarely try to accommodate newly arriving migrants. More often than not, the IDP population is not counted in planning figures. Even when municipalities do calculate IDPs in their population for budgetary purposes and ask for additional resources, the funds are allocated, if at all, for the following year, by which time the population is likely to have grown even more.

Of particular concern in this respect are the problems of health care and education, both of which should be free and available to IDPs. But in reality, IDP access to these services is very patchy. IDP informants nearly all denied that their children were receiving primary education free of charge, a fact confirmed in numerous national and international organizations' reports. Although not charged tuition in local schools, the children usually have to buy uniforms and school supplies and pay other bureaucratic costs that, for many families, prove prohibitive. Nor are there sufficient schools or teachers in the rapidly growing urban areas.

Municipal and departmental authorities lack motivation to productively incorporate the IDPs under their jurisdiction. A determination to incorporate IDPs in the social and economic fabric of a community, they contend, would attract even more arrivals. A second important impediment is the weakness of municipal institutions. Finance, health, education, and planning officials often lack the technical experience needed to "work" their respective national bureaucracies and obtain needed resources. As will be discussed below, international agencies have made it a priority to strengthen local institutions for this reason. A third problem lies in the persistent notion that the problems faced by IDPs can be solved with the mechanisms and institutional vehicles in place for assisting Colombia's poor. However, since the displaced population is so numerous and its members often lack fixed addresses, property, identity documentation, and even minimum sources of income, they are unable to meet the requirements that a stable population would meet for access to the services they require (such as social services, credit lines, health, and housing subsidies).

Internally displaced persons are held in disdain and stigmatized. Because they are unwelcome, they are not treated as citizens of the places where they reside, even if they have stayed there for some time. Unable to find work, obliged to take possession of property illegally, many eventually conform to society's negative image of them. Their conditions of life often lead them to treat public authorities with distrust and hostility, and their need to survive may drive many of them to illegal acts and criminal activities.

THE PERSPECTIVE OF DISPLACED PERSONS: THEIR ORGANIZATIONS AND THE EXPERIENCE OF ASSISTANCE

As previously described, the route from the former home to the place of refuge is seldom a straight line. If the immediate danger that produces displacement passes, people will usually return. Those who cannot return follow routes determined by a need for safety, a means of livelihood, and the possibility of social integration (CODHES 2000). They are likely to be following the former routes of family members, of friends, and of people who come from the same locality. The small municipalities that the migrants first reach, in most cases, are temporary stops. One third or more move on within a short time to a different, usually larger city, still seeking safety, livelihood, and social integration. The tendency has been for more families to migrate toward larger urban areas, in turn prompting other family members and friends to follow. In this sense, the displaced population is "floating," trying out different opportunities but finding no respite due to continued problems of security or lack of accommodation.

The places of arrival are typically either 1) existing neighborhoods where IDPs blend in with "historically displaced"—more traditional rural–urban migrants—and "socially displaced"—poor people who have been squeezed out of the inner cities by the recent processes of gentrification; or 2) new settlements on illegally occupied public or private land. The process of urbanization in these areas takes place, by and large, beyond the control of local authorities. The newcomers are exploited from the start. Often groups of middlemen, called "urbanization pirates," sell the right to build houses on the land, and the buyers receive receipts with no legal value. In Bosa, within the federal district of Bogotá, an estimated 50 percent of residents live on properties that have not been titled. On the employment side, *tinteros*, the ambulant hot coffee street vendors, are exploited by people who rent equipment to them, or who make them work in exchange for food or rent on land they own or control.

Urban accommodation is usually very insecure and substandard with little developed physical or social infrastructure. The authorities have difficulties in communicating with the newcomers, because of the lack of trust and confidence on both sides, and the fact that land invasion has been criminalized. Thus, the displaced cannot participate in the basic entities of local governance, the Juntas de Acción Comunal. Nor do they receive services, at least not without special and costly arrangements in their areas of residence.

A further significant source of insecurity is the ongoing rivalry of the armed parties for control over the population, which has reached the outskirts of the cities. "You never sleep peacefully here," as one IDP said. People are afraid that the parties that displaced them once will keep looking for them. Groups of 10–50 armed men, *los encapuchados* (hooded men), undertake "social cleansing" as they beat, threaten, or cause young men to disappear, on the excuse of a supposed theft or other crime. They frequently tax the inhabitants, especially the local traders. Community leaders are particular targets of threats, including, of course, IDP leaders. The displacements caused by the urban conflicts between paramilitary and guerrilla groups are not recorded, but are obviously a major factor prompting the growing inter- and intra-urban movements. The IDPs generally do not trust public security forces, and the latter do not attempt to intervene in these situations.

In some urban and semi-urban locations in Colombia, IDPs have formed what are called "peace communities." The idea was developed during the 1990s, often supported by the Catholic Church. One of the best known peace communities is the Nelson Mandela neighborhood in Cartagena. Peace communities have been established in contested areas such as Urabá and Chocó, in order to provide safety for returning communities. They are based on rules of neutrality and independence from any of the armed parties in the conflict. The members of peace communities are unarmed, unaffiliated and refuse all support from the armed groups. By and large, the latter have not honored these rules, however, despite the frequent presence of international observers. At times police or army troops have offered to protect the residents of the peace communities, but the latter not only distrust the security forces, they also insist that an armed presence will attract violence rather then control it.

Up until October 9, 2002, when regulations were relaxed, to enter the governmental system of humanitarian aid the IDPs had to register with the RSS within a year following displacement, and establish that they had been displaced by political violence. However, a large number of IDPs never have registered because they could not meet the requirements or chose not to register for other compelling reasons.

First, considering the stigma inherent in the label of *desplazado*, families often do not register if they are able to manage life in the city through their own networks and capabilities. Second, in addition to the general suspicion of government bodies, people are afraid that if it becomes known that they are living illegally on a property, or are part of an illegal land invasion, the authorities will forcibly remove them from the places they occupy. Third, the RSS determines eligibility on the basis of a long and intrusive questionnaire that includes questions relating to the reasons for displacement. Many IDPs fear that their statements will not be confidential and they will be identified to their pursuers. Rumors abound that the information is passed on to the paramilitaries. Many people view the risks of giving up anonymity and invisibility as too high, especially in view of the small benefits provided by the humanitarian system. Fourth, a large percentage of the IDPs do not have personal documentation. To remedy this lack, UNHCR has supported a mobile registration unit that can issue birth certificates. Finally, it seems that many people do not know about the possibility of receiving assistance, or do not know where to go and what to do. Therefore several agencies (e.g., La Defensoría, UNHCR, and WHO/PAHO) produce and distribute information on the definition, the rights, and the possibilities of IDPs.

By permitting registration only within the first year after displacement has taken place, the system excludes several categories of persons who might otherwise register: first, persons who became IDPs prior to the 1997 law; second, anyone who was displaced more than a year previously, whether or not that person received emergency assistance from ICRC; third, the large and growing number of people who are victims of multiple forced displacements. The fairly detailed registration form is passed on to the local "technical unit" of the RSS where screening is undertaken. In principle registrations are accepted on the basis of "good faith" since the RSS does not have investigative capacity. Officers interviewed in 2001 disagreed on how often applications were rejected, but agreed that the major reason was that the applicant was not judged to have been forcibly displaced by violence. In practice, it appears that only a small percentage is actually rejected. A new "single registration system" (the RUT: Registro Unico Tributario) which has been in effect since 2002 permits the RSS to detect if a person has received assistance in other places before.

Frequently it may take two or three months before families receive the three months' worth of assistance to which they are entitled. However, it is generally agreed that nearly all the families are vulnerable and three months is woefully inadequate. The arbitrariness and inadequacies of the system are exacerbated by the fact that there is little or no follow-up action. The majority of IDPs interviewed by the authors of this chapter maintained that the hospitals and clinics would turn them away. This was confirmed in a visit to a Médecins sans Frontières (MSF) clinic in the IDP community of Soacha. The MSF doctor noted that she had to intervene personally to convince the local medical facility to take even very grave cases. Schools would tell IDPs that there was no room or oblige them to pay for supplies and uniforms. The establishment of new schools in the migrant areas is far behind the needs. In any case, assuming they can reach a health facility and there are schools nearby, the IDPs usually pay both for health and education, albeit at reduced amounts. While a few municipalities and departments are keen on helping IDPs to establish themselves permanently within their jurisdiction, several municipalities have actively deterred access; at best the IDP population is ignored.

Projects for income-generation and training are few, and those that do exist tend to be short term and not sustainable. Many NGOs, reportedly, prefer to fund psychosocial projects. Psychosocial support is doubtless badly needed among all segments of the IDP population. Yet, when introduced as a stand-alone project, it is not always appreciated by the IDPs, whose priority is remunerated labor. "They bring us psychologists who tell us we are traumatized, but we are peasants and we need to work."

As in other places where relief assistance has been institutionalized, the humanitarian system in Colombia has generated attitudes and dynamics of distrust and mutual recriminations between the IDP organizations and the assistance providers. The registration practices and the project mechanisms seem to be based on the logic of limiting expenses by applying strict criteria, cut off points, and layers of control. The assistance agencies, which are nearly always understaffed, are confronted with overwhelming demands and huge numbers of needy people, and they therefore engage in what amounts to mob control.

This kind of experience of being kept outside, marginalized, and under control, yet receiving only minor contributions to their livelihoods has embittered the IDPs. As one leader put it: "In the countryside we worked all day, here we have nothing. We go asking people, we go knocking on doors, we are begging on our knees in order to have something to eat. But we are rejected, everybody sees us as thieves and *maleandros* (wrongdoers). We are disposable people." Relief workers have complained that the IDPs and their leaders show resentment, ingratitude and stubbornness, and are demanding and aggressive. Some of the relief workers point to such attitudes as diminishing the legitimacy of the IDP claims to be victims: "true" IDPs would be humble and grateful. The IDP leadership is typically blamed for inculcating bad manners among the group overall, and authorities tend to discount the assertion that the organizations actually represent the IDPs.

The IDP leadership and IDP organizations do face problems of representation, legitimacy and effectiveness. To the extent that the leaders are acknowledged, they are seen as the easily manipulated tools of one of the armed parties and as motivated by ideology or greed. The organizations are sometimes artificial constructs, created primarily in order to allow the IDPs to receive assistance. NGOs and government bodies are usually required to manage projects with legally recognized organizations. Most are precluded from entrusting individuals to manage funds, land, or small projects.

From the point of view of the IDPs and their leaders, the function of their organizations is to claim their rights as victims of the political situation. They insist that the government has a legal and moral duty to assist them: "We have analyzed the word 'migrant,' but no, we are not migrants because we were forced out—we are refugees of a war. But it is not an open war—the government covers the sun with the hand, saying there is no war, but we are the living testimony of this dirty war, we are living its effects every day." The organizations are well equipped with all the relevant laws, decrees, constitutions, human rights declarations, and statistics. They adopt the appropriate legal language and can differentiate among the legal options for holding authorities accountable for their responsibilities.

That the leaders have educated themselves about their rights does not signify that the average IDP is equally aware. Despite the numerous workshops and rights-based education events sponsored by community leaders, local and international NGOs and UN agencies and human rights offices, dissemination of such information remains limited. When the researchers asked why advocates for IDP rights did not publish popular education type flyers and simple-format literature for wide distribution among IDPs, they were told that the advocates feared the consequences of doing so. They believed that anyone found to be holding or distributing material explaining IDP rights would be at risk of reprisals from armed parties.

A few IDP leaders have contacted sympathetic legal experts to intercede with authorities on their behalf. In the universities and in private practice, there are lawyers who bring cases of IDP rights to the courts, help IDP communities obtain titles to the land they occupy, demand compensation for stolen land, and represent the IDP interests before national, departmental and municipal authorities. The IDPs make ample use of the government bodies put in place to defend citizen rights, especially the Defensoría del Pueblo, whose offices can be found in every department. IDPs and their advocates have brought thousands of complaints to these offices, but favorable legal decisions have rarely been translated into action.

However, the situation is further complicated by the fact that one or another of the armed groups identifies the large IDP concentrations as under its protection, even though most of the residents are committed to none. Depending on which of the armed parties caused the displacement of a particular group, the other will offer the group its "protection." Both guerrillas and paramilitaries recruit young unemployed IDPs in the settlements to spy and report on activities. The position of IDP leaders and representatives is especially dangerous, because both guerrillas and para-military units strive to eliminate any organization outside of their control. The staff of the UN Special Representative on Displaced Persons charac-terized Colombia as being "probably the world's most dangerous country for leaders of displaced persons organizations and for the local NGOs that help them" (UN-ECOSOC 2000: 10). Needless to say, this situation poses a painful dilemma for international agencies like UNHCHR and UNHCR, which have supported and encouraged IDP leadership, yet know that more effective leaders are also more vulnerable to assassina-tion.

In sum, IDP organizations lack strength both in political and opera-tional terms. The organizations are divided; they compete for resources, over leadership, and over the right to represent the IDPs. IDP unity is further undermined by political and ethnic differences among groups, who often coexist in the same settlements. There are no national-level coalitions of IDP organizations, although there is a national umbrella group of IDP organizations that includes representatives from 17 depart-ments. It has held two national assemblies, which called on the govern-ment to integrate the displacement issue into the peace process (Cohen and Sánchez-Garzoli 2001: 8).

The IDP population is drawn predominantly from rural areas where educational levels, health indices, and income are lower than national averages. Within this population, these indices are lower still for women. According to figures compiled by the UN, women are the heads of approximately 25 percent of IDP families in rural areas and 49 percent in urban areas (Sistema de las Naciones Unidas 2002). It is believed that many women migrate with their children in order to protect the latter from forced recruitment. Among the women displaced by conflict, 15 per-cent are estimated to be illiterate, as compared with 8 percent of those displaced for other reasons and 6 percent of women who are not among the displaced. Women lack documentation far more often than men, and therefore are unable to access needed services on their own.

In 2001, the Association for the Well-being of the Colombian Family (PROFAMILIA), a Colombian government agency, undertook a compre-hensive study of internally displaced women and their access to repro-ductive health services (Ojeda and Murad 2001). Within a broadly based representative sample of women studied, the IDPs were found during their reproductive years, to have more children (5.3) than the rural popu-lation overall (4.8) and to continue the pattern even after they had resided some time in urban zones—where the reproductive rate is approximately 3.4. The study found 8 percent of the women between the ages of 15 to 49 to be pregnant at the time they were interviewed, which investigators estimated to be double the national figure. Only one fourth of them had wanted the pregnancy at that time. Less than one half received prenatal care (Ojeda and Morad 2001: 45, 49–50). Of greater concern was the high level of pregnancy among adolescents: 30 percent of interviewees between 13 and 19 had been pregnant, 23 percent were already mothers (Ojeda and Morad 2001: 116). Among the interview sample, 9 percent reported having been raped since displacement (Ojeda and Morad 2001: 72–73).

There are few women leaders among the displaced persons organizations, but UNHCR and other agencies have made it a priority to support training workshops and seminars for women in order to engage their participation and encourage more female leadership. In May 2001, UNHCR held a national consultation with displaced women, to determine their specific needs in relation to age and situation, and to interpret the Guiding Principles from a gender perspective with reference to protection and rights (UNHCR and OCHA 2001).

According to Save the Children, some three million Colombian children and youth have been involved in or directly affected in some way by armed conflict: they may be armed combatants, demobilized combatants, internally displaced persons, or victims of kidnapping or of land mine accidents. As previously noted, it is estimated that children constitute over 48 percent of the IDP population. In the year 2000, 267 children were kidnapped and 600 killed in combat. Four out of every ten guerrilla combatants killed were minors, and over 5,250 minors have died in land mine accidents (figures from the Office of the Vice President).

Children's involvement in armed conflict has been marked despite broad international and domestic legal restrictions against it. While there are no firm figures on the number of children and youth either in the guerrilla or paramilitary groups, it is estimated that some 6,000 children directly participate in military actions (UNICEF 2000).

In the light of this situation, government prevention programs are focusing more on keeping children from participating in the war, as are the programs for humanitarian and legal assistance, rehabilitation, reintegration and treatment of children, supported by legal and humanitarian agencies. The effects on children as a result of their experiences in conflict undoubtedly are as varied as the experiences themselves. We do not yet know the scars that have resulted, or how these will affect their social lives and relationships in the future. A 2003 Human Rights Watch report, however, gives children's accounts of the effects of bearing arms and their reasons for joining (HRW 2003).

Local NGOs

The relationship between local NGOs and IDP organizations is sometimes problematic, with unavoidable competition for donor funding between NGOs and IDP organizations, fueling some of the common allegations and mutual recriminations.

Human Rights and Advocacy

A number of the NGOs that have long defended human rights have taken on internal displacement as a priority concern. Colombian human rights organizations brought internal displacement to the early attention of the Inter-American Human Rights Commission of the Organization of American States and invited the UN Special Representative for Internal Displacement to Colombia before the Guiding Principles on Internal Displacement were drafted. The several non-government entities that defend the internally displaced have prominently used the Principles in their efforts. Additionally, they typically collaborate closely with the government's human rights mechanisms and with international NGOs and UN agencies.

To date, these NGOs have devoted their efforts to three kinds of tasks: collecting and disseminating information about displacement and the effects of displacement on human rights; representing IDP rights and interests before local and national authorities; and accompanying threatened communities. Threatened communities include those where people are under pressure to leave their original homes, are living in settlements and attempting to resist incursions of armed groups, or are in a return process with no other source of security. The human rights organizations, for the most part, make it a priority to establish good relations with IDP leaders, and to follow their lead. Such advocacy is difficult in Colombia, and repeated failures to stem violent displacement have created frustration and disappointment even among those most committed.

IDP Assistance Projects

There is a much larger pool of local NGOs that implement relief projects of their own or of the international agencies, and have proven capable of making more serious contributions to the quality of IDP life. The international agencies working in Colombia report good results from the majority of the local NGOs with which they have been working.

Options for IDPs and Their Supporters

The possibilities open to IDPs to improve their conditions lie in 1) demanding rights, 2) returning to their homes, 3) finding an alternative place to settle and work.

Demanding Rights through the Courts

Legal channels are available to IDPs for asserting their rights. The usual procedure for IDPs is to bring a complaint to a Defensoria del Pueblo. This institution, created to uphold citizens' rights, has devoted a major portion of its institutional resources to making formal complaints to political authorities and the courts on behalf of IDPs. They have been successful by and large, but thus far the successes have not translated into visible improvements. The well-meaning judges who have heard the *tutelas* brought before the courts often have upheld the rights that the IDPs are claiming. They are not, however, well equipped to design the solutions, and instead have frequently placed unrealistic demands for action on the RSS or local authorities. When decisions are contrary to policy or previous planning, the efforts to implement them may even worsen the existing situation. As of 2004, the Constitutional Court issued a general sentence, on the basis of 200 *tutelas* that have not led to any government action, declaring that the general state of affairs regarding the IDPs was unconstitutional and that the government must take action to solve the problem of displacement.

Return Projects

International agencies and IDP advocates question the option of return as still dangerous in most cases, and the IDPs interviewed virtually all concluded that they would not be able to return in the short or medium term. The European Commission Humanitarian Office (ECHO) occasionally has supported returns, but only if the group returning is accompanied by a national NGO. As already described in this report, NGO accompaniment does not assure safety.

Those participating in a return project sanctioned by the government receive a package containing tickets for transport, food and a basic tool kit for reconstruction. Until the Uribe administration, they were not given any assurances of security and had to sign declarations that they would take on this responsibility themselves. Since President Uribe assumed office, a few return projects have been accompanied with security forces assigned to remain for a short period of time, and the government has put in place some local development efforts. Thus far, these initiatives have been few and small scale, affecting only a limited number of beneficiaries whose places of origin are amenable to government protection.

A key issue is whether a returning IDP can recover the family land. Thus far, authorities organizing the return movements have been unable to resolve the legal issues entailed in land and property restoration. UNHCR has taken on this task to a small degree, and the Uribe administration has been promoting a program of land and property registration in places vulnerable to displacement. Returnees' land, if not taken over by parties to the conflict, is likely to be occupied by someone else, in which case the original owners may have to pay rent for access to their own plots. A major gap in IDP protection is the absence of reparations for the losses related to displacement, despite the fact that these are stipulated in Law 387.

Resettlement

Since the majority of IDPs do not believe they will be able to return to their homes, many hope to be resettled in another rural area or, alternatively, have the possibility of working with people with similar backgrounds and values. When they are resettled, the agricultural land they receive is usually in relatively safe areas. Yet, for other reasons, the resettlement projects tend to fail. First, the Land Reform Institute, INCORA, has identified very few plots of land that the state controls and that can be turned over to IDPs. Consequently, INCORA usually locates the IDPs on privately owned and long-uncultivated properties. The IDPs are obliged to pay rent before they can produce anything and while they are clearing, preparing and planting the private land. This generally presents an unsustainable financial hardship, since the IDPs have already suffered the loss of personal property, and have usually exhausted their resources in the course of migration. Second, a large number of owners have reportedly demanded the return of their land after the first crop comes in, leaving the IDPs again without a means of livelihood. Third, the government limits its involvement to identifying the plot of land for settlement by IDPs. According to international agencies and domestic organizations working with IDPs who have been resettled under these conditions, very little planning goes into either the compatibility of the proposed residents, or the economic viability of the proposed productive activity. The state does not assist in marketing the products.

INTERNATIONAL HUMANITARIAN INVOLVEMENT

Unlike many of its Latin American neighbors, Colombia has previously had very little experience of international development assistance. Today, Colombia is a major recipient of relief and development funding, as well as the target of various international initiatives to adopt measures for cutting coca production, bringing the conflicting parties to the peace table, and revitalizing the much-deteriorated economy. With regard to the growing problem of internal displacement, many Colombians credit the international community for repeatedly raising the problem and maintaining pressure on the Colombian government to improve its institutional and political responses. At the same time, they criticize the relatively small overall presence of international agencies, and the uneven and unbalanced geographic coverage of UN programs.

The major international organizations now operating in Colombia have oriented their humanitarian programs to take account of the situation of massive nationwide displacement. On the UN side, the agencies involved in working on displacement have come together in the Thematic Group on Displacement, led by UNHCR and supported by OCHA. The members of the Thematic Group include UNHCR, UNHCHR, WFP, PAHO/WHO, UNDP, UNICEF, FAO, and UNDCP. The World Bank and IOM are also members. Additionally, ICRC, ECHO, and the Joint Technical Unit of the RSS attend meetings as observers. The Thematic Group is generally considered a reasonably effective mechanism, but not a coordinating body. Only in late 2002 did the agencies embark on a serious effort to develop a common strategy for addressing the IDP issue, but in the absence of a joint funding mechanism.

Because of the donors' priority for moving the peace process forward, they have shown a preference for supporting projects aimed at reconciliation, conflict resolution and early warning. Such projects, along with productive initiatives located in sending regions, comprise the essence of what the RSS classifies as "prevention" activities. An important example of how peace promotion and displacement prevention coincide is the "Peace Laboratory" in Magdalena Medio, to which the European Union has pledged €34 million over a period of eight years (EU 2002). Other donors as well—especially UNDP—are committed to this endeavor. Magdalena Medio is a major IDP producing region, whose capital, Barrancabermeja, is one of the largest and most conflictive of the IDP receiving cities. The project proposes to build a zone of peaceful coexistence sustained by local institutions and citizen participation.

The international agencies' programs for the displaced in Colombia have a limited reach both geographically and in time. Even in the regions where displaced persons are concentrated and where there are many programs for them, it is difficult to reach more than a small percentage of the population. A considerable—and certainly important—focus of international agency work has been devoted to advocacy and supporting IDP associations. There is relatively little international contribution to emergency assistance (deemed to be the responsibility of the government), and the international agencies have come to emphasize longer-term "stabilization" projects to help integrate IDPs economically and socially. The donors have also contributed to institution and capacity building projects aimed at strengthening the Colombian government's local and national response mechanisms, including those related to human rights. Most of the international agencies remain skeptical of return projects, in which the present government shows particular interest, on grounds of continuing insecurity. There is, however, support for strengthening local economic development in the regions that generate displacement.

It does not appear resources will be sufficiently increased to permit an expanded international humanitarian involvement. The combined operational budget of UN agencies for attending to IDPs was a mere $17 million in 2001 (UN Senior Inter-agency Network 2001). For 2003, the UN system budget for displacement was $47 million. The government depends on outside funding for over 50 percent of the cost of its IDP programs, calculated at about $78 million for 2002, up from $70 million in 2001.

All agree that the international presence and its support for multiple national programs have been grossly inadequate. The primary responsibility, they insist, belonged with the government, with international initiatives serving as supplemental and complementary to government action. The government shares this view, but insists that it cannot fund the needed staff levels and activities. Advocates for the displaced expressed their fear that international support will shrink rather than expand, as agencies become frustrated by the small results of their long involvement and by the continuing conflict.

The following agencies are prominent in protecting and assisting internally displaced persons. The activities and approaches elaborated below are illustrative of the various aspects of international involvement: protection/advocacy, emergency response, short and medium term assistance, capacity building and institutional strengthening, and social services.

United Nations High Commissioner for Human Rights, UNHCHR

The Colombian government invited the United Nations High Commissioner for Human Rights to establish an office in Colombia in 1996 in order to observe and advise the authorities regarding the formulation and implementation of its human rights policies and programs "in the context of violence and internal armed conflict that the country has been experiencing." The mandate of the office has been renewed yearly. Its international staff numbers 24, and it maintains a presence in the various regions of the country.

UNHCHR seeks to hold the state responsible for fulfilling its international obligations in human rights. In addition to monitoring the situation of internal forced displacement throughout the country, the UN Human Rights office has called on the government nationally and locally to act more forcefully in preventing it. Its prevention work involves collaboration with government authorities, other international agencies, especially UNHCR, and NGOs in order to enhance governmental and international protection in high-risk communities. The office devotes its expertise to strengthening the national institutions in the judicial and law enforcement sectors that are charged to defend rights, primarily by means of training for officials in the security and judicial sectors.

The UN Human Rights Office has established ongoing relations with Colombian officials at the municipal and departmental levels as well as at the national level. It also has pursued partnerships with and given support to human rights organizations, within and especially outside of the government. Organizations and individuals throughout the country bring complaints of human rights violations, including displacement, to UNHCHR.

United Nations High Commissioner for Refugees, UNHCR

In 1997, the government of Colombia invited UNHCR to establish an office in the country. At first UNHCR's major donors, primarily the US and Canada, were wary of establishing a national program with a caseload almost entirely devoted to internally displaced persons, but ultimately agreed on the formulation of a regional program that encompassed Colombia's internal caseload, along with the refugee caseload in Ecuador, Venezuela, and Panama. In 1998, UNHCR established its office in Bogotá, but with only one international official. This was an inauspicious beginning given the already large dimensions of the problem, but the office engaged in activities that proved useful both to Colombia's governmental and non-governmental sectors. Both the government and Geneva Headquarters came to support a stronger role for UNHCR in Colombia, and the staff presently consists of 18 international officials and 3 UN volunteers. UNHCR now operates suboffices outside of Bogotá, in Barrancabermeja (Magdalena Medio), Apartadó (Urabá), and Puerto Asis (Putumayo). In 2003 the agency opened another office on the Atlantic Coast in Barranquilla.

UNHCR concentrates its activities on promoting protection in the framework of the Guiding Principles on Internal Displacement, with particular attention to prevention efforts. It combines support, including material support, for national agencies that defend IDPs and IDP rights, and strengthening of national, departmental and local institutions that serve IDP rights and needs.

UNHCR supports IDPs directly through their representative organizations and indirectly through their advocates. It has organized encounters, workshops and seminars, often jointly with ICRC, UNHCHR, or both, for a wide range of sectors in Colombian politics and society. UNHCR has also organized documentation campaigns among IDPs, a large number of whom lack the basic identity cards needed to access nearly all state services. It has issued publications about indigenous rights and gender, jointly with advocates and other UN agencies, and gives priority attention to women and indigenous groups among the displaced. The agency confers with national NGOs. While some Colombian NGOs advocating for IDP rights believe that UNHCR's potential protection capacities have been constrained by its close relations with the government, most acknowledge that such relations are a necessity, and maintain that the protection support UNHCR affords is of value.[5]

Finally, UNHCR monitors Colombian borders, working closely with its offices in Ecuador and Venezuela, and a UNHCR representation in Panama, the neighboring countries that increasingly receive refugees from Colombia. As previously noted, cross-border flight grew rapidly after the demilitarized zone was closed in the latter part of 2002, and the conflict zone expanded.

International Committee of the Red Cross, ICRC

The International Committee of the Red Cross has 53 international staff members in Colombia, approximately 200 national employees, and operates 17 offices throughout the country. Although ICRC has been in Colombia for about 20 years, its presence and the range of activities it undertakes have grown during the last seven years due to war, displacement and generally deteriorating humanitarian conditions. ICRC now plays a very significant role in assisting IDPs, having established a response capacity in parts of the country where the government is not present. ICRC probably reaches the largest number of IDPs, thanks to its activities in the conflict zones, as well as in the previously guerrilla-controlled demilitarized zone, closed in 2002.

ICRC operates a combined program of protection and assistance. It verifies reports of executions, disappearances of civilians, hostage taking, threats and displacements. Its delegates dispense medical assistance to war-wounded people, visit detainees, disseminate humanitarian law and train government authorities, regular and irregular security forces, and other sectors, and they act as intermediaries among adversaries. ICRC policy is to respond to emergency needs in those areas where government assistance is not available in order to avoid duplicating government relief programs or taking over activities that the government should be managing. ICRC also finances small community-based quick-impact projects (QIPs), initiated in 2000, primarily but not exclusively for the benefit of the internally displaced.

In its direct assistance for IDPs, ICRC takes responsibility for responding quickly with emergency assistance when there are rural displacements of over 10 families or over 50 people. QIPs are generally limited to helping to build small infrastructure (schools, health clinics, etc.) or supporting a few food cultivation projects in rural areas.

ICRC plays a small role in facilitating the return of individuals to their homes. When people have fled due to threats against their lives, ICRC is sometimes able to negotiate their return, just as it participates in negotiations related to some kidnapping cases. These returns, however, are almost always individual in nature.

World Food Program, WFP

The World Food Program has been in Colombia since 1969. The Colombian government asked WFP to create a program in 2000 to directly benefit IDPs. The project, Extended Relief and Recovery, is being executed by WFP jointly with the RSS, the Colombian Institute of Family Welfare (ICBF: Instituto Colombiano de Bienestar Familiar) and a variety of national and international NGOs. Half of the approximately $20 million project budget comes from the government, with WFP contributing the other half. WFP works in 12 departments with high concentrations of IDPs. The Relief and Recovery program had four components: relief assistance, which operates under a joint agreement with ICRC; food for massive displacements; food for work, intended for resettlement projects and returns; and training. The Relief and Recovery program is intended to help people move beyond direct relief assistance to greater economic security. As is emphasized in its own publications, however, WFP is aware that so long as families can neither return to their homes nor resettle in zones that are secure, serious planning for a process of recuperation is unrealistic; hence the program focuses on project activities that can contribute to self-sufficiency and stability (WFP 2000). WFP has revised its initial approach to the food for work program as a support for resettlement and return. Concluding that the security conditions do not permit returns and finding that resettlement projects are few and generally unsuccessful (WFP 2001a), WFP began in 2001 to use its food for work resources to offer vocational training and support short-term agricultural projects.

In reality, food insecurity for the internally displaced is WFP's major concern. The government's emergency relief package of three months not only is insufficient, but leaves IDPs without resources during the period when they are probably most vulnerable, namely, after they have spent whatever resources they may have brought, used up the government-donated ration (assuming they received it in the first place) and find themselves with no employment prospects. A WFP study in May 2001 confirmed that IDPs are exposed to a prolonged period of hunger for between four months and two years after displacement (WFP 2001). WFP has oriented its programs for preschool children and pregnant women toward the displaced population by placing services in districts where the number of displaced is high. Agency representatives described the strategies it has developed for reaching beyond the school population to involve the most vulnerable families in its programs; this has included particular assistance for women.

International Organization for Migration, IOM

In the latter part of 2000, the International Organization for Migration initiated a Post-Emergency Assistance Program for the Displaced Population and for Receiving Communities. IOM has been one of the few agencies whose program is targeted almost exclusively to the longer-term stabilization components of IDP assistance, reflecting the orientation of USAID, which has furnished a major portion of the funds for IOM's IDP program. IOM has selected its work sites in departments where the impact of displacement is deemed to be greatest, including the more sparsely populated Putumayo, which is the primary site of US-funded coca fumigation carried out under Plan Colombia. IOM and UNHCR collaborate on activities in the frontier zone on both sides of the border with Ecuador, and the IOM's role in the countries bordering Colombia has grown as refugee flight has risen significantly.

IOM's activity in IDP receiving communities is based on the premise that the Colombian government's weak response to IDPs is due in large part to the inadequacies of its institutions at the local level. Acknowledging that municipal authorities are often unwilling to formulate and request projects on behalf of IDPs, IOM has initiated projects that provide both incentives and technical assistance for municipal offices. IOM has for example trained municipal hospital administrators on the bureaucratic procedures for obtaining subsidies from the national health system, which has a budget line for IDPs. IOM micro-credits and income-generation projects for IDPs also include a strong component of capacity building.

As a first step in preparing for the Post-Emergency Assistance project, IOM undertook the most comprehensive study to date of conditions in the six departments where the project is based. The study, initiated in late 2000 and completed in mid-2001, provides an inventory and database of the IDP situation and impacts, and documents the conditions many researchers have maintained to be the obstacles facing IDPs and their impacts on the receiving community (IOM 2001).

Pan American Health Organization/World Health Organization, PAHO/WHO

The Pan American Health Organization/World Health Organization has been supporting public health in Colombia since 1954. Its program for displaced populations has operated since 1998. Although PAHO/WHO works through the Ministry of Health and advises the RSS, its services are not limited to registered IDPs. Until 2002 the agency devoted its efforts mainly to the delivery of emergency health care but, as in the case of the other UN agencies, PAHO/WHO has acknowledged that delivering emergency assistance is inadequate and unsustainable. It is now embarking on an expanded IDP program titled Attention in Disasters and Complex Emergencies, with a focus on improving medium-term attention as well.

The program operates, first, to strengthen the response capacity of municipal and departmental public health facilities in the areas that have received large numbers of displaced persons. Secondly, on an ongoing basis, PAHO/WHO has been developing basic health information related to IDPs and improving the skills of health care workers. In the interest of helping local health officials obtain the resources needed to assist IDPs, the agency is building capacity among clinic and hospital administrators in budgeting and billing through the complicated national administrative mechanisms. Toward these ends, WHO/PAHO has set up small departmental offices in six regions (Cartagena, Medellín, Cali, Bucaramanga, Condinamarca, and Montería) and is supporting efforts to educate the population on health care and other rights, so as to empower those denied service to demand government compliance with Law 387 and other legislation.

Other UN Agencies

Three further UN agencies (UN Fund for Population Activities, UN Children's Fund, and UN Development Program) also have ongoing health, education, community development and feeding programs aimed at Colombia's internally displaced population. In addition, UNDP supports human rights promotion and conflict resolution projects including efforts to increase protection for community leaders. As noted, UNDP has taken a lead role in the combined governance, peace, and economic development programs in Magdalena Medio.

International NGOs

The major European NGOs include Save the Children, Rädda Barnen, Oxfam, Diakonia, Christian Aid, and the umbrella organization Project

Counseling Service, and are loosely coordinated in the Diálogo Inter-Agencial (DIAL) group. In Colombia, they devote their efforts in a variety of ways to advocacy (including international advocacy), building local capacities, increasing participation by working with local churches and other organizations and, generally, promoting solutions for problems related to displacement. To a lesser extent, most of these agencies support small-scale humanitarian projects, such as housing and income generation for IDPs and other vulnerable groups. ECHO is an important funding source for the members of DIAL. Although it considers most local development to be paralyzed by the effects of conflict, Oxfam continues to operate with its own and with local NGO and community workers for relief and capacity-building projects. The Oxfam representative commented to the researchers on the difficulties of grassroots efforts in Colombia and the risks of trying to combine advocacy with direct operations. She was conscious of the risks involved to their staff in defending human rights or advocating the kinds of changes that address the root causes of conflict. The international agencies are necessarily cautious in the politically lethal Colombian environment.

In a similar vein, US-based NGOs also support local capacities, education/information and participation, but they are involved more than the Europeans in small-scale development efforts aimed at vulnerable populations. The Jesuit Refugee Service has community projects, the largest of which is in Barrancabermeja. World Vision receives funding from USAID for what it calls "area development projects," combining short-term relief and longer-term assistance. The Catholic Relief Service, CRS, has established partnerships with the dioceses of Colombia and supports the work of the Human Mobility section of Pastoral in the Episcopal Conference, which has been a key source of data on displacement and an essential source of IDP assistance. CRS funds projects promoting peace building, justice, and legal education, but like the European NGOs tries to avoid political slant.

European Union and European Community Humanitarian Office, ECHO

Within the Commission, ECHO is mandated to respond to emergency needs, and the office channels between €8 and 10 million annually for humanitarian aid in Colombia. Its activities are limited to short-term relief projects for IDPs, which ECHO defines as being implemented within the first year of displacement. ECHO has established a network of 14 partner agencies, most of which are international NGOs that receive ECHO funding. ECHO also counts among its partners UNHCR and ICRC and supports some of their activities. Typical among the projects that

ECHO supports are water and sanitation, basic housing, psychosocial counseling, and some small QIPs. Beneficiaries of ECHO projects for IDPs do not require prior registration with the RSS.

In general, ECHO projects are placed in regions where governmental response is weak. One of the major objectives of the assistance is to curtail migration flows from the rural areas that generate displacement to distant urban centers. The strategy is to reach the IDPs immediately after the first displacement, extend emergency assistance so as to permit people to remain where they are, and to follow up with funding from the EU for more sustained assistance. Although committed to a prevention strategy and to policies that enhance the ability of people to return to their places of origin, ECHO rarely has directly supported the groups that attempt to re-establish themselves in their places of origin. ECHO's support for these return movements depends on strong guarantees regarding security and requires that the returnees be accompanied by a Colombian NGO.

As the ECHO partner agencies have grown more frustrated with the inadequacies of assistance limited to emergency relief and have sought support for more durable efforts aimed at income generation, ECHO has been drawn into involvement with some longer-term initiatives. The European Union has recognized Colombian displacement to be an enduring phenomenon and in 2002 established a funding line for medium- and longer-range IDP projects in the "stabilization" phase. For 2003 ECHO assigned €10 million for "uprooted populations." These funds are to be channeled mainly through UNHCR and NGOs for institutional capacity building and income generation. This will permit ECHO to move back to its core of short-term relief operations. In addition, the EU supports prevention and dialogue in two so-called "Peace laboratories" in Magdalena Medio and in Norte de Santander, Antioquia and the Colombian Massif. The first was granted €34 million in 2001, while the second, covering 62 municipalities, was granted €33 million in 2004 (ECHO 2004).

US Agency for International Development/Population, Refugees and Migration, USAID/PRM

In 1999, under the presidency of Andres Pastrana, Colombia proposed a six-year $7.5 billion comprehensive reform and development plan. The original concept of Plan Colombia was a program in which over half the funding would be devoted to anti-narcotics activities including strengthening of the security forces, and the remainder for social and economic improvements and governance. The US offered to provide the lion's share of funding for the drug eradication components of Plan Colombia, including military and police aid to enhance national drug interdiction capacities. The US and Colombian governments intended to attract other donor money for the Plan's development components, but until recently little has been forthcoming. Potential European donors expressed reluctance to associate with the Plan, viewing the anti-narcotics and military aspects as counterproductive and damaging to the peace process. Although still uncomfortable about Plan Colombia, the Europeans, as noted above, have increased their humanitarian activity, including assistance to IDPs.

The US agreed to contribute $1.3 billion to Plan Colombia over the years 2000 and 2001, about 20 percent of which for economic and social purposes; the USAID budget for 2002 was $104.5 million (USAID Fact Sheets 2002). Priority areas were defined as strengthening democracy, promoting human rights, supporting the elimination of coca and poppy cultivation with alternative development and providing assistance to the IDP population. Under the Democracy rubric, USAID has been supporting judicial reform and improved local government management; its support for the government's human rights structures has buttressed the protection of both the targets of human rights violations and human rights workers. USAID also has financed infrastructure projects meant to employ rural workers who otherwise, presumably, might cultivate coca.

Under Plan Colombia, $37.5 million was set aside specifically for assistance to IDPs. More than two thirds of this was channeled through USAID, and the rest through the Bureau of Population, Refugees and Migration. The latter has funded some emergency assistance projects through international organizations such as UNHCR, UNICEF, WFP, PAHO/WHO and a few international NGOs. USAID has used its larger share to support NGOs and international organizations engaged in longer term institution building and development projects. It has supported projects for physical and mental health services, shelter, water and sanitation, education and rehabilitation of former child combatants (USAID 2002).

As of 2003, Plan Colombia has been replaced with a similar package under the Andean Counter Drug Initiative (ACI), within which the funding is divided among Colombia's five neighbors. The amounts are higher but the increase is almost entirely in the security area. Although not determined at this writing, the IDP programs are likely to receive roughly the same levels of support as the prior programs, but will have larger components for the border regions. It is estimated that Colombia will receive some $456 million of the total from which a minimum of $25 million must be spent on rule of law and justice programs and $13 million for human rights protection (Colombia Program 2004).

EFFORTS TO IMPROVE THE SYSTEM

Colombia's impressive networks of human rights and national legal structures have repeatedly censured the state for failing to fulfill its obligations toward displaced persons. The combined judicial actions and the multiple decisions of the court have prompted a government review of procedures and some important steps toward improving them. The presidential statements and planning documents issued during the last years of the Pastrana administration, especially Presidential Directive Number 6, are in many ways the direct outcome of the literally hundreds of IDP-related judicial actions. There has been a stream of presidential decrees and legislation aimed at the government entities involved in health, land, personal identity documents, education, and housing. Together these initiatives have sought to improve emergency humanitarian assistance, provide support for juridical developments and enhance monitoring and evaluation of programs. Other legal decisions have served to direct attention to seek compliance with international standards, must notably the Guiding Principles, when framing rules and regulations on displacement.

In December 2001, the heads of the UN agencies, meeting in New York, requested that their offices in Colombia produce a unified plan for how the UN system would address internally displaced persons. Two OCHA officials and one member of the UN Staff College were sent to Colombia to work with the representatives of the various agencies on an action plan. The agencies identified several weaknesses in existing UN performance and suggested how to address them (UNHCR and OCHA 2002).

First, each of the agencies selected the municipalities or regions in which it would establish its presence using its own criteria. Only occasionally have agencies expressly combined forces in a single place. In some areas where displacement was high, nearly all the agencies were present, e.g., Antioquia, Bolivar, Cesar, and Cordoba. In others, equally affected, only one or two are found, or none at all. For example, few UN agencies work in Bogotá itself, or in Magdalena, Cauca, or Huila. Thus, the international efforts have been dispersed and, since the overall presence is small, the net impact has been less than if resources were systematically combined.

Second, neither the international agencies nor the Colombian government have targeted their programs systematically to gender, ethnicity or age, although nearly all have emphasized the importance of doing so. UN officials agreed that women suffer disproportionately from the consequences of displacement and are in particularly serious need of programs for reproductive health. They also noted a disproportionate impact of displacement on Indigenous Colombians. And, as the IDPs themselves emphasized to this research team, humanitarian officials had neglected programs for adolescents.

Third, the UN system has not been contributing sufficient resources and expertise to enhance the ability of the Colombian state to meet the humanitarian challenge of two million IDPs. Likewise, the international agencies should have established stronger links with grassroots entities, including IDP organizations and the groups in civil society working on behalf of IDPs.

Fourth, although the agencies in the UN system in Colombia have achieved a reasonable level of cooperation, there has been little formal coordination and few mechanisms for interagency action in priority regions.

The resulting Humanitarian Plan of Action 2002–2003 addressed these weaknesses, aiming to move the system from "strategic coordination" to more "operational coordination" focused in a few priority areas (UN Thematic Group 2002: 15). The Plan calls for programs aimed at women, ethnic minorities and age groups (elderly, adolescents) hitherto left out. To support the Colombian government more effectively, it calls for a stronger Technical Support Unit, direct assistance to administrative entities, and a more concentrated field presence, possibly with joint offices in key locations. The Action recommends strong human rights criteria, gender focus and a rights-based approach in UN programs and components of programs related to the internally displaced. Additionally, the UN called on its member agencies to use their influence to turn public opinion in a more favorable direction with regard to the displaced, so that society would sympathize with rather than stigmatize the population.

To have an impact, the UN programs need to be expanded. No matter how much they may improve, without a stronger resource base, the programs will continue to reach only a small percentage of people who need the services they provide. OCHA will present the Plan of Action to potential donors, much like a consolidated appeal. Unfortunately, funding is likely to be an obstacle to its implementation, as donor countries still allege that Colombia is a relatively rich country with an orderly and democratic government, which should shoulder the major responsibility for dealing with the internally displaced. This assessment of Colombia's political and economic potential is unrealistic. To recover its former prosperity, the country requires a massive reform of the tax system and a dramatic turnaround in the price of coffee and other exports—both highly unlikely for the foreseeable future. For the present, the government of Colombia is poised to reduce, not increase, its contributions to humanitarian action.

CONCLUSION

Displacement, Conflict, and Peace Negotiations

The tragedy of displacement is part of the tragedy of conflict in Colombia, along with massacres, assassinations, kidnappings for ransom, destruction of social and productive infrastructure and persistent fear. National and international efforts to "humanize" the war, that is, to persuade all sides to comply with international humanitarian law and to end the widely practiced atrocities on all sides, have not produced results. Neither access to, nor treatment of, IDPs were burning issues at the peace table before these negotiations ended in February 2002. As the government's policies now have turned from vain efforts to negotiate the end of the conflict to actions aimed at military victory, it must take stronger steps to protect the civilian population. Continuing murder, displacement and expropriation of peasant land and resources are inevitable unless security forces are made accountable not just for battling guerrillas, but also for seeing to the security of Colombian citizens. This implies taking more serious measures to curb paramilitary forces engaged in repression and criminal activities.

The Enduring Effects of Displacement

Despite evidence to the contrary, Colombians and their international supporters continue to treat displacement solely as a derivative of war, that is to say, a temporary problem that will go away when the war is over, and about which little can be done beyond palliative emergency assistance until it is over. The present government promises to address displacement with stronger actions to prevent it and more ambitious programs to bring the displaced back to their homes. But these compelling options are buttressed neither with the funding needed for economic revitalization and recovery, nor with essential security and protection mechanisms for the affected population. No serious observer or analyst encountered by this research team considers either prevention or significant return movements to be realistic or viable under present circumstances. Nor do the IDPs themselves.

Nevertheless, neither the government nor the humanitarian agencies have wanted to acknowledge the extent to which displacement is irreversible, and how its effects have changed the face of Colombia. The forced exodus of so large a number among the rural poor has brought about an accelerated and almost certainly permanent concentration in the hands of a few landowners of the numerous smallholdings once used for subsistence agriculture. And, on the other side, it has led to an unprecedented acceleration of urbanizing trends. Assuming, as we do, that a majority of the present IDPs and their children will be unable to return to their rural areas and are often uninterested in doing so, their presence will change the class and ethnic demographics, as well as the size, of many Colombian cities.

The IDPs originate in large part from regions once considered marginal to national interests, and formerly they received few benefits from the state. The government and some international agencies advocate investing in the economic development of these marginal areas in order to prevent displacement. The moment to do so has probably passed. Now many, perhaps most, IDPs are living in urban settings, and depend largely if not wholly on the state and outside benefactors to provide for them. The palliative emergency assistance is barely adequate for short-term survival and, as such, does not allow IDPs to establish the bases for self-sufficiency in the future. As the number of internally displaced persons increases and prospects of finding gainful employment in the present Colombian economy remain small, emergency assistance resources will be even more strained than is now the case. The result can only be an ever expanding, marginal, disaffected population that continues to drain the social and economic resources of the country.

The dearth of serious programs in place either to retain IDPs in rural settings or resettle and help integrate them into the towns and cities is a major gap. The UN Humanitarian Plan of Action of 2002–2003 recognizes this gap, but lacks presence and resources to make serious progress toward filling it, despite its pledge to devote more attention to needs during the "transition." It is essential to design and implement a comprehensive set of policies, backed by competent organizations and funding, and based on the premise that neither displacement nor the reasons for displacement will disappear when—as all hope—the conflict has been brought to a close.

Displacement and International Humanitarian Principles

Colombia is unusually compliant with international humanitarian law, including norms for protecting and assisting IDPs. The government has sought international involvement, has invited the UN to establish its agencies and mount its programs in the country, and has incorporated the Guiding Principles on Internal Displacement into its National Law 387. Along with a legal framework that codifies IDP rights, the government has established structures at the national, regional and municipal levels which, in principle, should assure full access of rights and services for IDPs. Yet a large number of international missions have passed through Colombia to assess the massive and growing displacement and almost invariably have criticized the Colombian government's responses. They cite the failure of the state to adequately assume its obligations to assist and protect IDPs and other victims. As this report has shown, while the Colombian government fulfills its obligations through legislation, legal recourse, and institutional venues for services, it *denies* its obligations at the same time by narrowly defining the eligible beneficiary group, limiting the attention available, and placing obstacles in the way of claiming rights and services. The result has been a highly developed but ineffective response to displacement.

The Capacity of the State to Respond

Since the late 1990s the government has taken steps to reinforce the legislative measures and to rectify many bureaucratic practices that have impeded the implementation of Law 387. It has accepted judicial rulings demanding policy changes and has collaborated with international agencies through the Joint Technical Unit and Thematic Group on Displacement. Humanitarian assistance is in no way a solution, however. The government has been unwilling—and partially unable—to protect this quintessentially vulnerable population, to employ its members productively and, most important, to end or even to reduce the rate of displacement. At issue is the demonstrated weakness of the Colombian government on the ground. In its March 2002 report on the prospects of peace in Colombia, the International Crisis Group concluded, pessimistically, that in the course of conflict, the state has been fatally weakened.

> Presently, the Colombian state neither exercises fully and legitimately its monopoly of force and taxation nor implements the rule of law to any satisfactory degree. As much as 75 per cent of Colombia's territory is either controlled or contested by insurgent and paramilitary forces (ICG 2002: 7).

The present government has shown determination to strengthen the state, to bring its presence throughout the nation and, especially, to greatly increase its capacity to impose security. The citizens of Colombia urgently need strengthened security. Pervasive violence impedes the most common acts of daily life, traveling short distances, and remaining neutral in the presence of conflict. Yet, in the short term, tougher security measures and the newly enhanced security sectors are likely to target the IDP population as potential threats, rather than to protect its members. President Uribe has imposed a state of emergency that permits preventive arrests and establishes networks of civilian informants to identify likely insurgents. The IDPs, already highly stigmatized, often lacking documentation, and under pressures from guerrilla insurgents as well as paramilitary elements, are potentially prime suspects for reprisals.

The International Organizations' Contributions

The donors, UN officials and multiple NGO representatives with whom the research team spoke have devoted a considerable proportion of their energies to educating IDPs about their rights, strengthening IDP leadership, and directly challenging the authorities on behalf of IDPs who were being denied their rights. It is equally important that assistance be directed to improving the will and capacities of government and non-government officials and service providers. Efforts to fortify the "demand side," that is, the ability of IDPs to claim their rights, must be accompanied by greater efforts to strengthen the "supply side"; in other words, to contribute to institution strengthening, capacity building and consciousness-raising among official organizations and authorities, especially at the local levels. This integrative function has been advocated by most international agencies and, fortunately, important donors as well. The new Plan of Action advocates a "rights based" approach to IDP attention. This notion moves in the right direction, if funding is made available to implement the plan.

An obvious corollary is to empower the IDPs themselves to claim their rights. Unfortunately, as the latter now depend largely on social generosity, it is difficult for them to exert pressure effectively or to come up with creative strategies for the future. The IDP representatives have few options but to assert their leadership by demanding what is their due. Nevertheless, the demands alienate other sectors of the poor, the authorities in cash-strapped municipalities, and even a number of well-intentioned humanitarian service providers. What the IDPs want and need is the kind of support that will help them to become productive citizens who contribute to the strength of the country.

For a brief update on developments in Colombia since this chapter was completed, see the editors' postscript, page 224.

SOURCES

This chapter is based on interviews with more than 30 representatives of Colombian government institutions, intergovernmental agencies, Colombian and transnational NGOs, municipal authorities, organizations of IDPs, and university departments. Interviews were undertaken in and around Bogotá, Medellín, Baranquilla and Cartagena in January–February 2002, and information was updated in 2003 and 2004. A more extended report can be downloaded from http://www.cdr.dk/working_papers/wp-03-6.pdf.

NOTES

1. In 1995, the official planning agency, the National Council of Economic and Social Policy (Consejo Nacional de Política Económica y Social, or CONPES), rec-

ognized the presence of a crisis of internal displacement caused by violence, and proposed government policies to respond to it (CONPES 1995). CONPES comprises the major ministries, banks and syndicates of the state, and answers directly to the president.

2. The government's Social Solidarity Network (Red de Solidaridad Social, RSS) is limited to those displaced by violence and is based on registration. The Church's Human Mobility Section of the Colombian Episcopal Conference counts persons who have come to the attention of the parishes. The Consultancy on Human Rights and Displacement (Consultoría para los Derechos Humanos y el Desplazamiento, CODHES), an NGO devoted to tracking displacement and documenting human rights associated with displacement estimated close to 3 million between 1985 and the end of 2002, based both on Church and NGO sources. ICRC has its own estimates also based on various sources. International agencies may use government figures for certain programs but their estimates of real numbers are more likely to rely on CODHES.

3. In February 2004 the Colombian Defensoria del Pueblo claimed that 13,000 sought protection in neighboring countries, while a UN press release on January 28 (Reuters) estimated that over 20,000 had sought asylum in Ecuador alone.

4. In the US annual arrivals went up from 15,000 (2000) to 18,845 (2002) while asylum seekers numbered 2,631 in 2000 and 7,144 in 2001 (Migration Policy Institute, http://www.migrationinformation.org/GlobalData/countrydata/country.cfm).

5. This statement is based on the views expressed in our interviews. A few were skeptical as to the value of the seminars, workshops and meetings that UNHCR regularly organizes, and lamented the absence of direct material assistance of the kind that is directed toward refugee populations.

Chapter 5

Afghanistan's Complex Forced Migration

Peter Marsden

The Afghan conflict produced one of the largest refugee flows recorded, with 6 million refugees crossing into Pakistan and Iran in response to the Soviet invasion of Afghanistan in December 1979 (British Refugee Council 1990). Over the 25 years since that event, Afghanistan has continued to experience large-scale displacements of its population, both internally and to other countries, in the region and beyond. The response of the international community has been complex, influenced by political and other factors. The purpose of this chapter is to document what happened and reflect on the many issues that have arisen.

This chapter starts by looking at the complexities of the various population movements relating to developments in Afghanistan since the coup instituted by the People's Democratic Party of Afghanistan in April 1978. It then considers a number of key issues including: the changing relationship between the aid community and those establishing themselves as the de facto government of Afghanistan, with or without international recognition; the difficulties faced by the aid community in working alongside international military forces engaged in offensive operations; the protection of refugees in the various political circumstances that have prevailed; the sustainability of return at different stages; the changing capacity of the aid community to assist during those same stages; and finally, the question of planning for possible refugee flows in situations of military intervention by members of the international community, whether or not sanctioned by the UN.

PATTERNS OF DISPLACEMENT

Over the early 1980s, 3.2 million refugees sought exile in Pakistan and 2.9 million migrated to Iran. The exodus was regarded by the refugees themselves and by the two countries that received them as a religious one: Afghanistan had been invaded by a secular force and a duty had thus been imposed on them to reject that invasion (British Agencies Afghanistan Group 1997). Both Pakistan and Iran therefore received the Afghans as religious migrants or *muhajirin*, although Iran, as a signatory to the 1951 Refugee Convention, could have given them refugee status. Consistent with this perceived religious duty, both Pakistan and Iran supported military incursions from their territory into Afghanistan to attack the Soviet forces. These incursions were organized from refugee camps.

Provision for the refugees was different in each country (British Refugee Council 1990). In Pakistan, the government agreed to the establishment of refugee settlements along the border, to be managed by the government of Pakistan's Commissionerate for Afghan Refugees. UNHCR took responsibility for the provision of services and for negotiating appropriate protection arrangements. Tents were provided which refugees gradually replaced by mud housing. The World Food Program supplied wheat and other food rations throughout the 1980s, tapering off from around 1992 onward until they finally ended in September 1995. NGOs were contracted by UNHCR to provide water supplies, sanitation, health care, education, vocational training and income-generating opportunities. Refugees were given exemptions from the provisions of the Foreigners Act so that they could seek employment or set up businesses. Many refugees also established themselves in the urban areas, especially after the start of an assisted repatriation program in 1992 which required the surrender of ration cards. Although many did return to Afghanistan, large numbers opted to remain in Pakistan and moved out of the camps into one or other of the cities. The ending of rations in September 1995 accelerated this process, with many men leaving their families in the camps while they sought work in distant urban centers.

In Iran, the government set up a limited number of camps in desert locations at some distance from the urban centers. However, most refugees were required to fend for themselves and thus to find their own accommodation. The vast majority went to cities such as Mashhad, Tehran, Zahedan and Isfahan but significant numbers sought work as agricultural laborers. Afghans were permitted to work but only in designated menial occupations. This entitlement was progressively withdrawn through a series of new regulations. Refugees were not allowed to operate their own businesses except through Iranian counterparts. The Iranian government provided access to health care and education at a much

Map 5.1.   Afghanistan: A Decade of Forced Migration and Return, 1992–2002
Source: UNHCR; USCR.

higher standard than was available to the refugees in Pakistan and also gave the refugees entitlements to the subsidies on basic essentials that were available to the Iranian population. These subsidies were gradually removed over time and the standards of health and education provision also declined. Refugees in Iran were subject to much greater controls than those in Pakistan. All were issued identity documents which had to be frequently shown to the police. From December 1992 onward, when Iran signed a repatriation agreement with the government of Afghanistan and UNHCR, the government placed increasing restrictions on the right of Afghans to remain in the country, manifested in a confusing array of different documents in use, with differing entitlements. Afghans in Iran have therefore felt extremely insecure about their status since 1992 and this has been aggravated by periodic arbitrary arrests, detentions and deportations of Afghans in large numbers. The insecurity has been compounded by a police practice of tearing up documentation, irrespective of the entitlement it has given, in the process of arresting Afghans.

Donor funding for the Afghan refugees in Pakistan was far in excess of that provided in Iran. In part this was because Iran chose not to set up large numbers of camps, but more significantly because Iran was reluctant to permit UN agencies and NGOs to arrive in force, and thus create a significant international and, therefore, western, presence. The Islamic Revolution in Iran was very new and there was strong resistance to any development which might permit western value systems to permeate Islamic society. Donors were also geared up to funding food and other relief supplies for distribution by humanitarian agencies, and were very reluctant to hand over cash to the Iranian government to fund its own assistance programs. Political factors will have similarly influenced the outcome. The new regime in Iran was viewed in a very negative light in many western capitals, whereas the government of Pakistan was seen as a key ally in supporting a resistance movement which, it was hoped, might significantly weaken the Soviet Union. The Iranian government has made it clear that it has very much resented the fact that it has hosted, at one time, the largest ever refugee population,[1] with minimal international support.

In addition to the initial exodus in response to the Soviet invasion, there have been many waves of Afghans fleeing to neighboring countries to escape renewed conflict or political repression. The period of the Mujahidin government, from 1992 to 1996, saw an armed struggle for power in which the western and southern areas of Kabul were reduced to rubble. In two particular episodes, in the summer of 1992 and January 1994, Kabul experienced particularly intensive bombardment which led tens of thousands of people to seek internal or external exile. Mazar-i-Sharif received the majority of those fleeing in 1992 and it proved necessary to set up various settlements across the city to receive the influx. At the same time, a camp had to be built to the east of Mazar to accommodate Tajik refugees who were fleeing civil war in Tajikistan. In January 1994, the scale of the exodus from Kabul was such that huge camps had to be set up on the outskirts of Jalalabad. Around 50,000 made it to Pakistan, where they were provided for in Nasirbagh camp near Peshawar. The capture of Herat by the Taliban, in September 1995, led large numbers of professionals and intellectuals to apply for visas for Iran, but these were not regarded as refugees. The subsequent capture of Kabul, in September 1996, did, however, result in an outflow to Peshawar where additional provision was made at Nasirbagh camp. This particular outflow occurred as a direct consequence of various restrictions placed on the population, notably on the right of women to work and on behavioral and dress codes. The climate of fear thus generated was an added factor. The subsequent Taliban advance into northern Afghanistan created initial instability but no major movement. However, their capture of the northeastern town of Taloqan in September 2000 led to major displacement, internally and externally, and 170,000 people traveled to Pakistan in the hope of finding protection and sustenance. Most of these were from minority ethnic groups, unlike the Pushtuns who had found support from fellow Pushtuns on the Pakistani side of the border in previous outflows. This may have been one factor in the Pakistani government's decision not to allow this group to be registered, and therefore provided for, but it was also true that the level of resentment within Pakistan over the large Afghan refugee population was increasing and there was strong political pressure on the government to resist any further influx. The new arrivals headed for a makeshift camp on the edge of one of the existing refugee settlements relatively near to Peshawar known as Jalozai. Here, refugees lived under thin plastic sheeting and bits of cloth under the intense scrutiny of the international media. Because UNHCR felt unable to organize food and other distributions in the absence of a registration process, the refugees were dependent on charitable handouts provided by, among others, the wife of the former cricketer and current Pakistani politician, Imran Khan. Finally, under pressure, Pakistan agreed to the creation of new camps in the tribal areas, at some distance from urban centers, in the hope that the difficult access to employment opportunities and the relatively poor security would deter many potential refugees. This agreement had yet to be implemented when the United States threatened military action against Afghanistan in response to the terrorist attack in New York of September 11, 2001.

The efforts of the Taliban to take additional territory also resulted in a high level of internal displacement from the Shomali Valley, north of Kabul, which was the scene of frontline activity between the Taliban and the Northern Alliance forces of Ahmed Shah Masoud from the autumn of 1996 until the overthrow of the Taliban. Around 200,000 people were displaced to Kabul in January 1997, following a particular Taliban offensive, and tens of thousands of others fled to the Panjshir Valley or to Mazar-i-Sharif. Toward the end of this period, after the frontline had moved back and forth, the Taliban adopted a scorched earth policy, destroying homes, irrigation and water supply systems and even orchards to make it difficult for people to return to their homes. Many of those who fled also sought refuge in Iran or Pakistan.

A further major cause of population movement was a serious drought from 1999 to 2002. This was particularly acute in the northwest, north and south of the country. A large camp was set up at Maslakh, near Herat, to make provision for over 100,000 displaced people from the neighboring provinces. This was initially run by the Taliban administration before responsibility for camp management was accepted by an NGO. Much smaller settlements were created in and around Mazar-i-Sharif to receive those affected by the drought in the provinces to the south of the city. Large numbers of nomads who had lost their livestock gravitated to Kandahar where a minimal level of provision was made by the Taliban administration and various external agencies.

Repatriation to Afghanistan did not commence on any scale until 1992. The international community had expected the Soviet-backed government to fall immediately after the withdrawal of Soviet troops in February 1989, and for refugees to return en masse thereafter. In the event, the regime remained in being until after the Soviet Union had itself collapsed in 1991, when the resources that the Soviet Union had provided to sustain it were no longer available. The emergence of a Mujahidin government in April 1992, following various deals between elements of the Mujahidin and of the Soviet-backed government, provided the signal for the end of the religious exodus and, over the summer of 1992, almost one million returned from Pakistan and a much smaller number from Iran. The return process from Iran accelerated after the negotiation of a repatriation agreement, in December 2002, between the governments of Iran and Afghanistan and UNHCR. Thus, while the rate of return from Pakistan slowed down as refugees became disenchanted with the new Mujahidin government because of the open conflict between its constituent parties, the spring and summer of 1993 saw the return of several hundred thousand Afghan refugees from Iran. However, the level of return from Pakistan dropped to around 100,000 per year over the years that followed and dropped even more from Iran, coming to an effective halt after the Taliban takeover of Herat in September 1995.

Both return programs were supported by assistance packages provided by UNHCR in the form of 50–100 kg of wheat per person together with varying levels of cash and additional items such as tarpaulin, kitchen utensils and tools. The content of the package varied from one period to another and was slightly different on the Iranian border from that on the border with Pakistan. The assistance package was handed over at processing centers within Pakistan and on the border with Iran. In Pakistan, this was given on surrender of ration books entitling the refugee to food aid in the refugee camps. On the Iranian border, refugees had to present specific documentation.

The assistance package was not intended to provide more than temporary support, equivalent to approximately three months' supply of wheat. There was concern that those who had never left their villages in Afghanistan might feel resentful of returning refugees if these ended up relatively better off. The focus of resource allocation was therefore on the provision of reconstruction assistance to the villages to which the largest number of refugees were returning. This took the form, typically, of the repair of irrigation systems and flood protection structures, the construction of shallow wells, the supply of improved wheat seed and the provision of health, education and veterinary services. Over the period of 1992–1999, substantial progress was made in large areas of the country in restoring the agricultural base and thus supporting the return of refugees. Regrettably, the severe drought which hit the country in 1999–2003 undermined the progress made and created a population in excess of six million that was vulnerable to food insecurity and dependent on food assistance.

The provision of reconstruction assistance was largely undertaken by NGOs, drawing on information provided by UNHCR as to the areas to which the greatest number of refugees were returning. The UN Office of Project Services (UNOPS) added substantially to this for several years during the mid-1990s through a program of intensive work, based on priorities determined within each district through a community consultation process, to improve irrigation systems, flood protection structures and water supply systems. Toward the end of the 1990s, UNHCR set up a similar program through which it identified groups of refugees in the camps in Pakistan who had indicated a willingness to return if their areas of origin could be rehabilitated. Working with NGOs, UNHCR provided a significant level of resources to each targeted area but it lacked the resources to cover more than a limited number of areas.

The repatriation process has been complicated by a long-standing tradition of economic migration to Pakistan, Iran and, to a lesser extent, the Arabian peninsula. Typically, farming families have sent one or more sons, at any one time, to work as laborers in neighboring countries for limited periods (British Agencies Afghanistan Group 1997). Varying levels of hardship brought on by the conflict and natural disasters have led this outflow to increase or decrease and it represented a particularly important safety valve during the period of the drought. Many of the families which sought exile in Pakistan, in particular, also kept their links with their original farms, sending the more experienced family members back to Afghanistan each spring and summer to look after their land.

However, those who had been landless prior to exile were not able to diversify their income-earning opportunities in the same way and have faced particular problems on their return. An important change arising from the conflict has been a significant increase in the population, brought on by better access to health care in Pakistan and Iran and also, as a consequence of NGO programs reaching rural areas within Afghanistan. This has meant that the agricultural economy has been less able to support the population than was the case prior to 1979, and those without land have tended to seek work in the urban areas or to try their luck in Pakistan or Iran, notwithstanding the growing difficulties encountered. There has been a marked urbanization process over the period of the conflict, and movement back and forth across the borders with Iran and Pakistan is likely to continue, no matter what controls are imposed.

THE US-LED MILITARY INTERVENTION
IN AFGHANISTAN

The US-led military offensive of October 2001 had two immediate effects. First, the bombing raids on Kandahar, in particular, led hundreds of thousands of people to flee toward Pakistan. Second, in anticipation of such an outflow, UNHCR put pressure on Pakistan to permit the entry of new arrivals and their registration. As noted above, the government of Pakistan had agreed, earlier in the year, to the creation of new camps in remote locations along the border. Most of these proposed camps were problematic with regard to both security and logistics and it took UNHCR much longer than planned to bring them into being. Fortunately, a planning figure of 1.5 million fleeing as a consequence of the hostilities did not materialize and the numbers who crossed were very much less. Further, those who had fled Kandahar returned relatively soon after the bombing ended. However, another two groups of displaced people did demand assistance in the new camps.

The first of these were Pushtuns fleeing violence in northern Afghanistan. The Pushtun population of the north had been settled in this area, as colonists, by a particular ruler, Amir Abdur-Rahman, at the end of the nineteenth century, as a means of consolidating his conquests of the non-Pushtun areas. These Pushtun colonies had existed in the intervening decades, side by side with other ethnic groups, on the basis of simmering resentment at their economically advantaged positions. The Taliban had been able to draw support from these colonies in their efforts to take control of the northern provinces and, although the Taliban brought about an improvement in the security situation in the north, they were perceived as an army of occupation by much of the population. This was aggravated by a massacre of thousands of ethnic Hazaras during the takeover of Mazar-i-Sharif in August 1998. Thus, when the Taliban forces were destroyed in the north in October 2001, through a combination of US bombing raids and military action, on the ground, by the forces of Jamiat-i-Islami and of Rashid Dostam, there was a strong desire for retribution on the part of the Afghan ground forces. Regrettably, the US Special Forces stood by as acts of retribution took their course and tens of thousands of ethnic Pushtuns left the area for the Pushtun south.

Large numbers crossed into Pakistan, where they were provided for in the new camps that were being established. However, many were held in what came to be known as waiting areas astride the border, in makeshift or temporary camps, and some 60,000 people were still waiting to be moved on when Pakistan refused any further registrations in March 2003, following the signing of a repatriation agreement with the government of Afghanistan and UNHCR. They therefore had to join with another group of forced migrants—the large population of nomads displaced by the drought—to survive the best they could in the border camps. Although the accommodation and facilities in these camps were extremely substandard, there were, at least, good income earning opportunities in the town of Chaman on the Pakistan side of the border. Thus, when, in August 2003, UNHCR negotiated with the Kandahar authorities the opening of a new camp in a remote desert location at Zhare Dasht, to the west of Kandahar, to relocate the population of the waiting areas, relatively few people were willing to avail themselves of the opportunity because they knew they would not be able to find work (UNAMA 2003).

The US-led military intervention eventually brought about an internationally-recognized government, following the signing of the Bonn Agreement on December 7, 2001, in which the international community had been heavily instrumental. The international community thus had a strong interest in seeing the new government succeed, in order to justify the military intervention and also achieve other strategic goals. European governments had an additional objective, which was to secure the return of the large number of Afghans who had sought asylum in Europe. The emergence of a government which could be presented as creating the conditions for sustainable return was, therefore, very much in their interests.

Pakistan and Iran were similarly concerned to take the opportunity of the fall of the Taliban to substantially reduce their own Afghan refugee populations which had swollen as a consequence of the drought. Both countries had in excess of 2 million Afghans at this stage and both had already started to put pressure on this population before the autumn of 2001. In the case of Iran, as noted above, this had started in the mid-1990s when it became apparent that the three-year repatriation agreement of December 1992 had not delivered the desired result of securing the departure of all Afghan refugees. Police harassment of Afghans became more frequent and young men, in particular, became vulnerable to being stopped by the police, detained and then deported. The pressures increased in June 2001 following the introduction of a regulation by the Ministry of Labor and Social Affairs which imposed heavy fines and imprisonment on those who employed foreign illegal workers. Afghans were also, as already noted, seeing a gradual reduction in their entitlements to health and education services and were having to pay increasingly for these services. The fall of the Taliban accelerated and accentuated these pre-existing pressures.

Pakistan started to harass Afghans more frequently from the spring of

2001 at a time when the Taliban were facing increasing difficulties recruiting young men to fight for them. There were suspicions at the time that the government of Pakistan, which had strong links with the Taliban, was deporting young refugees and handing them over to the Taliban to boost their fighting ranks. However, other than this, Pakistan, unlike Iran, had no organized process of deporting Afghans. The pressures from the Pakistani police increased considerably following the Bonn Agreement, however, with Afghans living in the urban areas being particularly targeted. It was clear from the various measures taken that the government of Pakistan was seeking to empty the cities of their Afghan populations, pending a concerted effort to reduce the camp population (Turton and Marsden 2002).

Afghans in both countries were also strongly encouraged to contemplate return by media coverage of an international donor conference held in Tokyo in January 2002, which gave the impression that there would be a significant level of international investment in Afghanistan and, therefore, plenty of jobs. The Iranian government went one step further through a sustained media campaign for return, advising Afghans that they would be provided with free transport to their home areas where the UN would be there to assist them (Turton and Marsden 2002).

Faced with this heavy pressure from the host governments, UNHCR felt it had no choice but to make the best of the situation and so provide assistance to those who chose to repatriate (UNHCR 2002). This was in spite of the fact that the new government had only been in power for a few months when the repatriation process started and the country was still recovering from three years of drought. It was therefore clear that the economy was not in a good state to receive a large influx of returning refugees and that the government had almost no capacity to provide for them. The security situation was also extremely poor. It could thus be argued that UNHCR should have actively discouraged return to a manifestly unsatisfactory situation (Turton and Marsden 2002). In the event, it set in motion the assistance program that it had been using since 1990 and provided wheat, cash and other items at processing units at various locations within Afghanistan.[2]

Donors were also prepared to provide relatively generous funding to UNHCR to support a large-scale return of refugees. UNHCR was thus used to help build an image of large numbers of Afghans returning voluntarily to their homeland and so add weight to the arguments being put forward to present the change of regime as a success. Whether or not UNHCR was a willing party to the creation of this myth, the international community made substantial use of the large-scale return of Afghan refugees from Pakistan and Iran over the spring and summer of 2002 as a prominent indicator of the success of the new government. The fact that the numbers who returned, at 1.8 million, were far in excess of the planning figures of 400,000 each from Pakistan and Iran, further enhanced this image that refugees were giving a huge vote of confidence in the regime (Turton and Marsden 2002). The image that the new government has been a success has also been used to reduce the protection accorded to Afghan asylum seekers in Europe and to justify deportations to Afghanistan from the UK and other countries.

The Afghan government has similarly wished to present its achievements in a positive light in order to attract donor funding. Speaking at a donor conference in Brussels on March 17, 2003, the Afghan Minister of Foreign Affairs, Dr. Abdullah Abdullah, stated: "As President Karzai has said on many occasions, Afghanistan is once again the home of all Afghans. Over two million returning refugees in one year have proven so."

HUMANITARIAN ISSUES

The Afghan conflict has brought up a number of important issues in relation to the capacity of the international community to support refugee and IDP populations. Some of these issues are unique to the Afghan situation. Others may be applicable to other situations which create internal and external displacement.

Relationships Between the Assistance Community and the Various Afghan Governments

The emergence of an internationally recognized government has forced UN agencies and NGOs to completely rethink how they relate to the authorities in Afghanistan and it has also brought other players into Afghanistan, including the World Bank, the Asian Development Bank, diplomatic missions and a multiplicity of technical assistance missions.

During the period of the Soviet-backed government, the UN had a very limited presence in Afghanistan. The development assistance earmarked for each country by UNDP from its budget could not be used in Afghanistan because it required an internationally recognized counterpart. The government survived on assistance from the Soviet Union, and the people in the Mujahidin-held rural areas largely had to fend for themselves, with limited supplies of relief goods being provided by what were known as cross-border NGOs, using Mujahidin commanders as intermediaries. NGOs were not willing to work cross-line, that is, from Mujahidin to government-held areas.

The period of the internationally recognized Mujahidin government,

1992–1996, was one in which the aid community significantly increased its level of provision to the rural areas, but it was heavily constrained in seeking to provide basic services in the cities by the high level of insecurity that existed in Kabul and Kandahar, in particular. However, Herat was secure from 1992 onward, under the leadership of Ismail Khan, and the aid community thus continued to work on the basis of relationships with regional and local power holders. An opportunity to work with the central government in Kabul was presented in 1995, when the conflict abated for over six months. During this period, UN agencies and NGOs set in motion capacity building programs to help strengthen the government infrastructure. Particular efforts were put into the Ministry of Public Health and the Municipality. UN agencies and NGOs also provided complementary services relating to health care, education, water supply and sanitation. These continued over the following year, in spite of the Taliban bombardment of the capital, but were brought to a halt when the Taliban took Kabul in September 1996.

Although the Mujahidin government was regarded as internationally legitimate, its extreme fragility meant that the aid community did not have to take it seriously into account in planning and operating the provision of basic services. The UN, in particular, operated as a parallel government and NGOs were able to run their programs with a minimum of official interference. It was as important for them to negotiate with the commanders controlling road blocks as to build relationships with the governmental and regional power holders.

The Taliban government was not accorded international recognition and the British government, for example, went so far as to prohibit any capacity building programs in support of the Taliban administration. The UN and NGOs, therefore, continued to operate with a considerable degree of freedom to determine policy and plan programs. They were only seriously constrained to the extent that their programs contravened the Taliban bans on female education and employment and the restrictions imposed on female access to health care and on female mobility. The Taliban also sought to impose a regulatory framework on both the UN and NGOs, but with limited success. This initiative built on work already started in 1995 during the Mujahidin government but took on increased importance because of growing tensions between the Taliban and the aid community, which was heavily associated with the West and therefore viewed negatively in the light of the US air strikes and two sets of UN sanctions (in October 1999 and December 2000). By the summer of 2001, these tensions were becoming particularly acute and there was a significant risk that international NGOs might find it impossible to remain.

Throughout the 1989–2002 period, the UN's humanitarian operations were overseen by a UN Coordinator for Afghanistan. For the first three years, until the fall of the Soviet-backed government, the task of the UN Coordinator was to facilitate joint working arrangements between the different UN agencies under the umbrella of the UN Office for the Coordination of Humanitarian and Economic Assistance Programs to Afghanistan (UNOCA). When UNDP became able to use its country program money with the emergence of an internationally recognized government in Kabul, UNOCA lost responsibility for reconstruction assistance and took on a purely humanitarian role. Its name was also changed to the UN Office for the Coordination of Humanitarian Assistance to Afghanistan (UNOCHA).

Simultaneously, a UN Special Mission to Afghanistan (UNSMA) took on the role of a peace mission in which a succession of Special Representatives of the UN Secretary-General explored options for bringing the parties to the conflict together to achieve a peaceful settlement or, at the very least, agree on a ceasefire.

In 1997, it was decided, at a conference in Ashkhabad, that a single UN Coordinator would be appointed to oversee UNOCHA, UNDP and UNSMA. This coincided with discussions within the UN aimed to create greater cohesion between the various UN actors through what was termed the Strategic Framework Process. Afghanistan was chosen as a pilot project for this initiative which resulted in the creation of a new coordination structure aimed to achieve what was termed Principled Common Programming. An Afghanistan Programming Body was thus established in Islamabad to bring together donors, UN agencies, ICRC and NGOs to determine overall policy and strategy for the aid program. This drew on the experience of, and information provided by, Regional Coordination Bodies in the key urban areas of Afghanistan. This program, despite inevitable shortcomings, was reasonably successful in ensuring an adequate degree of consistency of policy approaches and an avoidance of serious duplication.

The terrorist attack in New York on September 11, 2001, and the subsequent threats by the US government that it would intervene militarily if the Taliban did not hand over Osama bin Laden, led the UN to review its operations in anticipation of a possible collapse of the Taliban. There was concern to ensure that any new government that emerged had the necessary authority to run the country effectively and the concept of "a light footprint" was therefore adopted to denote a minimal UN presence (Conflict, Security and Development Group 2003). It was also decided that the UN Secretary-General's Special Representative would have overall control of all UN operations and that a new body, known as the United Nations Assistance Mission for Afghanistan (UNAMA), would be set up, with two separate pillars, one for humanitarian and reconstruction assistance and the other to focus on political affairs and human rights. UNAMA was finally formed in March 2002, after six months of organizational limbo in which UNOCHA was constrained in its planning by its limited life expectancy. At a time when strong leadership was needed, therefore, UNOCHA lacked the necessary authority (Office for the Coordination of Humanitarian Affairs 2002). In spite of this, it was able to orchestrate an effective operation, in conjunction with WFP, to ensure that food aid was delivered to high-altitude areas before the roads were blocked by snow following a severe curtailment of aid operations due to the US military intervention.

Because of its late arrival, UNAMA found itself having to deal with a business-as-usual situation in which individual UN agencies continued to operate with a high degree of independence (Stockton 2002). It was not possible, therefore, to bring separate agencies together in common premises in the regions or to encourage a streamlining of administrative systems and logistics resources. In the event, the "light footprint" proved to be a very heavy one, with individual UN agencies employing large numbers of international staff in support roles to carry out functions which Afghan professionals would have been well able to perform (Conflict, Security and Development Group 2003). The large international presence also required an ample supply of drivers, interpreters, translators and other English-speaking Afghans. NGOs, particularly Afghan NGOs, thus found themselves losing their Afghan managers to relatively menial jobs with the UN or the many diplomatic missions that had opened up. The end result was a highly visible international presence which sat very uneasily with a government starved of resources and which had to wait for some months before it was in a position to receive international funding at even a minimal level.

The UN was, however, not strong enough to stand up to the international community and, particularly, the US government to address governance and human rights issues. Thus, when it transpired that US Special Forces had allowed acts of retribution to happen in the immediate aftermath of the collapse of the Taliban in the north, the UN was powerless to intervene. Similarly, when the US government effectively selected the president of Afghanistan after the UN had spent a considerable amount of effort convening a Loya Jirga (grand council of tribal elders) to carry out an election process, there was nothing the UN could do. Moreover, in the wake of the killing of an international member of staff employed by ICRC, the UN was reluctant to encourage a withdrawal of NGOs from southern Afghanistan lest this undermine the stability of the government. The UN was, therefore, very much caught up in a nation-building process orchestrated by the US government, with other governments in a support role. It was also well aware of the fragility of the transitional government and of the strong possibility that the country could again descend into civil war if the government collapsed.

It has, nonetheless, continued to operate, in many respects, as a parallel government, notwithstanding its commitment to help the nation-building process. In part this has been because UN agencies have, over the years, become used to a government which has had limited capacity to govern. It is also because the government continues to have very little administrative capacity. The fact that the aid community has had to continue relating to regional and local power holders for the purpose of delivering assistance has also represented a major constraint on its ability to work through the central government. By the autumn of 2002, the government was becoming particularly aggrieved at its relative powerlessness and demanded that it should, at least, have the key role in determining policy even if it had limited capacity to operate programs. In fact, it went further and proposed that it should seek to contract out services to NGOs and private-sector operators. It was in a reasonably strong position to do this, having drawn up a National Development Framework and Budget earlier in the year which had laid stress on the role of the private sector and on lean government (Afghan Interim Government 2002). On the other hand, it had inherited a Soviet-style bureaucracy based on centralized control and government provision of services. It also inherited many thousands of relatively unskilled civil servants but lacked a sufficient number of professionals as a result of the departure of so many educated people to the West and to the UN and NGOs over the previous decade.

One particular ministry, the Ministry of Rural Rehabilitation and Development, has taken on responsibility for the coordination of relief programs and reconstruction assistance. This includes a specific program through which rural communities are allocated funds to be spent on priority projects to restore the local infrastructure. The ministry, which has received World Bank funding for this purpose, offers contracts to development NGOs to facilitate the prioritization process, using participatory rural appraisal techniques. The implementation of selected projects can then be undertaken by the communities concerned or be contracted out to other NGOs or to the private sector. This initiative is unusual in creating a contractual relationship, potentially, between a southern government and international NGOs. This is the first time, during the course of the conflict, that the Afghan government has been in a position to provide a significant level of support to rural communities, including those returning from exile.

This support provided by the World Bank is consistent with its current role in Afghanistan, which is to work to strengthen the efforts of the Afghan Transitional Administration to engage in long-term reconstruction and development programs. In this respect, its mandate is similar to that of UNDP but the World Bank is clearly the lead player of the two. The World Bank administers the Afghan Reconstruction Trust Fund through which donors provide funding for the Afghan Transitional Administration. This mechanism has been established as a temporary measure while the Afghan government establishes a capacity to manage large-scale funding. The World Bank has also taken responsibility for a number of major reconstruction programs including restoration of the major highway from Kabul to the border with Tajikistan. As in other post-conflict situations, it took about a year for the World Bank to be in a position to disburse funds.

Although the government has gradually increased its capacity, with some ministries better resourced than others, it has come up against a high level of popular criticism that there is little to show for its existence so far. This is in spite of significant success in addressing the humanitarian consequences of the drought. It can, therefore, be partly attributed to high expectations for the reconstruction of the country. The fact that there is little visible reconstruction activity is also likely to influence attitudes, even though the economy is gradually picking up and initial work has started on reconstruction of part of the national highway system. The population is also concerned at the poor security situation and at the slow progress being made to create a national army and police force.

In the face of these pressures, the government regrettably scapegoated the aid community and NGOs in particular, with frequent public references to their staff driving around in four-wheel-drive vehicles and drawing high salaries. This negative perception has not been helped by the fact that international NGOs arrived in very large numbers toward the end of 2001 and in early 2002 and only a relatively small proportion of these were registered with the principal NGO coordinating body, ACBAR (Strand 2002). There was, therefore, no centrally held record of which NGOs were operating in Afghanistan and coordination between the many NGO actors proved to be virtually impossible in a situation in which telephone communication was enormously frustrating and NGOs were scattered over a wide area of Kabul with no maps to show their location. The government was thus understandably concerned that many NGOs were operating outside its control and outside the control of the overall aid community. This was particularly unfortunate because, notwithstanding the usual difficulties that exist with coordination between aid actors, the NGO community had been sufficiently small, prior to September 11, 2001, to, at least, be aware of each other's programs and so minimize duplication. There had also been a high degree of consistency in programming approaches, for example on the use of community-based programming, and it had proved possible to bring new agencies into line reasonably easily based on common principles (Euronaid and VOICE 2002).

The hiatus created by the transition between UNOCHA and UNAMA contributed to this loss of coordination (Office for the Coordination of Humanitarian Affairs 2002). The Strategic Framework Process mechanism had included the employment, by the UN, of Regional Coordination Officers in each of the main cities of Afghanistan and it was their role to coordinate all the aid actors, including NGOs. While some were more effective than others, there was a system for ensuring, through the UN, that the contribution of NGOs was taken seriously on board. In contrast, UNAMA has not had a structured mechanism for linking with the NGO community and has accorded NGOs very little weight, in spite of the fact that they are the primary implementers of programs. This may be because UNAMA has been much more heavily focused on governance issues than UNOCHA was before it and has given relatively little priority to detailed programming in the various localities of Afghanistan. More concerted efforts are now being made by the NGO community to engage more actively with both the government and UNAMA and it is hoped that a reasonable way forward can be found through which the government, the UN system and NGOs can work effectively together to meet both humanitarian and reconstruction needs.

Consequences of International Military Involvement for Humanitarian Neutrality

UNAMA has also been preoccupied by complex relationships with the US-led coalition military and their wish to undertake humanitarian projects in order to win the hearts and minds of the population. NGOs have been particularly upset at this practice, which has threatened to undermine the neutrality and impartiality which has enabled them to operate for very many years in the midst of a fragmented and shifting powerholding situation. Initial concerns that some of the military were carrying out humanitarian projects, such as building schools and digging wells, out of uniform while still being armed have been met with a change in practice so that the military are now always in uniform. Discussions have subsequently been focused on an initiative introduced by the US military to create what are termed Provincial Reconstruction Teams (previously known as Joint Regional Teams) (Stapleton 2003a). Through these, the military aimed to negotiate a better security environment with the various regional and local power holders. The original concept was extremely confusing and included a proposal that the PRTs would seek to coordinate assistance in each area. NGOs were understandably concerned that they would be perceived by the population as acting under the direction of the military and that their cherished neutrality and impartiality would be undermined. Negotiations have resulted in the military dropping its plans to coordinate assistance, leaving this to UNAMA and the government. The military has also agreed to undertake reconstruction programs of a non-humanitarian nature such as repairs to government buildings or bridges, leaving NGOs to provide support to communities in relation to agriculture, health, education, water supply, and so on. UNAMA has played a key role in the negotiations with the US military. However, the US-led PRTs persisted in undertaking humanitarian programs, in spite of the agreements reached (Stapleton 2003b).

NGOs have also faced serious security constraints in the areas where the US-led coalition forces have been particularly active, notably in the southern and southeastern provinces. The US-led coalition forces have inevitably made mistakes in their bombing raids, while searching for Taliban and other radical elements, and there have been many civilian casualties. There has, as a result, been a high level of antipathy to the US military presence which the various radical elements have exploited. The murder of an international member of staff of ICRC to the north of Kandahar may have been one consequence of this. This incident was especially significant because the perpetrator had received a prosthetic from ICRC yet regarded it as more important to kill a foreigner, as a political act targeted at the West, than respect the neutrality and humanitarian role of ICRC. The perception of aid workers as associated with the West was therefore becoming greater than the perception of them as being neutral. This murder was likely to result in a significant reduction in the level of ICRC and NGO programming in the south of the country and, therefore, their ability to help returning refugees and IDPs.

The experience in Afghanistan since the Bonn Agreement of December 2001 has thus brought very much into focus the difficulties that humanitarian agencies face in operating in countries where the US has intervened militarily to secure a change of regime. The UN was already facing difficulties asserting its neutrality during the Taliban period as a result of the involvement of the UN Security Council in the issuing of the UN sanctions in October 1999 and December 2000. The endorsement given by the UN Security Council to the US military intervention of October 2001 further reinforced the image, in the eyes of the Taliban and other radical elements, that the UN was simply a tool of US foreign policy.

The US intervention in Iraq of March 2003 has led to a heightened level of threat from these radical elements to individuals associated with the West and the murder of the ICRC staff member is a tragic manifestation of this. This has been particularly profound in its impact on both ICRC and NGOs, which have been able to operate for over a decade in, at times, extremely insecure conditions in Afghanistan in the knowledge that their impartiality and neutrality would be respected by the various local power holders. The introduction of an added political element into the situation, that of aid workers being targeted by virtue of their association with the West, is a disturbing new dimension.

It becomes particularly difficult to maintain a perception of neutrality and impartiality amongst the population when the military are numerically far more visible and therefore more dominant. Inevitably, beneficiary communities will be on a constant lookout for where the greatest resources can be found and NGOs will be seen as relatively small players. The security of NGO staff, which prior to September 11 was seen by beneficiary communities as important, is now seen as being of less consequence. This clearly has long-term implications for the ability of the UN, ICRC and NGOs to provide support to refugees in conflict areas worldwide, particularly where the conflict has been generated by US military action.

The Protection of Returning Refugees

Refugees returning to Afghanistan over the 1992–1995 period did not raise serious protection concerns for the international community. They had been inextricably linked with the resistance movement and were returning to areas under the control of local resistance leaders. Although refugees were clearly political pawns in a wider game, they were in a relatively strong position within Pakistan, at least, in that rations continued to be provided and it was reasonably easy to move around in search of work or to engage in business activity. It would also appear that they felt able to resist pressures to return once it became clear that the Mujahidin government that had taken power in April 1992 was not able to provide an adequate level of security.

With regard to return from Iran, the protection concerns related primarily to the actions of the Iranian government in carrying out arbitrary arrests, detentions and deportations from 1995 onward. There were also concerns that refugees who were forced to return to Taliban-controlled areas would be at risk but these were mitigated by the knowledge that it was relatively easy for returnees to slip back into Iran. Refugees in Iran also tended to be from relatively impoverished backgrounds and were, therefore, not seen by the Taliban as posing a particular threat.

The protection needs of Afghans increased markedly following the US air strikes on Afghanistan in August 1998: professionals and intellectuals became clear targets of the Taliban and many sought exile in North

America and Europe. UNHCR also became concerned by the Taliban's growing resort to forcible recruitment. The Taliban had faced increasing resistance to their conquests from May 1997 onward, when they suffered very heavy casualties in an abortive assault on the northern city of Mazar-i-Sharif. This, and growing disillusionment, meant that the population in the Pushtun south, who had provided volunteers in large numbers during the early military campaigns, were no longer willing to provide their sons to fight. Thousands fled Afghanistan to escape such recruitment and many of these found their way to Europe, fearing that they might be handed over by the Pakistani authorities if they sought refuge in Pakistan. UNHCR was therefore concerned that returning refugees might be particularly vulnerable and monitored known groups of returnees to check that men of fighting age were not being forcibly recruited. They were also helped, at this stage, by the fact that refugees were returning as part of a controlled process through which UNHCR would provide intensive support to particular groups who had indicated a willingness to return if significant work was undertaken to restore the basic infrastructure in their villages of origin. There was, therefore, an established relationship with the local Taliban authorities which could facilitate a negotiation of protection concerns.

The US-led military intervention created a different set of risks. In particular, the assumption made by important elements within the international community that the change of regime had made the country safe for the return of all refugees heightened the overall level of risk to potential returnees. First and foremost, refugees have felt less able to decide for themselves whether the conditions for their secure return have been sufficiently conducive. The pressures from the various host countries, in the region and further afield, have meant that it has become increasingly difficult to contemplate more than a temporary and precarious future in exile. Refugees have thus felt that they had little choice but to return, whatever the conditions and whatever the risks. Second, the overthrow of the Taliban created a power vacuum into which a multiplicity of power holders stepped, ready to settle old scores (Johnson et al. 2003; International Crisis Group 2003b). The acts of retribution carried out against Pushtuns in the north were one important consequence of this. However, one particular power holder, Jamiat-i-Islami, gained very significant power through the military intervention and the subsequent Bonn Agreement and became the de facto power holder in Kabul. This meant that those who have good reason to fear Jamiat-i-Islami forces, either because of previous associations with the former Soviet-backed government or because of associations with the Taliban, were vulnerable to an arbitrary use of violence. This vulnerability was compounded by the absence of an effective army, police force and judiciary. A report by the International Crisis Group documented very well the prevailing climate of impunity in Afghanistan and made it very clear that the Afghan government was in no position to protect the individual from an arbitrary use of power (International Crisis Group 2003a). Returning refugees will feel particularly insecure going back to areas where they may have good reason to fear that they will be victims of violence based on previous associations. This includes those who have fled forcible recruitment by the Taliban as the latter remain a threat. Afghans in Europe, many of whom have been politically active in the past or who are perceived as intellectuals or professionals and, therefore, as a potential challenge to any power holders, are particularly nervous about their potential fate if they return. UNHCR is aware of these risks but is constrained by the limited resources at its disposal for the exercise of its protection mandate. It is also in a much more difficult situation than it was when dealing with known groups of returnees in that returnees are now widely dispersed and the numbers involved are very much greater. UNHCR is not, therefore, in a strong position to monitor what happens to returning refugees and ensure their protection.

The Sustainability of Refugee Return

Refugees returning during the early 1990s benefited from the important safety net accorded by economic outlets in Pakistan or Iran. Thus, while some family members would rebuild damaged homes and get the land working again in their villages of origin, others could be working as laborers in the countries of exile. The current pressures on refugees in both countries mean that this safety net was less secure and returnees were more dependent on their ability to survive within Afghanistan than was previously the case. Refugees who have gone back since 2002 have had to contend with the aftermath of three years of drought and with the fact that the economies of Kabul and Mazar-i-Sharif have been crippled for several years, Kabul by ongoing conflict during the Taliban period, in the Shomali Valley, and Mazar by the closure of the border with Uzbekistan when the Taliban took the city in August 1998. These micro economies have therefore had to restart from an extremely low base. Much of the aid provided by the international community at the January 2002 Tokyo Conference has, thus, been used to fund relief programs. It has also been on a much smaller scale, relative to the size of the population, than was allocated for post-conflict reconstruction in the Balkans and East Timor. Funding pledges made by donors in March 2003 were at a somewhat higher level and met most of the budget requirements set by the transitional government. However, reconstruction assistance only began to become significant in the spring of 2003, in the form of rebuilding of the major highway system, although progress on this may be undermined by the growing insecurity in southern Afghanistan. The economy is thus manifesting a gradual growth, helped by the easing of the drought, but returning refugees are not likely to find it easy to survive economically, in the short term, and their capacity to survive will be heavily dependent on their ability to have some family members working in Pakistan or Iran.

Returning refugees will also have to compete with demobilized fighters in their search for income-earning opportunities if the planned government/UN program of disarmament, demobilization and reintegration is effective. Efforts by the international community to find economic alternatives to opium production will be undermined by the demands placed on the economy by returnees and demobilized fighters.

The Capacity of the Aid Community to Provide for Returning Refugees

For as long as returning refugees were able to benefit from the safety nets accorded by Pakistan and Iran, the assistance provided by the UN, ICRC and NGOs to help restore agriculture was beneficial but not essential. Thus, typically, returning refugees would be able to rebuild their own homes, get their land back into use, clear irrigation ditches that had become silted up and build rudimentary flood protection structures. However, they would not necessarily have had the engineering expertise or resources to construct complex irrigation systems or more robust flood protection structures. NGOs and UN agencies such as the UN Office for Project Services, which has a community-based reconstruction mandate, were able to provide such support and thus help assisted communities take a significant leap forward.

The major difference at the current juncture is that returnees have felt a degree of compulsion in their decision to return or have been influenced by unrealistic expectations of the economic opportunities available and may, therefore, be in a more vulnerable position than earlier returnees. The aid community has been in a reasonably strong position to provide relief commodities to vulnerable households throughout the country, including returnees, but their efforts to help with the restoration of agriculture had to be largely put on hold for the duration of the drought. Thus, many programs aimed at reconstruction assistance have only restarted since 2002 and it has been a matter of luck whether individual returnee families have been going back to areas where reconstruction assistance is already being provided. With the exception of the Shomali Valley to the north of Kabul, the numbers of returnees in any given district have not been large enough to justify reconstruction assistance targeted specifically at this group.

International Military Interventions and Refugee Flows

The international intervention in Afghanistan was one of a series, following on from those in the Balkans and East Timor and preceding that in Iraq. In each case, there has been a need to provide for refugees or to plan for possible refugee flows. In the case of Afghanistan, UNHCR planned for a much larger population movement, in the event of military action by US-led forces, than proved to be the case. However, if an outflow had occurred on the scale planned, UNHCR would not have had the capacity to respond, because of the enormous difficulties involved in preparing the sites provided by the government of Pakistan. The question, therefore, arises as to how accurate UNHCR was in its planning forecast and whether it could have been better prepared. It can reasonably be argued that UNHCR had no prior knowledge of the US battle plan and would have had to weigh up the hope that the use of precision bombing against military targets would not create civilian casualties against the likelihood that mistakes would occur and that attacks on civilians might create panic. It had found itself under-resourced in previous conflicts and would have wanted to err on the side of caution in making appeals to donors. It would also have taken into account the relative porosity of the border and the size of the refugee flows in response to the Soviet intervention. There was, however, a clear underestimate of its capacity to bring the sites provided by the government of Pakistan into use and, therefore, of its ability to spend the resources for which it had appealed. Again, mitigating circumstances can be used in UNHCR's defense, notably a deterioration in the security environment in the tribal areas where the sites were located, as a direct consequence of an increase in anti-western sentiments arising out of the US-led intervention.

CONCLUSION

Over the 25 years of the Afghan conflict, we have seen clear shifts in the policies of the international community toward the refugee population. The feelings of solidarity felt toward Afghans who were the victims of an invasion by the Soviet Union led to a generous response toward the needs of Afghans who had sought exile in Pakistan, even though the complex relationship with Iran meant that that country was effectively forced to provide for the needs of refugees without international support. The fall of the Soviet-backed government in 1992 created the conditions for a formally negotiated repatriation program and, over the best part of a decade, refugees were progressively squeezed in both Pakistan and Iran through a withdrawal of entitlements and growing police harassment. The Bonn Agreement of December 2001 created a further dimension, that of media-induced pressure and encouragement of refugees to return in the hope of economic opportunities which failed to materialize. Refugees were also used as an instrument of western foreign policy to help legitimize a military intervention and present the emergence of an internationally orchestrated transitional government as a success by virtue of the scale of the refugee return—an apparent vote of confidence in which the push factors were not taken into account. The US-led intervention in Afghanistan did not result in a change in policy but it led to a deterioration in the security environment in Afghanistan which created a profound reluctance by Afghan refugees in the region, and within Europe, to return. In spite of this, the pressures from all host countries continued to increase.

Afghanistan has manifested many of the dilemmas that face the aid community when caught up in much larger scenarios over which it has no control. After over a decade in which it had been possible for the various aid actors to work reasonably well together (albeit with the usual tensions) because the scale of resources involved was relatively small, the decision-making process has become, to a significant degree, paralyzed by the multiplicity of actors. It could be argued that the UN system should have been far more ruthless in cutting the number of expatriate staff in Afghanistan to the absolute minimum, particularly in the administrative and other support roles, in the aftermath of the US-led intervention. On the other hand, the Bonn Agreement placed heavy responsibilities on the UN to organize an electoral process, establish various commissions and initiate a disarmament, demobilization and reintegration process, among other tasks, and it is clear that the UN staff have struggled to meet the resultant demands on their time. In some ways, therefore, a much stronger UN presence might have been beneficial, to achieve a greater level of effectiveness. A stronger UN might also have been in a better position to stand up to the US government and the wider international community and challenge some of the compromises that the US government has been prepared to make with regard to human rights abuses, and the existence of a government which falls far short of the democratic ideals enshrined in the Bonn Agreement. However, a stronger UN would have been an even more visible one and the relative weakness of the transitional government would have been even more apparent. It is unfortunate that the poor security and poor infrastructure that have characterized Afghanistan for much of the conflict have made it necessary for the aid community to allocate a high level of resources to the security of its staff, including the provision of four-wheel-drive vehicles equipped with radios. The resentment caused may result in even greater threats to agency security and may, in the end, force agencies to withdraw in an unplanned fashion, leaving the government in the midst of a governance process that still has a long way to run. For returnees and IDPs, these organizational strains could leave them unprovided for and at risk of a decline in security which could provoke further population movements.

For a brief update on developments in Afghanistan since this chapter was completed, see the editors' postscript, page 225.

SOURCES

This chapter draws on the author's long-standing work as coordinator of the British Agencies Afghanistan Group, which provides information on humanitarian needs in Afghanistan, and on the wider political, economic and cultural context.

NOTES

1. At the height of the war with Iraq, Iran was hosting 4.5 million refugees, including 1.5 million Kurds and Shi'as from Iraq.

2. The processing of UNHCR assistance within Afghanistan had replaced processing within Pakistan toward the end of the 1990s in order to avoid Afghans remaining in the country after encashing their ration books. The new system had not, however, prevented people traveling to Afghanistan to claim the assistance and then returning to Pakistan and this proved to be a major problem during the 2002 repatriation.

Chapter 6

Georgia's Forced Migrants

Matthew Karanian

Georgia is one of the three main states in the south Caucasus, along with Armenia and Azerbaijan. Hundreds of ethnic groups live throughout the Caucasus, which is perhaps the world's most linguistically diverse region (Thubron 2000: 147; Meyer 2001: 89–92). Georgia has a strategic geopolitical location between the Caspian and the Black Seas. It is situated on an important transit route for major oil and gas pipelines and communications along the corridor that links Central Asia and the south Caucasus with Europe. Prior to the tragedies of September 11, 2001, however, the individual countries of the region were not considered to be of great geopolitical significance. The countries that directly border them, Turkey, Russia, and Iran, were considered to be of much greater importance, but the war against terrorism has increased the geopolitical significance of the entire region (see Eurasia Insight 2001).

This chapter investigates the current situation in Georgia, examining specifically the causes and effects of displacements that have affected the country. Prolonged and diverse forced displacements in Georgia have been attributed to the inability of the authorities to reach a political solution to the region's sustained conflicts. As a result, an analysis of the political background is critical to any analysis of this displacement. This chapter describes the status and needs of the displaced, and addresses the humanitarian or short-term, and developmental or long-term responses by international, national, and non-governmental actors. This chapter also analyzes the effects of the displacement upon Georgia's entire population and upon the Georgian state as a whole.

HISTORICAL AND POLITICAL BACKGROUND

Historically the national identity of the Georgians has been subordinate to regional or tribal identity (Suny 1994). Russian authorities seized on these weaknesses of the Georgian state at the start of the Soviet era by drawing national boundaries in a manner that would ensure that Georgia would not develop a powerful central authority that could challenge Moscow. This manipulation of Georgia's borders was not unique in Soviet history. Internal boundaries throughout the USSR were fluid during the life of the Soviet Union and were changed for political reasons many times. The border changes in Georgia and the south Caucasus have fueled some of the former Soviet Union's most lengthy and bloody ethnic conflicts. Georgia was initially awarded the status of a union republic, which gave it the same official status within the USSR as was held by Russia. This newly formed Georgian Soviet Socialist Republic included within it the autonomous republics of Abkhazia and Ajara, and the autonomous region of South Ossetia as an enclave. After an attempt at merging the republics of Armenia, Georgia, and Azerbaijan into one republic (the Transcaucasian Soviet Federated Socialist Republic, 1922–1936), Stalin broke the countries apart and upgraded Abkhazia to the status of union republic (see Suny 1993: 141). Abkhazia's elevated status lasted for only about one decade, however, as Stalin just as abruptly downgraded it to an autonomous republic.

Conflicts

Inter-ethnic conflict dominated the internal politics of Georgia throughout the first half of the 1990s. This resulted in a massive displacement of the population from conflict zones.

Abkhazia

Upon the collapse of the Soviet Union, the Abkhaz constituted approximately 18 percent of the population of Abkhazia, whereas ethnic Georgians made up approximately 46 percent. Conflict in Abkhazia erupted in 1992 after the Abkhaz members of the region's Supreme Soviet voted for independence. Georgian troops entered Abkhazia but were defeated and expelled from the breakaway region the following year. The war led to displacement of more than 300,000 persons, most of them ethnic Georgians, and resulted in the devastation of this once thriving agricultural and tourist destination. In 1994 the Georgian and Abkhaz leadership, under the auspices of the United Nations and with facilitation by the Russian Federation, signed the Moscow Agreement on the Separation of

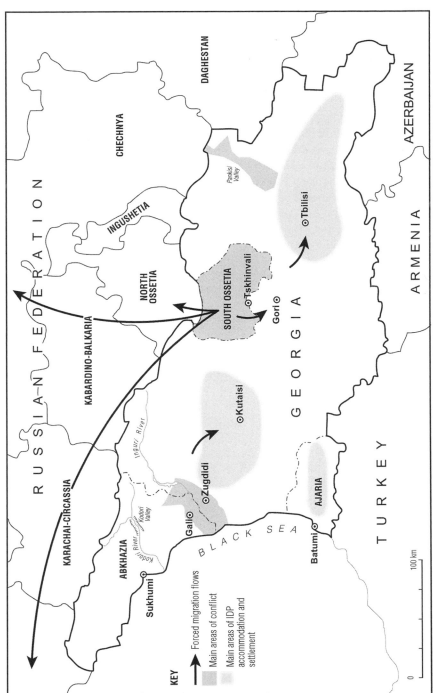

Map 6.1. Georgia: Conflict and Displacement, 1994–2003

Source: UNHCR; USCR.

Forces, bringing two years of fighting to a halt. Relations have continued to be tense, however, leading to resumption of hostilities, most dramatically in May 1998. The Commonwealth of Independent States Peace Keeping Force (CIS PKF) and the United Nations Observer Mission in Georgia (UNOMIG) are currently monitoring the Moscow Agreement.

A Quadripartite Agreement on Voluntary Return of Refugees and Displaced Persons was signed in 1994 by authorities representing the Abkhaz and Georgian combatants, as well as the Russian Federation, and the United Nations High Commissioner for Refugees (UNHCR). This agreement, however, did not encourage a large-scale return of IDPs to the Gali District. By 1996 and 1997, an increasing number of spontaneous returnees drew the support and assistance of international organizations.

During renewed negotiations in Geneva in 1997, Georgia and Abkhazia established a Coordinating Council which has since served as the primary negotiating body within the UN-led peace process. The council is chaired by the Special Representative of the UN Secretary-General (SRSG) to Georgia, and is assisted by the Russian Federation as a facilitator. International observers include the Organization for Security and Cooperation in Europe (OSCE), and the Group of Friends of the Secretary-General consisting of France, Germany, the United States, the United Kingdom, and the Russian Federation. The Coordinating Council comprises three working groups: on Security and the Non-Resumption of Hostilities; on IDPs and Refugees; and on Social and Economic Issues.

In 1998, within the framework of the Working Group on Social and Economic Issues, the UN-led Needs Assessment Mission visited Abkhazia. On February 19, 1998, four UN military observers were kidnapped in western Georgia during the mission. Despite this incident, the mission continued and was able to identify short- and medium-term needs in the primary production and social sectors. In addition, the mission reviewed food security issues, the status of de-mining operations, and facilities for post-trauma counseling and continuing humanitarian needs.

In the spring of 1998, the situation in Gali District and western Georgia deteriorated. From March 12 to April 29, 1998, a prolonged protest on the Georgian-controlled side of the Inguri River forced the closure of the bridge that had served as the only legal entry point into Abkhazia for vehicular traffic. The blockade severely hampered the movement of humanitarian aid workers and the delivery of assistance to civilians in need, as did several similar subsequent protests. In May 1998, fighting broke out in Gali District, causing the renewed displacement of approximately 30,000–40,000 persons, many of whom were returnees receiving assistance from international organizations who now became displaced for the second time. During those events, many of the homes and communal facilities that had been built or rehabilitated by UNHCR to support returnees were destroyed. Since the events of May 1998, security in Gali District has remained a serious concern to the international community. The safety and dignity of returnees have not yet been guaranteed and international humanitarian organizations have not resumed regular assistance programs in areas of return. Nonetheless, by 1999 many new spontaneous returns, with some encouragement by the local authorities, had been observed in Gali District. The living conditions of these returnees are poor, however. Security has not been firmly established, and there has not yet been a satisfactory rehabilitation of returnees' homes, community infrastructures, and socioeconomic conditions.

Since the declaration of independence by the de facto Abkhaz authorities, attempts to resume negotiations on the political status of Abkhazia have been unsuccessful. Despite protracted efforts by the international community, the peace process remains in deadlock.

Paralleling these efforts to resolve the political status of Abkhazia, the United Nations, in the framework of the 1997 Geneva Process, has addressed the issues of security, the return of IDPs and social and economic problems through the Coordinating Council and its three working groups. The Coordinating Council has not met since January 2001, however. The Abkhaz had initially suspended their participation because of an aggravation of tensions in the region which included hostage-taking and an increased presence of armed groups along the ceasefire line in April and May 2001. Later Coordinating Council meetings were also canceled by the two sides due to continued tensions and hostage incidents throughout 2001. Although—after several successful meetings of respective working groups in 2002—a tentative date for the next meeting has been announced on several occasions, the Coordinating Council has not yet met and there is no indication of when it will.

In late 2002, the security situation in Gali District and Kodori Valley, despite a number of minor incidents and at times heightened tensions in Kodori, had in general improved. The improved security conditions permitted the resumption of efforts by Working Group III to resolve social and economic problems. At its meetings in April, June, and November 2002, agreements were reached on further steps regarding such matters as education, provision of healthcare, development of electricity infrastructure, and agricultural projects. The parties had hoped to hold another Working Group III meeting in February 2003, but it was postponed.

Despite continuing efforts by the international community, little progress was made in 2003 to resolve the political aspects of the conflict. The UNSG's Group of Friends for Georgia met in Geneva in February 2003 and reaffirmed its commitment to securing a political settlement of the Georgian-Abkhaz conflict. The group also recommended that task forces be established to address: economic rehabilitation; IDPs and refugees;

and political and security issues. The Tbilisi-based "Friends" visited Suk-humi in March 2003 and, for the first time in four years, met with local authorities, the CIS PKF and UNOMIG. The parties hoped that the three task forces, which were broader-based than existing working groups, would help revitalize the political and the Geneva/Coordinating Council process. The Abkhaz side, however, objected to establishment of the so-called task forces recommended by the "Group of Friends" as part of the Geneva Process, since, they said, there already existed a Coordinating Council mechanism.

Security guarantees continued to be discussed by the groups in February and May 2004, in accordance with the recommendations that were made at the Geneva meetings. The Georgians and Abkhaz reiterated their commitments to a peaceful settlement of the dispute. Georgia's Minister of Foreign Affairs said that Georgia was committed to "[f]irst a dialogue, then other democratic methods" (*Georgian Times*, May 17, 2004). The parties agreed that they would meet again in Tbilisi in September 2004.

On July 30, 2003, following the Secretary-General's recommendation, the UN Security Council extended UNOMIG's mandate in Abkhazia until January 31, 2004 and endorsed the Secretary-General's recommendation to add a civilian police component to the mission to strengthen its capacity to carry out its mandate and to contribute to the creation of conditions conducive to the safe and dignified return of IDPs and refugees. The Council intended that the civil police would work closely with the Georgian and Abkhaz sides in building trust and cooperation in law enforcement, good governance and the protection of human rights. More concretely, the Council expected that the civil police would help to create safer conditions for the return of IDPs in Gali District. The first division of twenty international UN civil policemen was deployed to Abkhazia and Georgia in the last quarter of 2003.

The UN Observer Mission for Police Issues reported in May 2004 that a team of sixty UN civil police officers—represented in equal numbers by ethnic Georgians and ethnic Abkhaz—would soon enter the Gali region. It was the apparent intention of the Georgians to use these civil police as a replacement for the Russian peacekeepers who had been stationed in Gali. Georgian officials have complained for many years that the Russian peacekeeping soldiers have been guilty of misconduct, and that they have cooperated improperly with the Abkhaz partisans.

The civil war in Abkhazia led to mass displacement and economic collapse and this has impoverished much of the population. International humanitarian agencies continue to provide food and medical assistance to the most vulnerable segments of the population. International aid has steadily decreased since 1998, however, and the humanitarian situation has not significantly improved. Instead, according to most humanitarian organizations present in the region, living conditions have been aggravated for many people.

Although humanitarian aid is still required for vulnerable groups, it is a commonly shared view of many in the international community in Abkhazia that the underlying causes for the widespread impoverishment need to be addressed more proactively. There is, for example, much potential for local-level, participatory community mobilization projects designed to increase opportunities for self-help and community building, thus preventing further de-capitalization and destitution. Even though the political status of Abkhazia remains unresolved and the peace process is in deadlock, more concerted efforts by the international community should be directed toward low-level rehabilitation activities to improve basic living conditions and to create more income. There is also a need to encourage community development and mobilization.

In certain parts of Abkhazia, most notably in the Gali District and in the Kodori Valley, a lack of security complicates the delivery of humanitarian assistance. Many returnees migrate between Georgia proper and Abkhazia in order to harvest crops as they mature, while they continue to receive IDP allowances in Zugdidi. After assessing conditions in Gali District, UNHCR has resumed certain types of assistance, including support for the rehabilitation of schools, to address the needs of persons who have already returned. Recognizing that the security threat in certain parts of Gali District precludes regular programming visits by humanitarian actors, UNOMIG, in consultation with UNHCR and other humanitarian actors, has studied how it can help alleviate human suffering in those regions where the UNOMIG patrols are the only regular international presence.

South Ossetia

The South Ossetian Autonomous Region consists of the four districts of Tskhinvali, Akhalgori (formerly Leningori), Java, and Znauri. Tskhinvali, the capital of the region, is a half hour's drive north of Gori, the administrative center of the Georgian region of Shida Kartli. At approximately 70 percent of the population Ossetians are in the majority, but are considered by the Georgian nationalist movement to be relatively recent immigrants whose autonomy was artificially created by Soviet power. During the Soviet era the region was relatively prosperous. Its mines, factories, and farms supplied raw materials to markets across the Soviet Union, and the mountainous regions of Java were dotted with tourist resorts. Following the collapse of the Soviet Union in 1989, the South Ossetian Supreme Soviet declared its intention to raise its status to that of an autonomous republic within Georgia. The Georgian authorities annulled this decision and revoked South Ossetia's status as an autonomous region. A violent conflict ensued during 1989–1992.

As a direct consequence of the Georgian-Ossetian conflict, South Ossetia and the adjoining regions of Georgia proper, including Gori, suffered substantial material damage, and tens of thousands of people, mainly ethnic Ossetians, were displaced from their homes. Many of them crossed into North Ossetia, which is part of the Russian Federation, thereby becoming international refugees. At the same time, several violent earthquakes and aftershocks struck the region, causing significant damage.

As early as the summer of 1992, an attempt was made to seek an amicable solution to the conflict. A ceasefire agreement was signed, leaving the authorities of the former region in control of Tskhinvali, Java, Znauri, and parts of Akhalgori, and leaving the central government in control of Akhalgori and several isolated ethnic Georgian villages. A peacekeeping force was deployed, consisting of Russian, South Ossetian, and Georgian troops, and known as the Joint Peacekeeping Force or JPKF.

In 1992, a mission from the Conference on Security and Cooperation in Europe (CSCE; later renamed the OSCE) was requested by the Georgians and South Ossetians to help mediate a peaceful resolution to the conflict. With the OSCE's facilitation, the Georgian-Ossetian conflict settlement machinery has evolved. This machinery has two principal components: political negotiations between Georgian and South Ossetian plenipotentiary delegations with the participation of Russia, North Ossetian authorities, and the OSCE; and the Joint Control Commission (JCC), which supports confidence-building measures and serves as a mechanism to address issues of mutual concern while leaving the issue of the region's political status to the political negotiators.

The JCC has three principal working groups: on military and security issues; on economic issues; and on refugees and IDPs. All four parties (i.e. Georgia, Russia, North Ossetia, and South Ossetia) and the OSCE are represented on the JCC working groups. In addition, the JPKF is a participant on the working group on military and security issues, and the European Commission participates on the working group on economic issues. UNHCR is a member of the working group on refugees and IDPs.

In 1997, in light of progress on the political front, reduced tensions, and a steady improvement in the security environment, UNHCR began programming designed to create conditions for the return of IDPs and refugees to the region. Nonetheless, an overwhelming number of IDPs and returnees remain displaced. Vigorous efforts by UNHCR and its implementing partners to promote a voluntary, safe, and dignified return of refugees and IDPs to their places of origin have had only limited results. Until economic and income-generating opportunities improve, and until basic services such as healthcare and utilities are adequately restored, many refugees and IDPs will remain reluctant to return to their places of origin. Some progress has been observed, however: more returnees were registered in 2003 than had been registered in 2002.

In November 2001, local presidential elections were held in South Ossetia. The election, which was not recognized by the international community, resulted in the defeat of the incumbent and a relatively peaceful transfer of power to the new de facto president and administration. At present, the central authorities in Tbilisi exercise little direct control over the region, while its status continues to be the focus of negotiations as explained above. Pragmatism is evidenced in the attitude of the people who live on each side of the ceasefire line. Much of the adult population speaks Ossetian, Georgian, and Russian at varying degrees of proficiency, a sign of the close interethnic ties that prevailed prior to the conflict. The population on each side enjoys freedom of movement across the lines of de facto South Ossetian–Georgian control. A regular bus service operates between Tskhinvali and Gori. Georgian villagers bring their produce to the Tskhinvali market, and transactions take place in a variety of currencies, including the Russian ruble, the US dollar, and the Georgian lari. The economy is based primarily on the ruble, however.

Despite increased tensions during negotiations and the security repercussions on the ground, the Georgian–South Ossetian conflict settlement process continued in 2002 and 2003. As a result, some agreements were reached on important issues related to security, economic rehabilitation, and IDPs and refugees. Moreover, finalization of the Russian-Georgian Intergovernmental Programs on Economic Rehabilitation in the Zone of Conflict in December 2001 and work on the draft law on Return, Integration and Re-integration of Refugees and IDPs should be conducive to further deepening of confidence and rehabilitation between the two sides.

The humanitarian situation in South Ossetia is not critical, but it remains precarious and it certainly requires more attention by the international community. International aid has markedly decreased in recent years, while the humanitarian situation has slightly deteriorated and some basic rehabilitation needs have grown. Local authorities have no external support to their budget for social security programs and they cannot provide more than minimal and irregular assistance to their own needy population. There is a widely perceived need for continuing, and possibly increasing, humanitarian aid, especially in the medical sector, as well as for the rehabilitation of infrastructure.

International humanitarian actors on the ground agree that properly designed transitional assistance programs may build confidence, encourage the return of IDPs and refugees, and promote rapprochement at the political level. However, throughout 2002 and 2003 donors appear not to have been persuaded of this. The lack of progress in political negotiations, the overall donor fatigue in a wider, regional frame, as well as some misunderstandings between the local authorities and international NGOs, have resulted in closure of most international NGOs and a prolonged delay in the implementation of planned projects by others.

Most of the people in South Ossetia live on extremely low salaries or pensions. Some are involved in petty trade or the transit goods trade. Some enjoy Russian pensions, which are considerably higher than those that are provided by South Ossetia. Many working-age people are economic migrants and have increasingly become emigrants, principally to North Ossetia and Russia, who then provide remittances that support their relatives. The majority of the population, however, survives on subsistence agriculture. Because of the gloomy socioeconomic situation, crime rates, drug addiction, and suicide rates have increased and have become a significant concern.

Without adequate programs to stimulate the economy, the local population, especially the most vulnerable groups such as single elderly without family support, will remain dependent on humanitarian assistance. Unsurprisingly, the current situation is not encouraging to potential returnees. The low number of returnees to South Ossetia, even among ethnic Ossetians, caused UNHCR and its implementing partners to scale down their presence in the region. Still, it was encouraging that there were more returnees to South Ossetia in 2003 than there had been during the previous year, as well as to Georgia proper subsequently.

FORMS OF DISPLACEMENT

Internally Displaced People in Georgia

The conflict in South Ossetia in 1991, and the events in Abkhazia in 1992–1993, resulted in mass displacement. According to UNHCR data as of December 31, 2003, Georgia had 12,821 IDPs from South Ossetia and 247,394 from Abkhazia. Together they comprised 6 percent of Georgia's population (nearly 4.4 million according to the General Population Census of 2002). This did not count Ossetians who had been displaced from regions of Georgia other than South Ossetia and who had moved there, nor did it include those who had recently left the Pankisi Valley for Tskhinvali because of security concerns.

Statistics provided by UNHCR showed a male IDP population of 116,274 (45 percent) and a female population of 143,941 (55 percent). The population of children under age 18 was roughly equally distributed between boys and girls. The population of all children was roughly 58,860, of whom 29,434 were girls. Thus, among the adult population of

188,980, roughly 57 percent (108,629) were women, and roughly 43 percent (80,351) were men.

The concentration of IDPs and hence their pressure on the local situation, differs markedly throughout Georgia. The majority of IDPs live in Samegrelo, a region bordering Abkhazia (100,750 people), and in Imereti (29,916 people). The number of IDPs residing in the capital city of Tbilisi, however, has been steadily growing. Their population was 95,044 as of December 31, 2003. IDPs are moving from rural to urban areas, especially to the capital, in search of better employment, better living conditions, and better education opportunities for their children.

Types of Accommodation for IDPs

After more than ten years of displacement, approximately 40 percent of IDPs inhabit collective centers, while a majority of the remaining 60 percent live in crowded conditions with host families or in rented apartments. Living conditions of IDPs residing with host families are as variable as the economic capacity of their hosts. Providing shelter for these IDPs for more than a decade has put an obvious strain on the finances of host families, however. These hosts have generally not received humanitarian assistance or other benefits similar to those that have been provided to IDPs. A limited number of IDPs received private shelter with donor assistance, but such approaches are costly and not widely applied.

Housing conditions remain one of the main problems for IDPs. Those living in private accommodation are considered to be slightly better off, although no data exists on such IDPs and most studies cover residents of collective centers, since it is much easier to target them. Their ability to make gardens on attached plots of land means that IDPs housed by the private sector may enjoy better conditions than those who live in collective centers. On the other hand, living in collective centers offers a degree of safety and serves as a social security net.

Collective centers are universally considered to be inadequate. Since they were constructed for different purposes, often they do not meet minimum living standards for long-term stay. During May 2001 we visited ten collective centers. Three were located in Tbilisi, one in Gori, two in Kutaisi, three in Zugdidi, and one in Batumi. In Zugdidi, in western Georgia, two hospital wards and an atomic energy plant have been converted to accommodate IDPs. In most cases they have not been refitted appropriately. Originally, the lack of refurbishment was attributed to the transient nature of the need. However, after many of these facilities have been in use for more than a decade, this rationale is no longer persuasive.

Living conditions at collective centers are bad. It is not uncommon for collective centers to have broken windows, leaking roofs, walls in disrepair, and plumbing that does not work. At many centers, the rooms assigned to IDP families include interior offices or large storage rooms without windows. Disease from poor sanitation and substandard living conditions is the greatest threat to IDPs at most centers. Tuberculosis is endemic and dysentery is also a great risk. Most facilities lacked adequate sanitation or washing facilities. In one building in Kutaisi, for example, 125 families were living in a former hospital ward where none of the toilets was operable. In Tbilisi, IDPs were housed in the central railway station where in one instance, a single room served as sleeping quarters for twelve members of an extended family. Most of the rooms that we viewed here had no windows and were lit by a single bulb hanging from the ceiling. There was no running water in the building, and the 119 residents shared one toilet. Security conditions at most collective centers provide a flicker of good news. The residents, having lived side by side for almost a decade, understand who belongs in the building and strangers are quickly challenged in non-menacing ways by the IDPs. Weaker members of the collective thus live in relative security. At times such collective centers have elected committees to tackle various administrative issues.

It appears that most of the IDPs are women and children. Residents of the collective centers explained that the men had either been killed during the fighting in Abkhazia or had gone to Russia in search of work. In the absence of men, women have assumed leadership of the communities, and are elected heads of collective centers.

Although the government has recognized the IDPs' social and economic disadvantages, its meager resources have limited it to operating an IDP program that distributes state allowances, free electric and underground transport, a limited amount (100kw/h) of electricity per month, and free public utilities for residents of the collective centers.

Internally Displaced People in Abkhazia and South Ossetia

Population figures for Abkhazia and South Ossetia are difficult to obtain. Although Abkhazia remains largely closed to outsiders, certain UN agencies and international organizations carry out their programs there. Crossing into South Ossetia is easier for someone with Georgian license plates or Georgian ethnicity, but is also dangerous. Since the ceasefire there appears to have been considerable movement of peoples, including the migration of Abkhaz villagers into the urban apartments of Georgians who fled during the war.

Repeatedly Displaced and Seasonal IDPs

In addition to the IDP population, there is also a large group of ethnic Georgians from Abkhazia whom one might describe as itinerant. This group was displaced from the Gali region in Abkhazia, and relocated in the Zugdidi region just across the border in Georgia proper (see map). These IDPs stayed close to the conflict with the expectation that they would be able to return to their homes after a short while. Additionally, many of them had relatives across the border who provided them with shelter. Many of these IDPs are said to move back and forth between their old homes and their collective-center housing. Officials speculate that some maintain their IDP status so that they can remain eligible for government and international assistance, but return to their homes in order to tend gardens and small farms. This pattern of movement has been described as nocturnal displacement, which is common in the early stages of a conflict. IDPs leave their homes during the night in order to avoid attack and then return each morning to tend farms and gardens (UNHCR 1997: 105). In the case of Abkhazia, the elderly and infirm generally remained behind in their homes while their younger and able-bodied family members fled to Georgia proper. According to our informants, the elderly were considered the least likely segment of the population to be targeted by partisans and to become victims of violence. They were also the least able to move, and the most fatalistic in their attitudes, often expressing a desire to die in their own homes. The continued presence in Abkhazia of some of these elderly family members has encouraged the perpetuation of seasonal migration, whereby family members who have fled make periodic returns to check on the condition of their seniors. The political background for the existence of supposed "seasonal" IDPs is explained in further detail later in this chapter.

Refugees

Approximately 5,000 refugees were accepted in Georgia in late 1999 and early 2000 as a result of the civil conflict in the Autonomous Chechen Republic of the Russian Federation. Chechens who sought refuge in Georgia did so mainly in the border region of the Pankisi Valley. Although since the kidnapping of ICRC staff in August 2000 access to the valley has been sporadic, particularly to international staff, 2003 saw a marked improvement in overall security. Approximately 80 percent of refugees live with host families. The protection and assistance package targeted at refugees has evolved since the start of the operation but for the most part remains focused on essential, life-sustaining activities.

Assistance to Chechen refugees is administered through local NGOs and international organizations, including the ICRC, NRC, MSF, UNHCR, UNICEF, and WFP.

The war in Chechnya has caused an even more serious threat to stability in Georgia. Pankisi has become a constant concern for the Georgian government, owing to its limited control of the area and the increasing instability there, which is characterized by frequent kidnappings and drug trafficking. Accusations from Russia that Pankisi had become a base and training site for Chechen rebels were not formally substantiated by OSCE observers, but there appeared to be some evidence to support such claims. In 2000 there were cases of apparently accidental bombing of Georgian villages by Russian aircraft, and there were fears that, following the September 11 terrorist attacks on the US, the emerging internationalization of terrorism might serve as a pretext for the Russian military to attack Pankisi. Finally, following repeated accusations by the Russian side of an al-Qaeda presence in the Pankisi Valley, the US administration in February–March 2002 decided to help the Georgian military build its capacity for counter-terrorist operations through a special "train-and-equip" program. The situation in the valley continues to be uncertain and a number of families, most of them ethnic Ossetians, have left the region and moved to the Tskhinvali area.

Georgian Nationals Who Have Left Georgia

Georgia is also a source of refugees for some neighboring regions. Ethnic Ossetians from South Ossetia have in many cases sought refuge in the neighboring republic of North Ossetia, which is a constituent part of the Russian Federation. This migration is facilitated by the absence of proper border controls.

In Abkhazia, ethnic Abkhaz have mostly remained within the territory and large numbers of ethnic Georgians have fled to Georgia proper. But this territory has also produced refugees from among its Greek, Russian and Armenian population. Greece evacuated the ethnic Greek population of something under 15,000. Of the ethnic Russians and Armenians, who each comprised populations of roughly 75,000, some stayed in Abkhazia but most crossed north to the Russian region of Stavropol (Dale 1997).

There has been significant emigration from the Samtskhe–Javakheti region, located southwest of Tbilisi, as well as from other areas of Georgia.

The General National Population Census of Georgia in 2002 calculated that there were 4,585,700 people living within the internationally declared borders of Georgia—857,600 (15.8 percent) fewer than in 1989. The population decrease seen in the 2002 Census can be explained by such factors as the loss of control over breakaway regions, a low birth rate, a high mortality rate, a high emigration rate (mainly to Russia, Germany, Greece and the USA), and by the departure of former Soviet military personnel and their families, most of whom were Russians.

Trafficking

Georgia is primarily a source country for trafficking in persons and, to a lesser extent, a transit country. There are also indications that Georgia is targeted as a destination country. In 2000 and 2001, IOM conducted research into the scope and trends of trafficking in Georgia (IOM Tbilisi 2000, 2001). The research showed that trafficking was a serious problem. Traffickers frequently took advantage of their victims' limited and distorted information about the realities of going abroad in order to exploit them through indentured servitude, forced prostitution, and agricultural and industrial labor. It was shown that trafficking in persons in Georgia is tied to a lack of adequate counter-trafficking legislation and, above all, the poor socioeconomic conditions that affect the majority of the Georgian population.

Turkey, Greece, the US, and several EU member states such as France, Spain, the Netherlands and Germany are the primary destinations for people trafficked from Georgia. Other recent research has indicated that Georgian women are also trafficked to the United Arab Emirates (IOM Baku, 2002; 31). According to IOM's 2000 and 2001 research, typical trafficking victims are young women, often those who are single or divorced, and who are interested in study or temporary work abroad. Most of these women fall prey to traffickers who operate under the guise of tourism firms, employment agencies and visa brokers. IOM researchers discovered that men were also victims of trafficking, and were used for agricultural or industrial labor in Greece and Turkey (IOM, 2001).

Until quite recently, the government of Georgia demonstrated an apparent lack of concern regarding trafficking. It believed that trafficking was not a major problem in Georgia, and that other social and political problems were more urgent. However, the government has recently displayed a change of heart and has set up a national counter-trafficking policy, however. Some important results of this initiative are the government's adoption of a national counter-trafficking action plan and counter-trafficking legislation, as well as its creation of a special unit in the Ministry of Interior to deal with counter-trafficking issues. These developments have not yet resulted in a tangible reduction of trafficking victims, but the nature of trafficking makes it difficult to gather accurate data. Recently, a number of other intergovernmental organizations and international NGOs have expressed interest in helping their Georgian partners to combat trafficking. Their potential contributions have been discussed at informal meetings, regularly hosted by IOM since the end of 2002.

The Non-displaced Population

The economic deprivation that is endemic throughout Georgia makes it impossible to isolate the circumstances of the IDPs from those of the resident population. The social needs of the displaced affect the ability of the central government to assist other needy groups. Consequently, the government appears to have adopted an unofficial policy of permitting foreign aid workers to assist the IDPs so that scarce national resources can be devoted to the non-displaced. The net effect upon the resident population has been a matter of debate. Among the general population, IDPs are believed to receive special treatment and to live better than the non-displaced. This perception may be attributed to the high profile that many of Georgia's IDPs have involuntarily assumed. In Tbilisi, for example, IDPs were housed for almost a decade in the Hotel Iveria. During winters when most of the city was blacked out, this hotel shone like a beacon because the government paid the electricity bill.

IDPs are frequently in the news, and special programs directed at them, such as free healthcare and free public transport, cause disquiet. IDPs living in private accommodation are entitled to a monthly allowance of 14 lari ($7) per person per month, or 11 lari for residents in collective centers. The monthly poverty line for an individual is roughly $22, however. IDPs often complained of long delays, sometimes for months, in receiving payments. By the summer of 2000, for example, outstanding allowances that were owed to IDPs but still unpaid by the government, amounted to more than $7 million. IDPs also complained that their allowances were improperly reduced and that they had to stand for hours in queues. Although it is true that IDPs may receive marginally more benefits than the non-displaced population, this does not mean that they are a privileged group.

In Georgia, as in many other places where there are protracted emergencies, pervasive poverty and lack of economic opportunity make it difficult for aid workers to draw distinctions between IDPs and non-IDPs when providing humanitarian and development assistance. The ICRC, for example, reports that it is often impossible, and also undesirable, to distinguish between IDPs and their host communities. This is because "any available resources will often have already been shared [with the host community] so that every person affected is in a similar situation" (ICRC 2000). Despite this, however, a study by the World Bank finds that IDPs "face the lowest risk of extreme poverty of almost any population group" and that there is a need to limit eligibility for social benefits to those IDPs "who truly need it" (World Bank 1999, cited in NRC 2001).

Nevertheless, the *Georgia Humanitarian Situation and Strategy 2004* paper developed by OCHA-Georgia in November 2003 still identified the IDP problem as one requiring priority attention in 2004. The need to distinguish IDP status from IDP benefits and to link IDP status more with the legal right to repatriation was put forward in the *Study on IDP Rights* developed by the New Approach Support Unit (with staff jointly from OCHA and UNDP/UNV) and the government.

THE HUMANITARIAN RESPONSE

Following independence in 1991, Georgia's economic decline was one of the sharpest in the former Soviet Union. The country's GDP declined by approximately 70 to 75 percent between 1991 and 1994, leading to extreme hardship. The conflicts and mass displacement left a wake of poverty, unemployment and destroyed capacity. Reform programs in the mid-1990s protected the economy from further decline, but failed to create conditions for sustainable growth.

A decade after its complex emergency period in the mid-1990s, Georgia still presented major humanitarian challenges. At the end of the civil war in Georgia, the international community started providing massive relief aid, in parallel with some development-oriented support. Since the mid-1990s, the international community has been gradually shifting away from humanitarian programs and instead has emphasized more transitional and developmental programs. This is a reflection of changes in the society and in perceived priorities. Humanitarian needs have persisted, however, and Georgia has become a theater of extended emergency. Mediation attempts by the international community to reach peace agreements and security arrangements in the conflict areas have been largely unsuccessful. This, together with the limited progress in achieving political and economic reforms and achievements, such as the failure to establish full democracy or a full transition to a market economy, has stymied Georgia's development.

After more than a decade of displacement, IDPs are still unable to return home and they remain dependent on limited foreign aid and inadequate state benefits. It is obvious, however, that international assistance has reached the vulnerable population, and that the Georgian government is cooperating with the international community. The government, although constrained by its own lack of resources, is genuinely concerned for the welfare of its citizens.

The Georgian Government

Georgian government assistance flows through its Ministry for Refugees and Accommodation. Within this ministry there are subdepartments of Refugees and Asylum Seekers, External Migration, Internally Displaced Persons, Ecological Migration, Registration and Information Provision, Migration Control, and a Repatriation Service. These subdepartments are supposed to coordinate the programs that are offered to refugees and asy-lum seekers, to internally displaced persons, and to ecological migrants. Programs provide cash allowances, housing, and social welfare benefits to displaced persons. The Department of Registration and Information Provision is also responsible for tracking and registering the displaced population. In practice, however, coordination is achieved not by the sub-departments, but instead by the international organizations that are operating in Georgia.

A person can register as internally displaced by going to the regional subdepartment or regional (city) IDP service of the local administrative body of the Ministry for Refugees and Accommodation. To qualify, a per-son must actually have been forcibly displaced. A child who is born to someone who is already an IDP may be granted IDP status with the con-sent of both parents. A spouse who does not otherwise qualify as an IDP will not acquire IDP status merely upon marrying an IDP. This decision was reached in order to reduce the growing number of IDPs, since local spouses of IDPs were not forced to leave their habitual residences. According to the Law of Georgia on Internally Displaced Persons of June 28, 1996, a decision on status must be rendered within 30 days of filing an application, and an applicant who is denied IDP status may appeal to the court (Art. 5, para. 4).

IDP status is lost if a person acquires citizenship in another country or leaves Georgia to establish permanent residence abroad, or if the threat to life, health or freedom ceases to exist at the IDP's place of habitual resi-dence. According to a judicial decision that was announced in 2003 by the Constitutional Court of Georgia, IDPs no longer lose their status if they purchase property or register at their place of residence. Once recognized, an IDP is issued an ID card. The rules applicable to refugee status are similar. At present, there is no time limit for refugee status.

Health matters are managed by Georgia's Ministry of Health for the resident population and by the Abkhaz Ministry of Health in Exile for IDPs, though some responsibilities are delegated to international organi-zations. Health provision appears to be reactive rather than proactive, however. Preventive measures, such as screening for tuberculosis, and health education, although better than they were in the 1990s, are still not sufficient for IDPs. Thus, although physicians are sent to each collective center approximately twice yearly, it does not appear that they are able to address the root causes of tuberculosis, heart disease, or other illnesses that affect the people living in these cramped conditions. At the Ministry of Health in Tbilisi we were told simply that "if an IDP is not ill, he will not be examined. Doctors will only examine those who present them-selves." Cardiovascular diseases, respiratory diseases, tuberculosis and neurological disorders are said to be the most significant health risks to IDPs today.

The administration of health programs (e.g., provision of medicines and medical equipment) is handled by several international organizations (such as ICRC and UMCOR) rather than by the Ministry of Health. Government-sponsored health insurance is available to certain groups of IDPs (principally children, the elderly and single mothers), although it covers only overnight medical care, basic medicines and part of inpatient treatment if hospitalized. In practice, free overnight stay in hospital is the primary benefit enjoyed. All IDP children under the age of fourteen are subject to the Children Medical Care Program, which provides them with standard medical care. IDP women are entitled to the benefits envisaged within the State Obstetrics Program. The Program for Active Detection of Pathological Developments and Preventive Health Care is particularly important because it entitles IDPs who are not ill to have a preventive-care medical examination.

Despite the flaws in its handling of IDP issues, it is to the government's credit that it actively welcomes foreign assistance. After repeated meetings with government officials and NGO leaders, it became evident that the government is committed to resolving the humanitarian crisis within the limits of its resources, though one commentator states, "authorities may be more easily motivated to assist people who belong to the same ethnic group as the state's majority" (McLean 1998).

International Assistance

Emergency Relief: the Initial Response

International humanitarian assistance to Georgia was relatively swift and generous. The United Nations initiated an inter-agency appeal early in 1993 through which it was able to deliver more than $20 million in direct assistance (Rubins 1997: 37). UN involvement had actually begun the previous year, when it sent representatives to Georgia to help negotiate a ceasefire. Russia eventually mediated a truce in July 1993, and UNOMIG was established the following month.

But it was the UN information-gathering team, which had been in place in Georgia since January 1993, that launched the humanitarian assistance programs. The findings of the team formed the basis for the mandate of the newly established international "Georgia Fund." The UN mission included representatives of WHO, FAO and UNICEF, as well as other UN organizations such as the erstwhile Department of Humanitarian Affairs (DHA) (Rubins 1997). In addition, WFP provided food assistance, and UNHCR accepted a mandate to provide protection to IDPs and to organize shelter and clothing programs.

International NGOs were also active in Georgia early on, but their programs frequently lacked coordination. It is argued that in the initial phase of the response, the needs of non-IDPs were neglected by almost all NGOs, with the exception of the International Federation of Red Cross and Red Crescent Societies (IFRC) and the ICRC. Coordination among and between the main humanitarian agencies and the government authorities has been an ongoing concern, however, and is addressed in the following section.

The Integrated Response of the CIS Conference

Observers estimate that about nine million people were forcibly displaced upon the collapse of the Soviet Union. The huge scale of the displacement demanded a coordinated response. UNHCR set out the humanitarian challenge well in its *State of the World's Refugees 1997–98*: "It rapidly became evident that the problems emerging in the newly independent states were both complex and interrelated. The various tensions, conflicts, and population displacements in the Caucasus and Transcaucasus [south Caucasus] regions, for example, were so intertwined that none of them could be dealt with in isolation" (1997: 105).

It was against this background and understanding that the UN General Assembly adopted a resolution in December 1993 that launched a process for coordinated international assistance (UNGA Res. 49/173). In mid-1995 a group of experts convened to evaluate the problems facing the newly independent states and drafted a program of action which was presented for approval in May 1996 at the "Regional Conference on Refugees, Displaced Persons and Other Forms of Involuntary Displacement in the CIS and Relevant Neighboring States." The UN launched a plan for international humanitarian assistance to the region on an unprecedented scale.

The objectives of the CIS Conference—to provide a neutral and non-political forum for the discussion of migration issues; to establish better understanding of the problem both within and outside the CIS; and to devise a comprehensive national, regional and international strategy for coping with the problem—were ambitious and wide-ranging (UNHCR 1997). According to observers and participants, including UNHCR, however, the program failed to meet expectations. By mid-2000 no truly durable solutions for the displaced in the South Caucasus had been achieved. Obstacles to achievement included the limited resources and experience of these new states individually, and their failure to translate principles into practical activities.

Among the most significant of the principles adopted at the conference was that of equality of rights and treatment for IDPs. "Internally displaced persons are entitled to enjoy in full equality the same rights, protection and freedoms under internal and international law as other citizens," proclaimed the Program of Action (1996: para. 14). States were encouraged to adopt or revise legislation in order to ensure that IDPs received equality of treatment, and to make trafficking in migrants a criminal offense (para. 42).

UNHCR and IOM received a mandate for facilitating the repatriation and return of internally displaced peoples, "if so requested" by the relevant state, and integration was announced as an "immediate goal for repatriants" (paras. 76, 86). UNHCR and IOM were charged with developing a joint strategy for the implementation of the Program of Action during the next five years (para. 140). UNHCR, IOM and the OSCE were charged with monitoring the implementation of the Program of Action, and have produced a joint report each year since the adoption of the program.

According to the self-assessment of 2000, the "immediate objectives" of the Conference were met. These accomplishments include "recognition" of migration issues, the "improvement" of relations among CIS states, and the "strengthening" of inter-organizational cooperation (UNHCR and IOM 2000: 8). Each of these so-called accomplishments is of course subjective and is difficult to quantify. Among more concrete achievements, such as implementation of reforms, the success rate varied. Georgia was favorably cited for acceding in 1999 to the 1951 Refugee Convention and to the 1967 Protocol, but all of the governments, including Georgia, cited a lack of financial ability as a reason for failing to implement legislative reforms. NGO participation in the CIS has dramatically increased since 1996, however, and the Conference's self-assessment cites this as one of its accomplishments. According to the 2000 report, "a vibrant NGO sector is emerging, and civil society is becoming more involved" (UNHCR and IOM 2000: 28).

The United Nations

The UN agencies resident in Georgia undertake a comprehensive portfolio of activities in the areas of conflict resolution, monitoring of peace accords, relief assistance, support to health and education sectors, economic development, environment, capacity building in management and administration and respect for the rule of law. This portfolio shows significant efforts to meet the need for an integrated model of assistance.

The United Nations Emergency Relief Coordinator (ERC) was an active member of the relief effort in Georgia and has the responsibility to protect and assist internally displaced persons. Despite the establishment of the ERC, however, some experts believe there was still inadequate coordination within the UN (Cohen and Deng 1998: 126). The Department of Humanitarian Affairs (DHA), set up in 1994 in order to assist the ERC, was restructured in 1998 and renamed the Office for the Coordination of Humanitarian Affairs (OCHA), amid concerns about the effectiveness of the DHA. The DHA office was reported to have been incompetent, or at best inconsequential, during its tenure in Georgia (Rubins 1997: 41–42). Part of the reason was said to be resistance from other agencies (Cohen and Deng 1998: 145). Responsibility for overall coordination of the UN system lies with the office of the Resident Coordinator, who also holds the directorship of the UNDP office. The Resident Coordinator also serves as the Humanitarian Coordinator with support from OCHA, which aims to mobilize and coordinate the collective efforts of the international community, in particular those of the UN system.

The leading UN agency dealing with forced migration issues in Georgia during the past decade has been UNHCR, which began working there in 1993, upon the request of the UN Secretary-General and the government of Georgia. It was in this year that the UN General Assembly agreed that UNHCR programs could be extended to IDPs "when both refugees and internally displaced persons are so intertwined that it would be practically impossible or inappropriate to assist one group and not the other" (Cohen and Deng 1998: 129). Its earliest programs called for it to provide emergency relief assistance to IDPs in government-controlled areas.

UNHCR Georgia began to protect and assist Chechen refugees in late 1999 on a prima facie basis upon their arrival on Georgian territory. In 2003 UNHCR Georgia, either directly or through partners, met all the basic needs of the refugee population. Basic food was provided by WFP and distributed by UNHCR. A pre-school program and a community center with vocational classes were managed by implementing partners. Legal counseling was also provided. Psychosocial rehabilitation for war-traumatized refugees was piloted in 2003 and continued in 2004. A water and sanitation project has been implemented through partners and a small income generation project which had been initiated in 2002 was expanded in 2003.

In 2003, UNHCR's operation on behalf of returnees from North Ossetia to the South Ossetian region remained at the same level as in the past, although a greater interest in return, particularly by IDPs, was noted. Although UNHCR closed its offices in Tskhinvali and Gori, the project has been implemented through the Branch Office. More than 120 families were assisted in 2003.

The Georgian-Abkhaz conflict remains politically charged and unresolved. In recent years there has been repeated tension in the Kodori Gorge and elsewhere, making repatriation on a large scale unsafe and therefore impossible for UNHCR to support. Nevertheless, local sources indicate that as many as 40,000 persons had spontaneously returned to the Gali region as of 2001. For this reason, and to support the UN-led conflict resolution process, UNHCR initiated in 2001 and expanded in 2002 and 2003 a community-based school rehabilitation program. The program was designed to primarily benefit those communities where children were shuttling between Abkhazia and Georgia proper to attend school on the Georgian side. In 2002 and 2003, in the interest of a balanced approach, UNHCR also offered a small-scale assistance to the schools throughout Abkhazia which had been devastated by the conflict, but where it was apparent that children attended or went outside their communities to attend school in a more appropriate facility.

The United Nations Development Program (UNDP) is also an important actor in Georgia. The UNDP program in Georgia is shaped by the UNDP Global Agenda and according to the priorities of the Georgian government. Taking these priorities into account, the activities of UNDP Georgia are focused on poverty reduction, democratic governance, energy and environment, crisis prevention and recovery, information and communications technology, as well as the prevention and treatment of HIV/AIDS. Its programs have gained greater profile since 1999 because of the implementation of the "New Approach to IDP Assistance," a program that encourages sustainable development projects for IDPs and their host communities instead of traditional humanitarian assistance. The New Approach is discussed later in this chapter.

The presence of the United Nations Population Fund (UNFPA) was established in Georgia in 1999. Specific areas of UNFPA assistance to Georgia are: reproductive health, including family planning and sexual health; population information, education, and communication; population data collection and analysis; and prevention of sexually transmitted diseases and HIV/AIDS.

The "Women for Conflict Resolution and Peacebuilding in the Southern Caucasus" project is a United Nations Development Fund for Women (UNIFEM) initiative. It has operated in Azerbaijan, Armenia and Georgia since 2001. The project supports the capacities of women to participate in the peacebuilding process and stresses women's strong commitment to creating long-term peace in the Southern Caucasus.

The United Nations Volunteers (UNV) program in Georgia promoted community-based confidence and peace building measures. The program started in 1994 as a pilot project to address aspects of reconciliation and confidence building following the 1992–1993 Abkhazia-Georgia military conflict. Under the guidance of the UNDP in Georgia and the United Nations Volunteers Humanitarian Relief Unit in Bonn, the program covered the areas of NGO capacity building, confidence building, and peace building; youth development, professional training, independent mass media development, psychological rehabilitation and mediation.

WFP initiated emergency assistance to Georgia in 1993. Targeted beneficiaries during the years that followed were mainly IDPs and other vulnerable groups. In 1997, the emergency operation was scaled down, targeting was redefined and a recovery-oriented food for work program was initiated. The emergency operation terminated in June 1999.

The UNICEF office in Georgia was opened in late 1993 with a focus on humanitarian assistance in response to the conflicts and social crises during that period. Since then, UNICEF has shifted its emphasis from emergency work to rehabilitation and development. UNICEF has been active in the health and education sectors in Georgia, continuously providing vaccines and other supplies to carry out routine immunization programs, and has developed educational programs of assistance through providing school-in-a-box kits for children living in conflict zones. UNICEF has also implemented mine-awareness campaigns for IDPs living in Zugdidi region.

The WHO works with the Georgian government, particularly with the Ministry of Labor, Health and Social Affairs, to provide guidance on health policy, strategy and other health issues, with a focus on the whole population.

As explained earlier, the mandate of the UN Observer Mission in Georgia (UNOMIG) is to monitor and verify compliance with the Moscow Agreement, and to observe the operations of a CIS peacekeeping force (PKF), as stipulated in the Agreement. The CIS PKF comprises approximately 1,700 officers and soldiers from the Russian Federation, and maintains stationary checkpoints along both sides of the ceasefire line. UNOMIG operates independently from the CIS PKF, but maintains close contact with them.

UNOMIG staffs a political headquarters in Tbilisi, a mission headquarters in Sukhumi and a sector headquarters in Zugdidi and in Gali, on the Georgian and Abkhaz sides of the ceasefire line. Its primary tools for ensuring compliance with the Moscow Agreement are observing and patrolling, reporting and investigating, and close and continuous contact with both sides at all levels. UNOMIG patrolling teams observe and conduct liaison, and promote dialogue among CIS PKF, heads of local administration, security personnel and local residents.

The safety of the unarmed military observers and civilian staff figures high on the list of the mission's concerns. UNOMIG patrols have come under direct fire and have been ambushed. The greatest threat they face arises from the risk that they will be taken hostage. There have been six hostage-taking incidents since the beginning of UNOMIG operations. The four most recent incidents each occurred in the Kodori Valley, in October

1999, in June 2000, in December 2000, and in June 2003. On each occasion the release of UNOMIG military observers was arranged after the intervention of the government of Georgia.

UNOMIG's Tbilisi office is the political head office of the mission where the Secretary-General's Special Representative (SRSG), who is simultaneously Head of the Mission, has a duty station. The meetings of the Coordinating Council, organized in the framework of the Geneva Peace Process, are regularly held in Tbilisi and Sukhumi, under the auspices of this office. The office is also responsible for the coordination of political work with the Georgian government, the Group of the Friends of the Secretary General, the OSCE and the Russian Federation as a facilitator.

UNOMIG Headquarters is located in Sukhumi and hosts the Chief Military Observer and his Deputy. This is the operational nerve center of the mission, where daily and periodic patrols are planned and controlled, including to the Kodori Valley north of the Gali Sector. Members of the team also liaise with local authorities, with local and international NGOs, and with the CIS Peacekeeping Forces. In addition, they deal with humanitarian matters reported by the patrols and ensure information exchange on these issues with NGOs. Similar activities are carried out in the Zugdidi and Gali sectors. The UNOMIG Working Group investigates incidents in the field, in cooperation with representatives from Georgian and Abkhaz law enforcement bodies.

As described earlier, perhaps up to 40,000 IDPs have returned to the Gali Sector on a provisional or intermittent basis. One of UNOMIG's main goals is to facilitate permanent return for all the IDPs. Good policing is considered essential to restoring the sense of security that IDPs need in order to return and prosper. According to their mandate, the new UN police officers will monitor and provide on-the-job training and advice to local law enforcement agencies and facilitate cooperation across the cease-fire line through joint activities.

Although UNOMIG is not a humanitarian agency, in the last year several projects have been funded in Gali and Zugdidi with UNOMIG assistance, partly to help create conditions favorable for returnees. Projects in Gali include education programs for local children, a legal aid office, teacher and local NGO training, and the creation of a youth center in the Gali House of Culture. In the Zugdidi area UNOMIG financed or supported such projects as road and bridge repairs, well digging and a water pump installation at Anaklia, as well as a computer center.

The United Nations Human Rights Office in Abkhazia, Georgia (HROAG), which is an integral part of UNOMIG, was established according to United Nations Security Council Resolution 1077 of October 22, 1996, and is mandated to assist the population of Abkhazia whose human rights protection cannot be guaranteed following the loss of control over the Abkhaz territory by the Georgian authorities. HROAG staffing consists of both UN personnel and human rights officers seconded from the OSCE. HROAG conducts protection activities both by monitoring the situation on the ground, especially in the Gali District where it participates on UNOMIG patrols, and by maintaining a city office in Sukhumi. At HROAG, the local population may receive legal advice and assistance on human rights issues, of which the most prominent are the right to liberty and security, the right to lawful arrest procedures, and the right to property and housing. Moreover, to promote respect for human rights, HROAG develops and maintains permanent contacts with the authorities and law enforcement agencies, CIS Peacekeeping Forces, NGOs and international organizations based in the region.

The International Organization for Migration (IOM)

The IOM cooperates with the UN agencies and is one of the most significant organizations working on migration issues in Georgia. The organization was a major participant in the CIS Conference and was one of the first international organizations to establish its Capacity Building in Migration Management Program in 1996 in collaboration with the Georgian government. The program aims to strengthen the capacity of the government of Georgia to establish a unified system for the management of migration processes in the country. This objective is achieved through integrated projects in the areas of policy and management, migration information systems, refugees and internally displaced persons, legislation, and procedures.

The IOM likewise aims to strengthen Georgian NGOs through its NGO Migration Sector Development Program, which it has operated in the country since 1997. The key component of the program is the operation of the Small Project Fund to support the activities of the national NGOs in the priority areas of migration.

Since the beginning of 2000, the IOM has been working to prevent and combat trafficking in Georgia, as described above in the section on trafficking. The organization is now conducting a preventive information campaign. Its outreach to potential victims is by means of advertisements, hotlines and consultation centers in the three Georgian cities of Tbilisi, Kutaisi, and Gurjaani. In addition, the IOM is assisting the government of Georgia to build its capacity to combat trafficking in a manner that is compatible with international standards. For example, the organization is helping to develop a comprehensive trafficking law, and is working to determine the organizational and legal grounds for the prevention and combating of trafficking in persons.

In light of increasing emigration from Georgia and the growing numbers of asylum seekers, the IOM is active in the field of assisted voluntary return and reintegration. It has conducted a general overview of unemployment and income levels and other statistical data. In addition, it has investigated employment opportunities, state employment creation initiatives, state-sponsored training and further education programs and private sector opportunities. A survey of credit institutions, including both commercial banks and NGOs, has been undertaken. The availability of micro-credit for returnees who wish to engage in entrepreneurial activities has been assessed in view of returnee need and status. The IOM also provides job counseling and employment placement services to the returnees in close cooperation with the State Employment Service and Employers' Association.

The International Committee of the Red Cross (ICRC)

The ICRC is the most significant of the non-UN international humanitarian organizations in Georgia. It is broadly trusted for its commitment to impartiality, neutrality and independence and for its exclusively humanitarian mission to protect the lives and dignity of victims of war and internal violence. This trust is attributable partly to the organization's early arrival and steadfastness on the scene: it was the first international humanitarian organization in Georgia, and the only one to remain in trouble spots when others left. An exception occurred in the notoriously dangerous Pankisi Valley, where even the ICRC was forced to withdraw its staff in August 2000 after three of its employees were kidnapped. It did not interrupt its programs, however.

The ICRC, which has been working in the country since 1992, assists the most vulnerable people in Abkhazia and the internally displaced people and needy residents in western Georgia. Throughout Georgia the ICRC visits detainees, collects and distributes Red Cross messages, organizes family reunions and actively supports the Georgian and Abkhaz commissions for tracing the missing. ICRC runs a tuberculosis control program in Georgian prisons and it supports emergency surgical and blood transfusion services in Abkhazia and western Georgia. ICRC prosthetic and orthotic activities are aimed at building local capacities for physical rehabilitation. Programs to promote international humanitarian law among the authorities, the armed forces and civil society, are underway.

Today the ICRC has a staff of roughly 370 nationals and 24 expatriates in Georgia. It is represented by the Delegation in Tbilisi, by sub-Delegations in Sukhumi (Abkhazia) and Zugdidi (western Georgia), by offices in Kutaisi and Gali, and by orthopedic centers in Tbilisi and Gagra (Abkhazia).

Other International Non-governmental Organizations

The principal role in providing protection and care for the affected populations, and in creating conditions for effective delivery of relief throughout Georgia, falls to the Georgian government. UN agencies, the ICRC, the NGOs, the OSCE and some other international organizations active in Georgia complement the government in addressing the country's humanitarian and related needs.

More than 20 international NGOs and more than 4,000 registered local NGOs provide assistance and expertise in protection, rule of law and human rights, food, agriculture, shelter and non-food items, health, water and sanitation, education, mine clearance, and economic recovery. Most international NGOs are based in Tbilisi, although their activities cover a large part of the country. Many have been operating in Georgia since the early 1990s and have exceptional experience and institutional memories. International NGOs are a vital resource for a country facing extended transitional difficulties and arrested development. They offer a support base to local NGOs and they assist with capacity building and growth. Community mobilization projects and grassroots civil society structures are also part of a social coping network for vulnerable people. This section describes the activities of key international organizations that are implementing projects for the displaced population in Georgia.

In July 2003, after ten years of assisting Georgia's internally displaced and vulnerable populations, the International Rescue Committee (IRC) Georgia Program suspended its operations and transferred responsibility for remaining project activities to the IRC Azerbaijan Program. Large numbers of people have benefited from the IRC's activities over the past decade.

Accion Contra el Hambre (ACH) is implementing projects both in Abkhazia and in the rest of Georgia. The aim of its ECHO funded agricultural program is to enhance the food security of the most vulnerable households from Ochamchire town (Abkhazia) and of IDPs from Ochamchira currently living in Samegrelo region in western Georgia. The project targets more than 13,000 vulnerable families and involves both food security and community-building components. By running projects on both sides, ACH introduces a peace-building component in Ochamchira and Samegrelo, and tests Abkhaz attitudes toward prospective returnees. A new ACH community development project, financed by the Swiss Agency for Development and Cooperation, will be implemented in both Abkhazia and Samegrelo regions. The project intends to create a favorable socio-economic environment for families living in Zugdidi, Ochamchira, Gali and Tkvarcheli districts.

The Norwegian Refugee Council (NRC) has had a continuous presence in Georgia since 1994. In the beginning its programs were aimed at providing immediate humanitarian assistance to IDPs through such means as teaching about mine hazards, distributing non-food items, assisting with the rehabilitation of shelters, and arranging for psychosocial support. Gradually, the focus of NRC has shifted to development projects which involve education and teacher training, community mobilization, information, counseling and legal assistance, the rehabilitation of collective centers and block houses for IDPs, and income generation. Since 1999 NRC, as an implementing partner of UNHCR, has started assistance to Chechen refugees in the Pankisi Valley of Georgia.

The Danish Refugee Council (DRC) South Caucasus program covering Georgia and Azerbaijan targets IDPs, refugees, host populations, and local NGOs that provide assistance to displaced and vulnerable people in both countries. DRC covers 16 urban and rural districts in western Georgia, and hosts approximately 50,000 IDPs. Its program has three main directions: social rehabilitation; micro enterprise development; and institutional development, which seeks to consolidate the capacity of Civil Society Organizations (CSOs) so that they can promote and support social and economic activities for the target population.

Save the Children is implementing five projects in Georgia: the STI/HIV Prevention Project; the Healthy Women in Georgia Project; the Caucasus Tolerance Education Project (which introduces conflict resolution concepts and cross-cultural communication skills for youth, educators and caretakers); the Citizens Advocate Program (which is aimed at civil society development through the promotion of strong and capable CSOs); and the Communal Centers Renovation/Rehabilitation Project for IDP Families. Save the Children, IFRC and World Vision implemented the WFP program of food distribution to the people living in six drought-affected regions, without regard to their IDP status.

Care International in the Caucasus is currently implementing four projects: Community Investment Program West, to secure the sustained socio-economic development of communities affected by the western part (Tsalka, Borjomi, Akhaltsikhe, Adigeni) of the Baku–Tbilisi–Ceyhan Pipeline Company and South Caucasus Pipeline projects; Sustainable Livelihoods in Adigeni and adjacent areas, to reduce poverty in the rural highlands of Georgia; and West Georgia Community Mobilization Initiative, to enhance the capacity of vulnerable communities to address their own needs and attain self-reliance.

In 2001, because of uncertainty over the leadership of the Georgian Red

Cross, the presence of the International Federation of Red Cross and Red Crescent Societies (IFRC) in Georgia was reduced and all ongoing operations were suspended. It maintained a small office to ensure liaison between the Federation and the Georgian Red Cross, international organizations, and Georgian authorities. In early 2002, however, new leadership of the Georgian Red Cross was confirmed, and in 2003 the Federation reestablished its operations.

The United Methodist Committee on Relief (UMCOR) Georgia began its humanitarian operations in 1993 to address the needs of women and children affected by conflict through the provision of essential medicines and training in preventive medicine. Since its inception this mission has grown to implement a number of transitional development projects throughout the country. UMCOR Georgia completed programs in agriculture and agribusiness and in rural infrastructure and it continues to work in youth development and informal education, in conflict transformation and education, in pharmaceutical distribution and primary health care, and in humanitarian assistance to children. UMCOR Georgia's operations are based in Tbilisi with a sub-office in Kutaisi assisting the vulnerable populations in central and West Georgia. UMCOR operates four youth houses in Tbilisi, Zugdidi, Ochamchire and Sukhumi which provide informal education and skills development activities for affected children and youth.

Oxfam GB in Georgia is currently working to improve access to sustainable livelihood and to primary health care in Samegrelo region; to increase institutional accountability (supporting CSOs); to reduce violence against women and to provide free psychological and legal consultations to victims of domestic violence. Finally, World Vision International in Georgia implements five programs: Children in Especially Difficult Circumstances, Micro Enterprise Development, Human Rights, Food and Community Development and HIV/AIDS Prevention and Education.

CONSTRAINTS UPON ASSISTANCE PROGRAMS

Providing assistance to populations in need is a difficult task in Georgia, mainly because of political instability and the absence of a political resolution to the conflicts that have produced most of the displaced. Other difficulties arise because of misperceptions on the part of the international assistance organizations, many of which are perpetuated by poor communication between leaders in Tbilisi and displaced populations in outlying areas.

Poor Security and Lack of Information

The security situation is generally stable and calm in much of Georgia, but remains volatile in Abkhazia and South Ossetia. In most of Abkhazia the security situation was generally calm throughout 2002 and 2003. In June 2003, however, four UNOMIG staff were kidnapped, and UNOMIG responded by suspending patrols in the area. This was the fourth time UNOMIG staff had been kidnapped since the mission began.

The two exceptions to a generally relatively quiet situation in Abkhazia are the Kodori Valley and Gali District, which are widely considered insecure areas both for the local population and for humanitarian agencies. Violent incidents with criminal and possibly political motivations continue to take place in Gali District. Individuals from CIS PKF and UNOMIG have themselves been victims of crimes and partisan attacks, as have some NGOs. Even the Abkhaz de facto authorities have been targeted. In 2003, a rise in criminality was also observed on the Zugdidi side of the Inguri River. The latest reports of the Secretary General on the situation in Abkhazia acknowledged that the level of tension in Gali District has decreased relative to the same periods in previous years because of a moratorium on partisan activities. Figures concerning criminal actions are in general also lower, although "cross-border" crime remains a serious problem, particularly in lower Gali. Criminal activities typically increase during the hazelnut and mandarin harvest seasons. Increasingly, incidents are criminal rather than political in motivation.

By comparison South Ossetia seems quiet. The OSCE continued to monitor the JPKF in the Georgian–Ossetian zone of conflict, with an emphasis on ensuring the transparency of their activities and encouraging further co-operation among the parties. The JPKF monitors the ceasefire and also maintains a rapid reaction force, which has proved able to respond quickly to threats to the peace and to help defuse tense situations.

Nevertheless, crime remains an acute problem in South Ossetia, in part because of the lucrative trade in goods that are shipped between the Russian Federation and Georgia proper via South Ossetia. Robbery and theft—particularly car theft—are common. Law enforcement officers from both sides are suspected of involvement in criminal activities. So-called escort fees by the South Ossetian de facto authorities and supposed customs fees by the Georgian authorities cause resentment. Officers in the zone of conflict have been assaulted. It has also become common for frustrated villagers to block the major road for hours in protest against various events. There have been constant concerns among the international community that the present trend of rampant crime could incite ethnic tension and violence.

Although the security situation was generally calm throughout 2002 and 2003, it deteriorated in mid-summer 2002. This was a period of heightened tension between Russia and Georgia culminating in an ultimatum to Georgia by Russian President Vladimir Putin to either take action against Chechens—whom he called "terrorists" within Georgia's borders—or face military intervention by Russia. This tension was compounded by local fear of the Chechens who were said to be seen near South Ossetia's eastern border, and of the Georgian government's anti-crime operation in the area. Although no major incident was recorded, these events resulted in some genuine safety concerns among the population and also in partial mobilization of South Ossetian military reserves by the local authorities. By late October 2002, tensions regarding the Chechens were somewhat lessened, and the South Ossetian de facto authorities had become more concerned about the Georgian military operations in South Ossetia. The mobilization of Ossetian troops in South Ossetia was retained for some time mainly because of their fear that Georgians might use an anti-terrorism operation as a pretext for taking South Ossetia by force. In late 2003, tensions again became heightened in Georgia proper and prompted the local de facto authorities in South Ossetia to declare a state of emergency.

These security problems are not only suffered by IDPs. Members of host communities are just as susceptible. In most cases, IDP communities have been established in what appear to be safe locations, and the IDPs who live there do not find themselves preyed upon by combatants. IDPs and non-IDPs alike may nevertheless find themselves caught in the crossfire in the event of new hostilities.

Changes in Personnel

The conflicts that created the displacement in Georgia are now more than a decade old, and foreign assistance to Georgia has been in place for several years. During this period there has been a high turnover of personnel in many organizations, with a consequent loss of institutional memory. As a result, organizations have not always been able to learn from their previous mistakes or to have the opportunity to observe best practices. An example is the perennial emphasis on repatriating displaced populations to their homes in the Gali region of Abkhazia and elsewhere in western Georgia. Some local aid workers have reported that international actors needed to learn and relearn about the intractable nature of hostilities among the Abkhaz and Georgians. Newly arrived aid workers invariably expressed the attitude that returns of IDPs would prove to be successful once they had become a fait accompli. In 1994 the UN supported such a plan, the "Quadripartite Agreement on the Voluntary Return of Refugees and Displaced Persons," which cost about $4 million. Only 311 people actually repatriated under the plan (Hunt 1995: 30). Nevertheless, UNHCR supported another abortive attempt at return in 1998 as is discussed in greater detail below in the section on "Prospects for Return and Repatriation."

Coordination of Activities

The coordination of relief activities and of other assistance to displaced communities was initially inadequate but has improved over time. From the outset, coordination within the UN system was handled by the Office of Resident Coordinator for the United Nations in Georgia, who had responsibility for information sharing and organizing regular meetings facilitated by OCHA. Coordination of UN activities on the global level has been facilitated in part through a Consolidated Inter-Agency Appeal and this has provided additional cooperation, at least in the past, through Georgia's participation. Sometime in 1999, in recognition of the trend of annually reduced humanitarian funding, OCHA stopped holding its monthly sectoral humanitarian meetings, though some were later assumed by other key actors such as WFP, which started to hold food meetings. OCHA also arranged monthly information sharing and coordination meetings in Zugdidi at UNOMIG premises for local and international NGOs working in western Georgia. Because of decreased funding, OCHA stopped this initiative in the summer of 2003. Responsibility for organizing these meetings was delegated to local authorities as a part of their capacity-building program. OCHA still hosts information sharing meetings for the international community each month in Tbilisi, though.

In the western town of Kutaisi, where there were roughly 14,000 IDPs (with an additional 30,000 IDPs estimated to be in nearby Imereti) according to December 2003 UNHCR statistics, coordination among international organizations is limited. Various meetings and conferences were held for Imereti NGOs at Imereti NGO House, which was supported by the DRC. There was nevertheless no comprehensive plan of action and programs were often implemented without the benefit of prior consultation with the other organizations in the region, with the local authorities who might be knowledgeable about the needs of the local population, or with the beneficiaries themselves. Assistance workers tend to select regions for assistance based upon expediencies such as the ease or safety of making deliveries, their previous acquaintanceships with the recipients, or the availability of certain supplies. The lack of coordination is not limited to the international organizations. Local NGOs also report poor cooperation among themselves. In Batumi, on the Black Sea coast, where roughly 6,600 IDPs are residing, NGO leaders report that they all work separately.

Others have reported that NGOs are more competitive than collaborative when they seek to obtain grants for projects (Rubins 1997: 56).

PROSPECTS FOR THE FUTURE

Collective Self-Help by IDPs

Despite many obstacles, the IDP population in Georgia is well organized and vocal, and members of the IDP community frequently mount demonstrations to draw attention to their plight. However, they are often not aware of many of their rights or of the opportunities available to them as IDPs. Their ignorance is often used to their disadvantage by dishonest government officials. For example, IDPs are generally exempt from paying the land tax, but in most cases it is up to the goodwill and honesty of the local authorities to exempt them.

IDPs living in collective centers have frequently formed cohesive communities and have provided each other with psychosocial care and support. Such community-initiated therapeutic ventures include the organization of music lessons and concerts, and art classes for children. Adults gained satisfaction from teaching, and sometimes from participating. Although the children at collective centers lacked many basic materials, they improvised with what was available. Despite the poor physical condition of their shelters, the psychological needs of these IDPs were addressed. Displaced people have also formed NGOs to advance their interests. Among the pool of strong NGOs created by IDPs are the charity humanitarian center "Abkhazeti," the IDP Women's association "Consent," the Sukhumi Foundation, and Abkhazintercont.

The active participation of many IDPs in the NGO sector is partly a result of the availability of grant money, but it also signals a genuine interest in reforming Georgian society. NGO political activism is limited, however, and has not resulted in concrete improvements in IDP participation in government. The community of displaced persons has largely been excluded from active political participation at the level of the state. In November 2003, however, for the first time since their displacement, IDPs participated in general elections. This was possible only because of amendments that were made to Georgia's election law.

Prospects for Return and Repatriation

Repatriation has always been a major priority of UNHCR in Georgia. Beginning with the failed Quadripartite Plan in 1994, and continuing in late 1996 and early 1997, UNHCR focused on repatriation of ethnic Georgians to Abkhazia's Gali region. UNHCR's mandate continued to expand in 1998, when it increased its field protection monitoring in areas not controlled by the government. UNHCR also began programs of self-reliance to help IDPs wean themselves off humanitarian aid. UNHCR established 2001 as a cut-off for its assistance programs, which were intended to be entirely replaced by development projects.

Efforts to enforce the political and civil rights of IDPs had long been neglected, mainly because of political considerations. However, there has been progress. In the November 2003 parliamentary elections, for instance, IDPs could for the first time exercise their right to vote and to run for election in local and national government. On the other hand, IDPs cannot exercise some of their social rights. Property rights, for example, have been ignored. Governmental bodies fear that if IDPs are entitled to privatize collective centers, they will lose the incentive to return to their former places of residence once conditions for return are met. Despite the difficulties, several groups of IDPs have indeed managed to privatize several rooms of collective centers through auction.

Temporary integration is still a political issue. The government wishes to see IDPs temporarily settled where they are, and prefers not to integrate them permanently by, for example, allowing them to privatize their temporary residences. Thus, temporary integration is prevented from growing into a more stable situation. At the same time, many IDPs fear that even temporary integration may lead to their loss of their legal right to return and the loss of their right to claim future compensation for lost property. Another controversial point is whether there should be an absolute link between IDP status and the entitlement to IDP benefits. Many observers ask whether all IDPs should receive benefits regardless of their different circumstances when there are many vulnerable local people who are not eligible for assistance. IDPs are not a homogeneous group. Their social needs are varied and their individual circumstances are often quite disparate.

The government's policy has regarded the IDPs as passive recipients of humanitarian aid, and has assumed that they will soon return to their homes. The government has not given them the tools they need in order to create better futures for themselves, nor has it sought to achieve a durable solution for them. Although IDPs report a strong desire to return to their homes, they nevertheless deserve the opportunity to live productive lives in their current places of residence in the meantime. Some sources suggest that the government has deliberately avoided integrating IDPs socially and economically because to do so might reduce their desire to return, and might in turn undermine the government's ability to restore its territorial integrity. While government pronouncements and actions convey the message that return is imminent, exile is a permanent situation for many, inasmuch as Georgia's political and military conflicts appear intractable (Deng 2001: 24).

Some Georgians fear that if the IDPs return to Abkhazia and South Ossetia before a comprehensive settlement of the disputes, then Georgia will be deemed to have accepted the de facto status of those two regions. For Georgia, it appears, IDPs are a political currency. The safe and dignified return of IDPs should be a carefully planned and gradual process that is supported by development projects. If so, the IDPs may be better able to generate income and to restore their home economy once they return.

The Abkhaz authorities proclaim their willingness to accept returnees to Abkhazia. But they also place severe restrictions on whom they will admit. The Abkhaz refuse to accept as returnees anyone who fought in the war, anyone who may have fought in the war, or anyone who supported Georgia in the war. Return programs to Abkhazia have been very difficult to sustain. For example, ethnic Georgians were encouraged by the Abkhaz authorities to return to their homes in the Gali region in 1998, and roughly 40,000 IDPs briefly returned. A resumption of fighting forced them to flee once again in May 1998, however. Their return had been encouraged by UNHCR, and was supported by roughly $2 million from the international community. Georgians claim that the Abkhaz initiated the hostilities in order to exact revenge from ethnic Georgians who they believed were responsible for wartime atrocities. The Abkhaz claim that Georgian partisans initiated the hostilities because of fears that a peaceable repatriation of ethnic Georgians to supposedly hostile Abkhazia would contradict Georgian claims of moral superiority over the Abkhaz. The Georgians are also said to have feared that a stable return process would give added credibility to the de facto government in Abkhazia. The actual reasons for the hostilities may be a mix of these reasons.

There is some evidence that IDPs, in pursuit of both protection and a livelihood, have adopted a seasonal pattern of IDP settlement and return. For example, Georgian IDPs who are living in the Zugdidi region outside Abkhazia are returning to Gali as itinerant farm workers. It appears, though, that most of the estimated 40,000 IDPs who have returned to Gali either temporarily or permanently have not returned to their original homes. The statistics are generally unreliable. It is likely that, to give the impression of increased normality, the Abkhaz de facto authorities tend to exaggerate the scale of the return, while the Georgian authorities understate it (UNOMIG 2000). Regardless of whether the IDPs in this group are still considered to be part of the IDP population or are instead considered to have returned to their homes, they remain at risk from the same perils that originally uprooted them nearly a decade earlier.

The New Approach to IDP Assistance—Finding a Durable Solution

In light of the harsh conditions faced by displaced persons, the UNDP, UNHCR, OCHA and the World Bank forged an innovative partnership aimed at substantially improving their living conditions, and those of their host communities. They did this in 1999 by seeking reforms in government policy and by supporting the transition from humanitarian assistance to development-centered activities through a program called the New Approach to IDP Assistance.

This New Approach recognizes the right of IDPs to return to their homes in secure conditions, and also their right to be treated the same as other citizens (Deng 2000). Categorization as an IDP need not result in social, political and economic marginalization. The New Approach, therefore, favors the provision of humanitarian aid to IDPs only within the overall context of vulnerability in Georgia. It seeks to raise awareness within the government, the IDP community, and society at large, to engage IDPs more fully in their communities without prejudicing their right to return. The Approach also aims to give IDPs an opportunity to build skills and to develop self-reliance to enable them to exercise their rights.

Guided by an emphasis on sustainable development, the New Approach aims to achieve these objectives by: overcoming legislative obstacles to the participation of IDPs in civil society; creating capacity building programs for IDPs; implementing a comprehensive assessment of vulnerability; and opening development-oriented assistance to the displaced.

In order to determine the types of assistance programs that will help both displaced people and their host communities, the New Approach partners established the Georgia Self-Reliance Fund (GSRF) to test potential projects. The Fund is currently capitalized by contributions from the Swiss Agency for Development and Cooperation and from UNDP, UNHCR, USAID and the World Bank, totaling approximately $1.2 million. Through a series of competitions, the Fund was to award a maximum of 20 grants, ranging from $10,000 to $100,000. Three selection rounds were held in 2000–2003, and funds have been disbursed to 15 projects run by individuals, by IDP groups, and by NGOs. These projects include programs to develop agriculture, housing, micro finance programs, access to health care and vocational training.

In 2000, the New Approach began a series of assessments to learn more about the conditions faced by IDPs and their hosts. These studies addressed concerns about shelter, access to social services, participation in the job market, community resources, and the law—all of which were assessed from the perspective of IDPs. In addition, in 2000 the International Federation of Red Cross and Red Crescent Societies conducted a detailed study to learn more about how displaced and non-displaced households live, and about the difficulties they face.

Starting from 2003 the New Approach Support Unit sought through its research work to provide a sober analysis of the consequences of long-term displacement, representing a serious advance in the development of the New Approach vision. Substantial work has been accomplished in commissioning and compiling research on different aspects of the situation of IDPs. These aspects include vulnerability, health, education, financial instruments, the rights of IDPs, IDP voting trends, a public awareness strategy, information campaign planning, IDP assistance partners and privatization of IDP collective centers. The research fills gaps in information and analysis on the current situation of IDPs, since previous studies rather fell into a "humanitarian needs assessment" approach and did not deal with the effect of long-term displacement.

The focus of the New Approach in 2004 and 2005 is on advocacy and policy together with the implementation of the GSRF small-grants projects. Beneficiaries in Georgia today include a mixture of more broadly understood humanitarian-related groups, some of which are still highly dependent and require targeted relief aid. But other beneficiaries require a more proactive and grassroots approach, self-help schemes, community mobilization, or income and employment generation projects. These relief projects should target not only the basic needs of IDPs, but also the underlying causes of their vulnerability. To adequately respond to the complexity of Georgia's humanitarian crisis, it is important to continue to promote creative approaches to linking humanitarian programs and development projects.

CONCLUSION

Georgia is in a period of transition from an era in which it received generous humanitarian assistance to one in which a combination of donor fatigue and international frustration has prompted donors to place a new emphasis on durable solutions. The international community has recognized the intractable nature of the conflicts that have produced more than a quarter of a million IDPs and thousands of refugees (USCR 2003). It has begun to emphasize programs that will integrate the IDPs and encourage them to become self-reliant. The New Approach thus appears to be a step in the right direction. A lack of security is still a principal obstacle to effective assistance, however. It is advisable for the UN to maintain an active military presence in the area until the government of Georgia is able to ensure law and order. International observers have in the past identified lawlessness as the most fundamental problem in Georgia (Open Society Institute 1995: 33). Lawlessness is still a problem today. Commentators have queried whether Georgia is a failed state (Carnegie Endowment 2001) in which endemic civil conflict renders the government incapable of asserting territorial control. The question remains unanswered. Regardless of Georgia's political situation, however, the international community should provide assistance to help protect its internally displaced people, just as it would have if those individuals had managed to leave the country.

The Georgian authorities, for their part, must continue to work toward domestic implementation of international human rights obligations. This means enacting legislation and pursuing practices that are consistent with international norms. This also requires Georgia to facilitate measures that underpin sustainable livelihoods and conditions of living for those displaced by the protracted conflicts.

For a brief update on developments in Georgia since this chapter was completed, see the editors' postscript, page 226.

SOURCES

During fieldwork in Georgia in May 2001, interviews were conducted with the Georgian Deputy Minister of Refugees and Accommodation and with representatives of the following organizations: DRC (Kutaisi), ICRC (Tbilisi), Georgian Ministry of Health, UNDP, WHO, IOM, NRC (Tbilisi), IRC, IFRC, UNOMIG. Additional interviews were conducted at the US Library of Congress in Washington, DC; and in Georgia at: the Office of the Mayor of Akhalkalaki; government offices in Ninotsminda; UNHCR (Tbilisi, Gori); BPRM (US Embassy, Tbilisi); USAID (Tbilisi); International Rescue Committee (Tbilisi, Zugdidi); American Bar Association Central and East European Law Initiative—ABA CEELI (Tbilisi); Georgian–Abkhaz Two Side Coordination Committee (Tbilisi); United Nations Volunteers (UNV, Tbilisi); OSCE; Georgian Young Lawyers Association; and numerous indigenous Georgian NGOs. The author first traveled to Georgia in 1996, and journeyed throughout the country in 1998, 1999 and 2000, prior to his research for this project. Thanks are due to Tamuna Tsivtsivadze for her contribution to this chapter.

Chapter 7

Displacement, Return, and Justice in the Creation of Timor Leste

Christopher McDowell

As they entered their third year of independence after 26 years of military occupation and rule by Indonesia, the people of East Timor looked back on the tumult and violence precipitated by the UN-backed independence ballot held on August 31, 1999. The ferocity of the violence that racked East Timor in 1999 is particularly memorable because of the scale of the human displacement it created. It is estimated that almost two-thirds of the territory's population of 750,000 people were forced from their homes as a result of the deliberate burning of houses and the calculated destruction of places of refuge such as churches, schools and government buildings. An unknown number of people who opposed self-determination opted to flee the territory and return to Indonesia, uncertain about their future in the newly independent country. The dispersal and scattering of so many people in such a short space of time and with such intensity presented an enormous challenge to the international community.

The citizens of the millennium's first new state are currently assessing the contributions and legacy of the international community as embodied in the various UN administrations and military intervention forces constituted to make possible East Timor's separation from Indonesia. This chapter contributes to that assessment by considering the extent to which forced population displacement—both within and beyond the borders of

East Timor—along with the international community's response to that displacement and return, characterized the complex nature of the East Timor emergency and by extension influenced the nation-building process.

The United Nations, having initiated the ballot for independence, was under considerable moral pressure to provide protection for those who had put their faith in the international community and its legal processes. The displacement of such a large proportion of the population demanded a range of responses from the UN, including a guarantee of protection and the provision of appropriate assistance. At the same time it was required to establish an administration capable of managing reconstruction and a peaceful transition to democracy. In effect, and in the context of the UN's more enlightened approach to administration and nation-building, the resolving of the crisis challenged the UN to seek solutions in accordance with obligations set out in Security Council resolutions, along with its own promise of transparency. This chapter will suggest that in many important respects, the UN Transitional Administration in East Timor (UNTAET) made significant progress in achieving its objectives; however, in relation to its obligations to those forcibly displaced by the conflict, it fell somewhat short of that challenge.

The forced migration issues examined in this chapter relate to the response to the initial emergency phase during which hundreds of thousands of people were deliberately displaced by a militia intent on intimidation and the destruction of private property and public infrastructure. Displacement took a number of forms in East Timor. The towns, the capital Dili in particular, were considered too dangerous by thousands of internal refugees; thus urban streets remained eerily quiet for many weeks following the post-referendum violence. Thousands sought refuge for varying periods of time in rural, often mountainous areas above the island's main towns, waiting until the militia had passed through their villages. For those prepared to risk their lives by returning to put out fires and reclaim their lands and the remnants of their property, flight and refuge were relatively short-lived. Many, on the other hand, elected to remain in their forest hideouts for weeks, confident to re-emerge only when the international peacekeepers had arrived. For some 240,000 people, displacement took the form of a swift and sometimes brutal eviction across the border into camps in West Timor. For those refugees, the experience of displacement turned into a form of captivity that lasted for several months or even years, in extremely dangerous circumstances and with only minimal assistance from international agencies. Indeed, as this volume goes to press, some 40,000 of the original evacuees in the West Timor camps remain in limbo, their fate yet to be decided.

These then are some of the forced migration dynamics examined in this

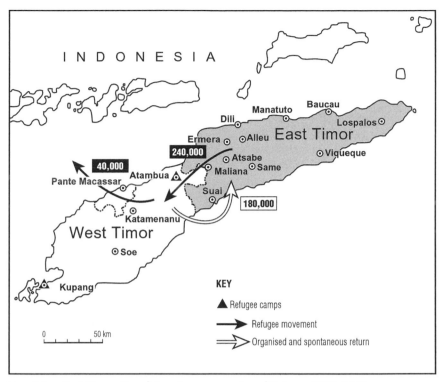

Map 7.1.   East Timor: Expulsion, Encampment, and Return, 1999–2003
Source: UNHCR; USCR.

chapter, which assesses in some detail the events leading to the evacuation—with varying degrees of coercion and voluntariness—of refugees into West Timor and their effective imprisonment. The chapter examines the responses to the humanitarian challenge as people left the safety of the forests and returned to their burned-out villages to begin the process of rebuilding. It demonstrates how the types of humanitarian response preferred by the gathering international military force and humanitarian agencies were not always appropriate to the situation on the ground. In effect, the displacees' urgent need for assistance in securing key basic needs, such as housing, health care and food, were only partially met, in some cases reflecting short-term political and media agendas rather than practice based on best humanitarian principles and learned experience.

The chapter further analyzes the UN's attempts to resolve the West Timor refugee crisis in the context of its obligations under international law, the timetable for UN handover, the humanitarian needs of refugees, and demands from the East Timorese leadership-in-waiting that the imperative for reconciliation should drive any resolution. The pressures that led to a final, albeit incomplete resolution of the cross-border refugee situation are described, and their implications for the refugees themselves are considered, as is the nation-building program. It is shown that the return of refugees in East Timor is linked to the broader issues that impact on efforts to create stable and secure independent states. Key concerns include the modalities of the repatriation program, the role accorded to former militia leaders, and the apparent sidelining of formal justice commitments by the UN and the East Timorese political leadership.

AN EFFICIENT BUT PAINFUL TRANSITION

The creating and maintaining of conditions necessary to rebuild East Timor, following the brutal destruction triggered by the announcement of the overwhelming vote in favor of independence, was an extremely ambitious undertaking on the part of the United Nations. In a number of important respects, while the East Timor experiment built on and developed earlier post-conflict reconstruction and state-rebuilding operations, in other ways it represented a new departure in post-conflict administration. Any evaluation of the international community's response to the complex forced migration emergency in East Timor has to take into account the challenge of addressing the complex political, social and economic issues, the resolution of which was vital to the new nation's post-conflict development.

In order to meet this challenge, the UN set itself an ambitious agenda in East Timor, furnishing itself with an enormous range of powers and competencies that amounted to a form of sovereignty over the new nation state. In the interim period between Indonesia formerly ceding control over the territory and independence in May 2002, the "national" transitional bodies (such as the Council of Ministers) which were established to facilitate the handover of UN powers to evolving East Timorese authorities, were in reality little more than shadow delegations. Throughout this period the UN remained in control. There was no formal transfer of the administrative, legislative and executive authority granted to UNTAET under the United Nations Security Council (UNSC) Resolution 1272 until after independence.

This meant that while laws establishing new East Timorese institutions empowered those institutions to frame and debate government policy and supervise public administration, they could only do so under the ultimate executive authority of Sergio Vieira de Mello, the Transitional Administrator. In what some regarded as a neo-colonial arrangement, decisions made by East Timorese bodies during the transition phase were always subject to the Administrator's review and approval. While this arrangement frustrated some in the East Timorese political leadership who were anxious to assume authority quickly and stressed the importance of evolving democratically and constitutionally mandated institutions of government, the administrative transition was remarkably smooth and was accomplished in under 3 years.

This was achieved in part because the UN Administration preferred to wield its colonial powers in a lighter fashion than many imagined would be the case. Indeed, from the outset the UN Administration in East Timor worked hard to maintain the momentum for handover. The process, which became known as "Timorization," ensured that governance and responsibility for shaping the new state was gradually transferred from UNTAET/UN and its partner (mainly international) NGOs to the Council of Ministers (and the ministries they headed), district, sub-district and village-level authorities, church-based organizations and national NGOs. Together these adaptations of gradually rebuilt former authorities and wholly newly-created bodies (some foreign, some local) were encouraged—albeit they were neither fully trained nor equipped—to act as representatives of the East Timorese. The UN regarded Timorization as a "new approach" to the administration of territories in transition. It was committed to the promotion of consultation with the people of East Timor, to permit their views to take precedence, and to encourage the progressive delegation of authority to the East Timorese through democratically constituted civil and political institutions.

In effect, Timorization was designed to create the conditions under which a democratic culture could emerge in parallel with the very visible construction of the architecture of a new government. The driving force behind the vision was mainly imported foreign expertise and capital, and success was dependent upon sustained security (guaranteed by a large foreign military presence and the cooperation of former liberation fighters who remained in their barracks), and the accelerated training of East Timorese to assume new positions.

The political construction of the new nation, however, remained a process that was to a large degree an elite exercise remote from the majority of the East Timorese population. UNTAET was housed in the first building to be comprehensively repaired and refurbished after the scorched earth campaigns. Its staff, who were billeted in floating hotels on the harbor and were whisked around town in an ever-expanding fleet of four-wheel-drive vehicles, appeared "other worldly" to those whose livelihoods had been destroyed. Meanwhile, the displaced were left to wait anxiously (and increasingly less patiently) for tarpaulin and wood to build temporary shelters. The distance between UNTAET and other international organizations and the people of the territory widened, as the latter's impatience for independence and actual self-determination intensified.

The massive obstacles that worked to obstruct the rebuilding of East Timor included the near total destruction of infrastructure, massive population displacement, and an economy in disarray, all of which culminated in widespread unemployment and intensified poverty, particularly in the rural areas. Notwithstanding, considerable progress was made between the establishment of UNTAET in October 1999 and the formal independence celebrations in 2002.

East Timor quite quickly became a far more secure country than it was when the International Force for East Timor (INTERFET) troops arrived in September 1999. Without international military intervention, East Timor may well have entered a prolonged period of civil war that would have created an even larger and more complex emergency. Against some of the worst predictions, an atmosphere of calm and stability was achieved; most notably in the sensitive border areas that separated East Timor from West Timor, permitting the early development of a border economy and sufficient confidence to re-establish cross-border familial and other contacts. Such normalization was essential in building confidence across the territory.

East Timor will, however, require an international peacekeeping military presence for some years to come. It will also require international financial aid to ensure the gains made recently are not reversed. After three years of unprecedented international presence and more than $1.3 billion spent on post-conflict reconstruction and nation-building, and a further $3.281 billion[1] spent on peacekeeping in the first two years of operations alone (UNSC October 18, 2001), the reality for the majority of East Timorese is that while independence is embraced, fears about further violence persist. The fact remains that most East Timorese today are experiencing the same (if not a greater) level of poverty they faced prior to the 1999 ballot.

To some extent, the UN and the broader international presence failed to connect with people on the ground from the outset of the operation. This failure, combined with their lack of ability to bring about visible and clear gains in people's everyday lives, contributed to the tensions that exist between the administered and the administrators. UNTAET became the target of the urban youth that regularly demonstrated outside UNTAET headquarters for jobs, and for greater participation in the political process. Some have argued that the UN was never fully committed to Timorization as a genuine program to democratize at the local level and encourage wide-scale participation. For those critics, Timorization and the inclusion in the Consolidated Appeal Process (CAP) document of Sphere Project commitments to human rights standards in the humanitarian response were little more than empty gestures.[2] The non-realization of these standards and principles was seen as proof of their redundancy. For this author, however, the idea that UNTAET was disingenuous in its stated commitment to international humanitarian principles, and that it in some way acted as a folly obscuring the imposition of a free-market western model of democracy on an Asian-Pacific society with no regard for indigenous values, history or aspirations, seems wide of the mark.

Rather it was the case that UNTAET and the East Timorese leadership-in-waiting reached a consensus on important issues for the new country's evolution. In particular they shared the view that East Timor needed to quickly establish for the first time strong centralized governance institutions in order to secure its position in a very troubled and unstable region and to avoid the exploitation of its vulnerabilities. The scale of rebuilding was massive, the entire Indonesian bureaucracy had left, there were barely five doctors, and no judges or police. Basic infrastructure was severely damaged and its re-establishment a priority. Timorese civil society, albeit fast growing, was immature and lacked capacity. Neither UNTAET nor the NGOs were in a position to adequately address the complex and deep-rooted social and political divisions and poverty, the legacy of East Timor's colonization by Indonesia. The task of providing a means by which local populations could assert themselves in a new political dispensation was explored through various Trust Fund–supported Community Empowerment Projects to fund village councils and other community grants, and further capacity building initiatives for NGOs. However, these initiatives were to some degree premature. The East Timorese leadership and others felt that such constitutional reforms could not be accomplished within the timeframe of UNTAET's authority, and were anyway the principal responsibility of a new government, rather than a temporary, non-elected international administration.

With independence, the outgoing UNTAET and the incoming leadership were in unison proclaiming that the message of the recent East Timor experience was the overwhelming desire of the East Timorese to put past differences behind them and embark on a democratization process. The role of the UN in East Timor's independence was pivotal, and its new approach, with emphasis on the capacity to govern and preparation to govern at the national level, was seen to be vindicated and a difficult and delicate balance struck.

Indeed, the UN and the international community in general remain positive about the medium-term effects of the emergency and development response to East Timor, the prospects for sustaining a democratic culture, and the strengthening of institutions. Following the ending of UNTAET's mandate in May 2002, the UN has maintained a large presence in East Timor through a UN Resident Coordinator (who doubles as a

Deputy Special Representative of the Secretary-General) and the United Nations Development Program (UNDP) Resident Representative. The primary task of the Resident Coordinator system in East Timor is to coordinate different UN agencies, programs and funds to improve the effectiveness of operational activities at the country level. The post-UNTAET budget has seen continued support in sectors (i.e. justice, finance, customs, procurement, power and telecom) previously most directly under Indonesian control—and subsequently lacking expert staff and infrastructure—and in the all-important health and education sector.

The full fruits of this assistance are yet to be seen; however, the World Bank believes that over the coming decade the new East Timor government will have a sustainable income base through foreign earnings from coffee, possibly rice, and tourism (though it will be difficult to compete with established locations in a declining market). The most important source of revenue will come from natural gas and oil production in the Timor Gap scheme, which should, on an annual basis from 2006/2007, cover all recurrent budget needs and leave a surplus for investment and capital works projects. However, while oil and gas revenues may last up to 25 years, concern remains about East Timor's negotiating position in relation to powerful industrial investors and the Australian government. Opportunities for alternative long-term sources of growth once the oil and gas income declines are not yet clear.

The distortions in the economy brought about by the international presence are still felt in Dili where the concentration of staff, offices and by extension hotels, shops, restaurants and associated services drew in labor and inflated prices and salaries. Many jobs, once dependent on the international presence, disappeared with UNTAET's withdrawal. In some places salaries dropped by more than 50 percent. Whereas UNTAET initiated schemes to assist its staff to find new positions, the World Bank disproportionately invested in rural areas to counter the urban bias created by humanitarian investment. But the bursting of the "relief bubble" continues to deliver negative repercussions.

Overall, the UN-led response to the East Timor crisis was deemed a logistical and bureaucratically administrative success. Humanitarian coordination was strong, the humanitarian institutions responded effectively, international staff were highly committed—indeed the emotional connection of individual aid workers with the people of East Timor was palpable. Headline achievements would include the fact that there were no major outbreaks of disease, and with the exception of border incursions in 2000, minimal violence occurred in what was unarguably a volatile situation.

Important questions, however, remain about decisions that were taken in the late 1990s prior to embarking on the referendum process in East

Timor. Larger issues to do with the UN's preparations for the 1999 ballot, including the mandate of the United Nations Assistance Mission in East Timor (UNAMET), the organization of the elections, and the absence of an armed monitoring presence have become particularly pertinent as further evidence emerges about prior knowledge that large-scale violence was planned, and, some argue, inevitable (see Human Rights Watch 2001; International Crisis Group 2001a). The political accommodations the UN reached with the government of Indonesia to allow the ballot to go ahead on the government's terms, and the UN's failure to act on the known complicity of the Indonesian Military (TNI) Special Operations units, political officers and the police in intimidation and violence, have all been raised as areas of concern that should be addressed. Subsequent human rights tribunals and investigations in Indonesia, East Timor and through the UN have fallen well short in providing answers to these questions. In the same way they have failed to convince the families of victims that perpetrators of violence at the highest levels are being pursued. Despite calls for it to do so, the UN has not sanctioned an independent review of its engagement in East Timor during the period leading up to the 1999 ballot. And as time passes, such an investigation becomes less likely.

Operational weaknesses identified in the international response to the East Timor crisis generally relate to failures to fully address the humanitarian needs and rights of displaced populations. McDowell and Ariyaratne (2001) have suggested that the emphasis on building, coupled with supporting the few pre-existing political and civil institutions, served to deflect attention away from pressing humanitarian needs and may have prematurely cut short essential relief assistance. Weaknesses identified were not matters of coordination. Rather they derived from policy decisions to shift the emphasis of the operation from one of emergency relief to one that focused on longer-term development in accordance with a political timetable for handover, and available resources as the October 1999 CAP pledges ran short. Displacement-related needs stubbornly persisted beyond the official "emergency period" but the necessary funds or institutional mechanisms were not in place to address them.

THE EMERGENCY RESPONSE

This section examines the international response to the East Timor crisis during the emergency phase of the humanitarian operation which ended in mid-2000, the period in which functions of the Humanitarian and Emergency Rehabilitation (HAER) Pillar in UNTAET either came to an end or were taken over by other UNTAET "desks" or UN agencies with an explicit focus on development.

This chronology of the emergency response outlines the mandates of the main agencies and coordination arrangements between them. It describes aspects of the military build-up, the deployment of INTERFET and military support for the humanitarian operation, and the displacement of more than 500,000 people as a consequence of the referendum process and post-ballot violence. The forced removal of people across the border into West Timor is examined.

From the Ballot to Stabilization

The days leading up to the August 1999 ballot were marked by violence and intimidation carried out by about a dozen pro-Indonesia militia groups, which to varying degrees were armed and trained by the Indonesian military (TNI). By contrast, voting day with a 95–98 percent turnout, was relatively quiet and declared a "triumph" by the UN. Immediately following the vote, when more than 75 percent of the population supported independence for East Timor, a campaign of intimidation and violence against the civilian population resumed. The militia also targeted the UN, leaving volunteers besieged in their vehicles and residences. Five UN officials became some of the earliest victims of the violence.

On September 3, General Wiranto, Head of the TNI, assumed responsibility for security in East Timor. His view was that culpability for the violence lay with "rogue elements," acting independently of formal TNI structures. The announcement of the ballot result was brought forward to Saturday, September 4. The UN restated its commitment to remain in East Timor, at the same time guaranteeing not to scale down its activities.

Escalating violence overshadowed the historic ballot result and increased pressure on the Indonesian government. President B. J. Habibie imposed martial law in East Timor, thereby sanctioning control of the territory by the military. At the same time, however, and in response to international pressure for an armed intervention, Xanana Gusmão, the East Timorese resistance leader, was freed from detention. APEC Foreign Ministers meeting in Auckland on Wednesday, September 8, endorsed the Australian government's demand for the creation of a multinational peacekeeping force (PKF). The United Nations sent a delegation of UNSC ambassadors to Jakarta to negotiate terms for the introduction of the PKF.

On Thursday, September 9, because violence had once again escalated in Dili, the UN announced its mission in East Timor would be largely withdrawn. On September 10 some 350 staff, observers, medical personnel, ballot officials and refugees from the UNAMET compound fled Dili for Darwin. However, a number of local and international UN staff volunteered to remain in Dili to offer what protection they could to the 1,500–

2,000 Internally Displaced Persons (IDPs) who had sought protection in the UN compound.

Economic and diplomatic pressure brought to bear by the international community paid off. While UNAMET prepared to leave Dili, UNSC commenced negotiations with the Indonesian government on how any PKF should be constituted, and what its mandate and terms of engagement should be. Meanwhile, British, American and New Zealand warships arrived in Darwin and by September 13 the Indonesian president finally agreed to a PKF in East Timor and access for the evacuation of the refugees in the UN Dili compound.

Following consultations with the United Nations Office for the Coordination of Humanitarian Affairs (OCHA), UNSC diplomats defined the immediate priorities of any international response. In no specific order, any force would be variously charged with the delivery of humanitarian aid to the refugees in the mountains, the early deployment of a UN PKF, and the mobilization of the international community to start the task of rebuilding East Timor. Immediate humanitarian needs of the displaced were assessed to be shelter, sanitation, water and health.

The UN decision to go ahead with an operation comprising a projected overall contingent of 8,000 troops was received on September 16, and by September 18 some twenty countries had pledged support under the command of Australia. The food drops (provisions for 14,000 people for one day) that took place around Dare, Ermera and Bobonaro over the weekend of September 18 and 19, were subsequently suspended for three days to allow for the military build-up.

An initial force of 2,500 UN peacekeeping troops—which had received a subdued welcome in Dili—secured the port and airport without opposition. Towns distant from Dili, however, remained out of reach of the Stabilization Force. But despite the presence of the troops, the forced evacuation of East Timorese to West Timor continued unabated, in Indonesian military trucks and by sea.

Establishing the East Timor Operation

During the first 18 days of September, international military, humanitarian and media activity was concentrated in Darwin and by September 18 some 25 Australian and international NGOs were present in the city. The arrival of larger and better-resourced European NGOs coincided with the gathering of the multinational PKF and signaled an internationalization of the response, the injection of larger amounts of cash, and a greater degree of complexity.

There were three main streams of activity in this period. The first involved the build-up of the international humanitarian presence in

Darwin. The second involved activities leading to UN Security Council resolutions and the creation of a multinational peacekeeping force. The third stream was the local response in Australia to the refugee crisis, an exceptionally well-handled effort evolved to offer refuge, protection and assistance to the UN refugees who were evacuated to Darwin.

Despite the fact that all three streams of activity were directed at responding to the crisis, synchrony between them was not always apparent. A lack of initial coordination contributed to concerns of NGOs that the UN, the Australian government in Canberra, and the international political community were, in general, allowing the government of Indonesia an undeserved and disproportionate role in directing the course of events.

In part, tension arose because of conflicting timetables for the respective components of the upcoming operations. The humanitarian community stressed the need for an immediate response. In contrast, the political process, based as it was on the need to include the government of Indonesia in negotiations and to work through UN channels, was largely not in the public domain and appeared to grind unnecessarily slowly. At the same time the military, preparing for its own contribution, seemed insulated from the diplomatic and humanitarian realms.

Political insistence that peacekeeping could only be effective with the backing of the government of Indonesia and, on the ground, working alongside the Indonesian TNI, also raised a series of concerns among agencies. The first was that it would be more difficult to hold the TNI accountable for their actions in East Timor. Second, the task of delivering aid where convoys were accompanied by the Indonesian military would be compromised. And lastly, the seeds sown in this earliest phase of East Timor's reconstruction would make harder still the task of fostering a climate of trust and security for both the civilian population and aid workers.

The situation improved with the arrival in Darwin on Saturday, September 18, of OCHA. The establishment of the OCHA office provided a focus for the relief effort for East Timor. Publicly, the Australian Council for Overseas Aid (ACFOA), UNHCR and UNAMET (up to this point the lead UN agency) were extremely receptive to OCHA, and looked forward to a "stronger response."

One of OCHA's first tasks, with the support of UNHCR, was to assess the humanitarian needs in East Timor, including an audit of the humanitarian capacity in Darwin and East Timor and an assessment of NGO capability. Important groundwork for OCHA was undertaken by ACFOA. In addition OCHA shared with UNHCR the responsibility for liaison with the military, particularly over the issue of reserving space on flights for relief supplies and personnel.

Stability, Displacee Return and the Delivery of Assistance

On September 20, Ross Mountain, the newly appointed UN Humanitarian Coordinator, along with five humanitarian advisers, made a first visit to Dili, the purpose of which was to conduct an initial survey and to evaluate logistics, the condition of the airports, and storage facilities.

During this time, General Peter Cosgrove, Commander of the UN peacekeeping force INTERFET, informed the media that INTERFET had three clear priorities: a primary task to establish security in East Timor; a secondary task to support UNAMET; and a final task to support the humanitarian operation. Cosgrove had interpreted the mission priorities as sequential and informed UN and other humanitarian agencies that military resources would only be diverted to humanitarian tasks as and when the primary and secondary tasks allowed. In the following period, INTERFET, anxious to demarcate the military role, repeatedly emphasized that the delivery of assistance was the responsibility of the humanitarian agencies. Large-scale distribution could not be undertaken by the military and would not proceed without there first being a climate of peace and security. Meanwhile attacks by the militia and the TNI Kopassus special operations unit continued.

UN responsibility extended beyond East Timor to the newly erected camps in West Timor and a UN mission announced that conditions for the 240,000 refugees were deteriorating due to a lack of food, clean water, medicine and shelter. It was reported also that militia, while not present during official visits, were thought to be controlling the movement of people and supplies in and out of the camps, and that refugees were, according to East Timor's influential "roving Ambassador" Ramos Horta, "hostages." In the following days sporadic confrontations occurred between the INTERFET troops and the militia.

Meanwhile, in New York on September 22, UN debate centered on Indonesian cooperation in East Timor, and the accelerated establishment of a Transitional Administration in Dili. At the same time reports emerged from West Timor that the Indonesian authorities had well-developed plans to forcibly resettle the majority of refugees in other parts of Indonesia. Speculation increased that the government of Indonesia was seeking to partition East Timor by extending the West Timor border eastward and populating the area with pro-Jakarta residents.

In Darwin and Dili relations between the military and the humanitarian agencies were strained. NGOs expressed frustration at the lack of access to space on military flights. In addition, they were frustrated by the perceived slowness in transporting supplies already stockpiled in Dili, or pre-positioned in Darwin, to displaced people outside the capital. Frustration further increased with the repeated looting of food stores in Dili.

The military again asserted that troop reinforcements had priority on the 25–30 daily flights between Darwin and Dili, and that the situation was not yet conducive for a large-scale civilian-led relief effort.

Despite confrontations, humanitarian relief operations gradually gathered momentum in and around Dili from September 25. Limited quantities of rice, baby food and other foodstuffs, plastic sheeting and medicines were delivered by UN agencies and NGOs. As the number of people re-entering Dili increased in advance of the TNI's official withdrawal on September 27, UN and other agencies developed a contingency plan to cope with the influx of IDPs. INTERFET increased its profile on the streets, and aid workers were given higher levels of protection, as were food warehouses.

Following their formal take-over of military control from the government of Indonesia on September 28, the 3,800 INTERFET troops stepped up confidence-building patrols. Responding to localized reports of militia attacks, they extended their presence in towns some distance beyond Dili, and provided limited escorts for humanitarian convoys.

The many residents who remained cautious, however, spent the daytime hours in Dili, returning to the hills at night. The relief effort continued to be hampered by a shortage of staff and suitable vehicles, a lack of safe warehousing, and severe problems with distribution to those who had sought refuge in the hills. The strategy of food parcel airdrops was deemed to be ill-advised and unsuccessful following several high profile failed operations, despite the new "snow drop" technology and newly-equipped aircraft. In West Timor, where makeshift camps were being erected, the situation remained tense, with access to the camps for UN agencies and NGOs limited.

Back in New York, the UN voted for an international inquiry into human rights abuses which was expected to be the first step toward a full war crimes tribunal for East Timor. The International Commission of Inquiry reported its findings to the UNSC on January 31, 2000, detailing widespread human rights violations and providing evidence of TNI and Indonesian police complicity in the violence. The government of Indonesia declared the UN investigation "unnecessary" and instead announced its own investigation.

On September 28, OCHA issued the preliminary inter-agency and NGO needs assessment for both East Timor and West Timor at an estimated cost of $114 million for the six months to February 2000. The broad objective of the humanitarian agencies was described as "providing assistance to IDPs and other vulnerable populations in East Timor, while creating conditions for more sustainable development." The report further recognized that only very limited relief had been delivered to the most vulnerable.

By the end of September some 70,000 people were thought to have returned to Dili, though the estimate was later reduced to nearer 45,000. On October 2, OCHA opened a UN Operations Center in Baucau from where the National Council of Timorese Resistance (CNRT), Commission of Humanitarian Affairs and church groups facilitated the distribution of assistance for the most vulnerable.

As the security situation stabilized in and around Dili, INTERFET made available two platoons to support UN humanitarian operations and together with OCHA developed a schedule for future assessments and operations using military escorts. Elsewhere, however, most notably at the eastern end of the island, 80 percent of residents remained too afraid of the militia to come down from the mountains.

While the gradual return of IDPs to their towns and villages continued, instilling confidence among the civilian population still proved difficult. On the weekend of October 10, INTERFET troops arrived by helicopter in the eastern town of Suai, scene of some of the worst reported atrocities. An overwhelming majority of the town's population up to that point had received no food aid or medical assistance.

Coordination

The humanitarian agencies involved in responding to the crisis in East Timor, and the individuals within those agencies, worked to a common set of objectives laid down in UNSCR 1264 of September 14, having agreed that their main priority was to "protect and ensure the survival of the people of East Timor." Other objectives, not necessarily shared by all, were nonetheless understood. These included rebuilding a constructive relationship with the government and people of Indonesia, and retaining the unique identity of a particular organization while at the same time being fully a part of a common effort.

Inter-agency emergency planning sessions were loosely controlled and coordinated from a central point according to OCHA's contingency plan. OCHA's manuals describing the need for Joint Logistics Centers (JLC), On-Site Operations Coordination Centers, the Military, Civil Defense and Civil Protection Assets Register, contained complex guidelines on their "activation" and use. Robust timetables for the emergency response were drafted; in practice, the phasing was not a tight planning tool but rather loosely predicted what was anticipated to happen.

In the absence, then, of a rigid and formal command structure, the pattern of the humanitarian response during the period covered by this analysis was largely created by the players themselves through their dealings with one another in a relatively deregulated environment. Those dealings were frequent, both official and social, and conducted by individuals who, in the main, were veterans of Rwanda, Bosnia, Sierra Leone or Kosovo. Experienced aid workers brought to discussions previous experiences, both professional and highly personal, and meetings within the humanitarian network were relatively swift with much shared understanding.

The situation in East Timor was different from previous emergencies. Certainly there were militia on the ground and INTERFET had to deal with the Indonesian military and police. However, the fighting had all but stopped and the problems faced by relief workers and the risks to which they were subject could not easily be compared to those experienced in some other countries.

Before the establishment of OCHA in Darwin, UNHCR, UNDP and World Food Program (WFP) vied in friendly fashion—and not for the first time—for the position of dominant agency alongside OCHA, their goal being to assume coordination responsibility once OCHA left East Timor. As a consequence, other NGOs felt pushed out from the inside track, which led primarily to the military and, by extension, the capacity to move relief supplies.

There was a general acceptance, however, that OCHA's coordination role was essential and largely successful. OCHA and other UN specialized agencies directed and shaped the overall pattern of relief. OCHA staff were clearly aware of the need to act sensitively in light of the different power relations between UN agencies and NGOs.

The "Military Side" and the "Humanitarian Side"

While coordination between agencies was well managed, and mandates generally understood, coordination and understanding between INTERFET and humanitarian agencies, including the UN, was slow in developing. The military was noticeably uncomfortable with the relatively unstructured style of working. More importantly, it came to the Timor operation with the concept of a relationship between humanitarian and peace-enforcing activities, which was different in important respects from that of the UN humanitarian agencies and certainly different from the expectations of the NGOs.

General Cosgrove, in his first meeting with Ian Martin (UNAMET), Ross Mountain (OCHA) and other UN representatives on September 20, referred to the "humanitarian side" and the "military side" as if in opposition. Mountain outlined to Cosgrove the basic elements of an integrated and unified approach to military/humanitarian operations, as OCHA understood them:

- the use of military assets to support the humanitarian operation (not diverted);

- the need to coordinate activities—particularly in relation to air movements to ensure that humanitarian movements would not be impeded unnecessarily;
- the need for the military and humanitarian agencies to share information for the purposes of planning;
- the need to work together on reconnaissance.

However, Cosgrove was determined to adhere strictly to his understanding of the tasks and to do so in a military way, without interference, with set resources and within a timeframe. Though denied by the military, NGOs felt that INTERFET was relegating the distribution of relief and that humanitarian workers were regarded as both encumbrance and impediment to the military-defined "mission success."

By the end of September, and with increasing agency presence in East Timor, the level and content of communication between the military and the humanitarian agencies in both Darwin and Dili, effected through the Civil Military Operations Center, had improved. INTERFET shared increasing amounts of intelligence, and joint logistical activities and planning were improved through coordination. Participation in joint operations (reconnaissance, warehouse security, food distribution) created a relationship based increasingly on trust and common understanding.

NATION BUILDING AND REFUGEE REPATRIATION

The violence which led to the forced evacuation of some 240,000 East Timorese across the border into West Timor broke out immediately after the August 31, 1999, ballot to decide East Timor's future relationship with Indonesia. Despite the arrival of an international armed force under Australian control on September 18, forced evacuations—many of which were captured on film—occurred throughout that month. People were transported across the border in Indonesian military trucks, by boat, or crossed on foot. Subsequent UN human rights investigations confirmed that the militia and TNI were involved in these relocations of refugees, among whom were many women and children.[3]

A number of refugee camps were hastily set up close to the East Timor border. Political leaders, including Ramos Horta, were quick to describe the refugees as "hostages," stressing the urgent need to bring about their return to East Timor once the security situation had stabilized. Between the establishment of the camps in September 1999 and the publication of this volume, a number of attempts were made by the UN to return the refugees to East Timor. There were initial movements across the border between October 1999 and February 2000. During this period, some

50,000 people left the camps and returned spontaneously to East Timor; a further 135,000 people returned as part of organized programs.

UN-led initiatives to facilitate return during this period included family reunion weekends on the border (some of which were attended by many thousands of people), "come and see visits" that enabled refugees to assess first hand the conditions for return in East Timor, and information campaigns often conducted by the Catholic Church. At the same time, the West Timor authorities applied their own pressure on the refugees, repeatedly threatening to cut off assistance to the camps and to close them down by force if necessary. However, despite the assurances from Dili that security on return would not be an issue, and that reconstruction—especially house rebuilding—was progressing well, the refugees either chose not to leave the camps and re-enter East Timor or were prevented from doing so.

It is still unclear why so few refugees voluntarily returned to East Timor after February 2000, seemingly opting to remain behind in camps in which conditions rapidly deteriorated throughout 2000 and 2001. As far as policy toward the refugees is concerned, it is clear that repatriation strategies were shaped by differing perceptions of the refugee population. Non-governmental organizations with links to the camps in West Timor tended to agree with Ramos Horta that the majority of refugees were there against their will, being forcibly detained. The UN view, however, was somewhat different. The official understanding was that a large proportion of the 240,000 "refugees" who fled across the border into West Timor at the end of 1999 were either pro-Integration supporters or family members of militia or civil servants. They were perceived to have voluntarily boarded trucks and boats or walked across the border because they feared retaliation following independence. The general analysis within UNTAET, therefore, was that the refugees could have returned to East Timor had they wished to, and that the slow trickle of returns provided evidence for this. The majority chose not to return because of quite genuine fears.

The first of these fears was rooted in concern about their personal safety on return. The UN perception was that there were East Timorese among the refugee population who had been involved, in various ways, in the post-ballot violence and who feared retribution on return. Stories were circulating in the camps to the effect that former civil servants or others close to the Indonesians during the period of their rule in East Timor were being lynched and/or murdered on return to their home villages. In truth, there was no evidence to support these claims. The second main concern involved the loss of pensions and income for those refugees formerly on the Indonesian payroll. It was generally thought that a number of the refugees in West Timor opted to remain there in order to continue receiving this income. The third level of concern was related to the targeting of resources. A general belief prevailed that in the event of their return, former refugees, on the basis of suspicions regarding their motives, would not receive aid, particularly new houses. They may even find that their lands and property had been reallocated to pro-independence supporters, or had been seized in settlement of previous long-standing feuds between families and business rivals.

The UN sought to address these fears through information campaigns, but with little success. During this period, the UN had only limited access to the camps, and while assistance was available through the West Timor authorities, along with two local NGOs and international NGOs including the Jesuit Refugee Service and Save the Children Fund, conditions in the camps remained appalling. The provision of clean water was infrequent; there were reports of malnutrition (particularly among children), and regular outbreaks of tuberculosis and other infectious diseases. The camps remained largely under the control of the pro-Jakarta militia and other political figures held responsible by many for creating the camps in the first place.

UN initiatives to repatriate the refugees received a further setback on September 6, 2000, when three UNHCR workers were killed close to one of the camps in Atambua. The reasons for the attacks are unclear, but they graphically revealed the very high levels of insecurity and danger that had been a feature of life in the camps since their establishment. The September killings increased the resolve of the UN in Dili, Geneva and New York to bring about a speedy resolution to the problems of the camps, and to find new ways of accelerating the return of refugees who had so far proved reluctant to leave.

There were other pressing political reasons to kickstart the stalled return program. The so-called "residual" refugee population was becoming an obstacle in the path of improving relations between Dili and Jakarta, and indeed between the government of Indonesia and the UN. The UN was applying pressure on Jakarta to take back control of the camps from the local West Timor authorities and the TNI, and in turn to reduce the influence of the militia. Despite the setting up of a refugee "Task Force" to be headed by senior military and other government officials in Jakarta, the West Timor authorities proved resiliently autonomous and retained their independent influence over the camps. When claiming an allowance from Jakarta for each of the refugees under their care, the West Timor authorities were given to over-estimating the numbers of refugees in the camps. Thus because they directly benefited from the refugees' continued presence, they may not have been the most reliable of partners in the UN-sponsored return initiatives.

In East Timor itself, the timetable for the handover of responsibility for the main functions of government—from UNTAET to the East Timor government-in-waiting—was moving on apace. The UN was seeking a resolution to what was rapidly becoming a refugee crisis at a crucial time in East Timor's transition from a UN Administered Non-Self Governing Territory to a fully independent nation-state.[4] The repatriation of refugees from West Timor should, therefore, be seen in the context of UNTAET's Administration-through-Partnership approach and its overall stated objective to secure democracy in East Timor, underpinned by formal justice processes (particularly for serious crimes) and human rights, and achieved through consultation. As stated earlier in this chapter, these objectives were contained in a series of Security Council resolutions, which set out UNTAET's mandate and obligations.

With elections to appoint ministers to the important Council of Ministers held in August 2001, and presidential elections in April 2002, the end of UNTAET's mission in East Timor had been signaled. The UN was anxious to bring about the closure of the camps and the return of refugees. But the continued presence on the border presented an on-going security threat. There was the ever present concern that former militia, intent on resuming their pro-Indonesia campaign, would (a) recruit from the remaining refugee population, (b) use the cover of the camps to launch cross-border incursions, a threat that would necessitate the continued presence of a peacekeeping force, and (c) accelerate the lucrative smuggling of sandalwood and other valuable commodities. Already the UN was experiencing difficulties maintaining a large presence in the area: the events of September 11 required large numbers of troops to be committed elsewhere.

In 2000 and 2001, a further and significant factor contributed to increased political pressure for the accelerated return of refugees. Xanana Gusmão (soon to be East Timor's first president), along with other senior figures, insisted that East Timor should pass through a process of reconciliation in order to heal the wounds of the past. Gusmão and other Council members were determined on a policy through which a general amnesty would be granted to former militia and other pro-integrationists involved in the pre- and post-1999 ballot violence (Radio National Australia 2000a, 2000b). It was argued that such an amnesty would enable the people of East Timor to be reconciled and begin the process of nation building before a formal justice process was implemented.

This amnesty-driven reconciliation process, which placed healing before formal justice, provided a boost to the repatriation effort. It was a key feature of the new East Timorese leadership's efforts to hasten the return of refugees. While not formally endorsing the amnesty, and privately acknowledging that it "didn't sit well" with its obligations to prosecute persons who had committed serious crimes, UNTAET nonetheless participated in repatriation negotiations predicated on the promise of amnesty. At various times in 2001 and 2002, Gusmão, Mari Alkatiri and other senior leaders made visits to the West Timor camps. They assured both former militia and refugees that a general amnesty would guarantee them a place in East Timor and provide them with an opportunity to participate in the rebuilding of the country. It was symbolically significant that Gusmão was seen receiving the first groups of returnees and embracing them at the border. Some of these returnees were known to have committed serious crimes during the period leading up to the ballot, and immediately afterwards, but they were not detained on arrival in East Timor and remain free today.

In a parallel process, UNTAET's Chief of Staff was present in West Timor, holding discussions with refugees and those who controlled the camps. It is unclear precisely what these negotiations were leading to. However, the impression was that the UN was active in promoting a repatriation policy. Former militia—who were involved in the initial forced evacuation of the refugees, and who controlled the camps and the camp populations—were now given what was regarded as the "legitimate authority" to control the return of the refugees to East Timor. In effect, however, it was a strategy that arguably contravened UNTAET's obligations to justice and human rights.

RETURN AND JUSTICE

The evidence suggests that the strategy to facilitate the return of refugees had clearly negative implications for the re-establishment of returnees' livelihoods, their security and protection. The strategy was founded on misplaced notions of pre-existing self-regulating rural communities that would, in an unproblematic way, permit the reintegration of returnees.

Of immediate concern to returnees was the problem of homelessness on return. A series of reviews of the international humanitarian response to the East Timor emergency criticized the shelter program and the shortfalls in the provision of replacement housing. The UNHCR and NGO programs, which distributed 50,000 shelter kits (not targeted at former IDPs or returnees) out of an estimated need of 80,000 units, ended in March 2001. No further kits were available to those returning from the West Timor camps. The World Bank estimated that 15,000 returnee families would be in need of shelter (McDowell and Ariyaratne 2001). The focus of UNTAET in East Timor had shifted from an emergency response to a development response in early 2001 and neither the budget nor the mechanisms were in place to respond in an adequate and timely way to the housing needs of the returnees. This led to a situation in Aileu District, for example, where more than 100 out of 600 returnees who returned to the Sub-District of Lequidoe were forced to find refuge in school buildings, being unable to return to their villages.

The lack of preparedness and the lack of attention to returnees' needs had serious implications for the health of returnees and the communities that were expected to absorb them. In 2001 there were a number of cases where returnees with serious health problems were sent back to areas which did not have the means to care for them. There were reports of tuberculosis sufferers being sent back to areas that were formerly free of tuberculosis, thus placing healthy populations at risk. Children suffering malnutrition were returned to subsistence economy areas where food productivity had not recovered to its pre-1999 levels; host families did not have the means to support new households.

Protection was a further major concern for returnees and one that made the whole undertaking of homecoming extremely uncertain. With regard to the protection of returnees, we have previously described how the repatriation program invested militia leaders—some of whom were implicated in serious crimes—with the power to direct returns. An aid worker with experience of returns to the town of Ainaro, for example, described the way in which "former militia, who were members of powerful local families, had reinvented themselves as Moses figures, bringing their people back from the wilderness." The return strategy had the effect of legitimizing the former militia's control of the refugee population both in the camps and on return to East Timor. A Jesuit Refugee Service official described the ways in which previous feudal arrangements, whereby militia families assumed authority over villages, had been re-established; thus the relationships of dependency created in the camps (including prostitution and illegal trading) continued on return.

Refugees were returned to a situation where their protection and security could not be guaranteed. An Amnesty International (AI) report criticized the UN for "failing in its primary task of ensuring that the new state of East Timor has protection and promotion of human rights at its core" (AI 2000, 2001b). AI was aware that with independence fast approaching, the new judicial system was only partially functioning and was fragile and vulnerable to interference. Judicial officials, AI argued, lacked the necessary support and training to make up for their lack of experience and had been subjected to threats and intimidation. Among East Timorese in general, but on the part of returnees in particular, there was little confidence in the formal judicial procedures, and concern that accelerated repatriation without necessary safeguards was placing refugees at potential risk. Returnees were far more vulnerable than others in the population, either because of their genuinely pro-Indonesian and anti-independence views or because of misperceptions about their views and their involvement in the 1999 violence.

In effect, there were no mechanisms in place to monitor and act on potential protection problems once people had returned to their villages. UNTAET and UNHCR officials argued that up to February 2000, 185,000 people had returned from West Timor with very little reported violence, and that future returns could be expected to follow the same pattern. The UN was confident that the civilian police and the new East Timor police force presence on the ground alongside the District Administrators and Sub-District Administration would be capable of receiving reports about any problems associated with return, and had the means to report any incidents to the UN. However, such "reactive monitoring" was very limited in scope. No arrangement was put in place for UNHCR to hand over returnee protection monitoring to the new Ministry of Justice. There was no guarantee that the ad hoc arrangement with the civilian police to receive complaints would continue, or that there was acceptance of the fact that returnees constituted a particularly vulnerable section of the population.

Taking these factors into account, the assumption that refugees were returning to rural communities with a social fabric that was effectively unchanged by the 1999 violence, and that existing community structures and institutions would serve to return the community to the status quo that existed before the violence, was unfounded. Returnees posed a whole series of difficulties, and fundamentally their reappearance in the villages altered social relations and placed an additional strain on available resources. The genuine fears of returnees about their personal security, the manner of their return tied as it was to an amnesty for former militia, and the complexities of reconciliation at the village level in coming to terms with past acts, together meant that return was fragile and the outcome uncertain.

CONCLUSION

This final part of the chapter briefly outlines recommendations for addressing some of the identified weaknesses in the international response to the protection and assistance needs of East Timor's displaced populations.

Coordination and Participation

While OCHA's positive role in coordinating the initial emergency response was commendable, it is argued in this chapter that the initial momentum which led to a relatively speedy and effective response to humanitarian needs was to some extent lost prematurely despite the continuing need for an emergency response in a number of areas. A Humanitarian Coordinator working through an Inter-Agency Committee should have been in place to ensure that the focus on humanitarian needs was maintained beyond the institutional change which downgraded an emergency-focused response in favor of a development-oriented response. This would have been particularly useful in the shelter sector, which experienced the greatest unmet need, especially for IDPs and returning refugees.

It has been acknowledged positively that the East Timor operation marked a "new approach" in the UN's administration of territories; however, consultation—with the East Timor view taking precedence—and the gradual handover of responsibility to national and local bodies, was limited in scope particularly during the emergency phase. Opportunities for joint activities in food distribution, reunions, needs assessment, and community consultation should have been pursued from the outset, and involved the civil society. In East Timor this would have included the church, the National Council of Timorese Resistance (CNRT), Commission on Humanitarian Affairs, and local NGOs.

The OCHA CAP for East Timor stated that all agencies involved in the response "are committed to incorporating the core humanitarian principles of neutrality, impartiality, transparency and accountability" (CAP 1999: 14). But there should have been a coordinated strategy to monitor the realization of these principles, particularly in regard to the CAP's guarantee to "work through local institutions and networks to help people regain their sense of dignity."

The UN and Protection

The larger question whether the UN in East Timor misread the political and security situation before, during and after the referendum, and hence failed in its duty to protect the people of East Timor, is beyond the scope of this analysis. It can be said, however, that in the period after the referendum was announced, the UN operation and the actions of its staff contained elements that were unique. While these elements may have set *positive precedents* for future operations, at the same time they revealed the *limitations of humanitarian intervention.*

A positive legacy of the UN's involvement in East Timor arose out of the commitment and responsibility of UN staff toward the people of East Timor in the immediate aftermath of the September/October violence. When given the option by the UN in New York to leave their posts due to the rapidly deteriorating security situation, a large number of UN staff and volunteers refused to go, opting to sign waiver forms indicating their willingness to remain in Dili and to see the mission through. Second, despite the destruction of the UNAMET compound and direct militia threats against overseas and local staff, the UN retained throughout a presence in Dili, which was symbolically important for the citizens of the territory as well as for the overall mission. Third, when the decision was finally taken to reduce their presence in Dili, UNAMET, for the first time in a UN mission, evacuated its local staff to Darwin. Finally, and perhaps most important of all, among those evacuated to Darwin by the UN were a large number of displaced people who had sought UN protection in the compound.

However, the issue of protection in the post-announcement period is more complicated. One of the greatest challenges facing the UN was to secure access to—and the return of—East Timorese refugees who had been forcibly removed to camps in West Timor. UNSC Resolution 1264 made no mention of West Timor, and, without a mandate, the UN had very limited leverage to protect those refugees. In addition, the resolution offered no mandate for INTERFET to accord protection to those East Timorese who continued to be forcibly removed from their homes and sent to West Timor or elsewhere in Indonesia after the multinational force had arrived in Dili. The credibility of INTERFET and UNAMET was damaged by news film, which clearly showed the TNI, the Indonesian police and intelligence services rounding up and deporting people in sight of INTERFET troops.

Among those leaving would have been individuals involved in violence that may become the subject of a war crimes inquiry. Whatever the case, while there was a large contingent of TNI in Dili, the INTERFET Stabilization Force and the UN did not regard intervention in these deportations as an option. While the decision was primarily a political one, in part it was a result of INTERFET's inability to intervene because of its initial small presence on the ground. Over East Timor, once again, the international community was forced to confront the limits of humanitarian protection, and the Security Council's inadequate attention to humanitarian and protection concerns. In East Timor, ordinary people suffered the consequences of the political vacuum in a situation with a clear imperative for action. The PKF should have created a liaison office with responsibility for humanitarian, human rights, and protection issues to ensure ongoing coordination and a capacity to respond to changing protection needs.

In defining the priorities for military-led humanitarian interventions, UN Security Council resolutions should emphasize the need to establish a safe environment, including direct interventions in actions designed to forcibly displace civilian populations.

Military-led Humanitarianism

This chapter has described how the senior command of INTERFET, in the period immediately following its creation, appeared not to share the humanitarian workers' vision of an operation in East Timor in which the military and the humanitarian agencies worked alongside one another, and at various points combined to respond to relief needs. In the opening stages of the operation, humanitarian workers believed that a combination of approaches was possible. But with time, a number of NGO and UN agency staff who visited East Timor privately thought that the conservative military approach had unnecessarily prolonged the suffering of East Timor's victims by obstructing access, offering insufficient protection to convoys, and committing insufficient resources to the relief effort. They argued that the military underestimated the capacity and capability of the agencies to respond in insecure environments.

Questions remain about the tasks set out in UNSCR 1264. Through correspondence, diplomats at the UN confirmed to the author that the tasks were not, contrary to General Cosgrove's understanding, intended to be sequential. The drafters did not intend the facilitation of humanitarian assistance by the multinational force to be dependent upon first re-establishing UNAMET and restoring peace and security. This raises the issue of INTERFET's resourcing. If operational difficulties limited the involvement of INTERFET in relief delivery, then it may have been possible for the large number of UN civilian police waiting in Darwin to have been deployed sooner. It has been noted with sad irony that one week after UNSCR 1264 "called for the immediate end to violence, and demanded that those responsible for such acts be brought to justice," UN staff and members of the multinational forces were forced to stand by as "those responsible" left defiantly aboard ships from Dili Port and by road on looted trucks, some of which carried refugees.

The priorities for military/humanitarian operations should be set only after consultation with all the main agency players, including local NGOs and, where possible, other representatives of civil society including refugees. This requires the establishment of effective lines of communication between military, political and humanitarian agencies to facilitate both coordination and a speedy response to changing circumstances. Agreement on the interpretation of Security Council resolutions and the timetable for action is essential.

Human rights investigations should be initiated as soon as security conditions permit, to enable the gathering of forensic evidence, to forestall tampering with evidence, and to allow victims and witnesses to recall their recollection of events readily. Military–civilian cooperation is vital to such investigations.

Relief Strategies

Airdrops of humanitarian relief supplies over East Timor were generally regarded as ineffective and were used largely as a short-term, stopgap response to public and political pressure for a speedier humanitarian response. Airdrops make good television. They present strong images, but with insufficient intelligence about the whereabouts of beneficiaries (despite assistance from CNRT and the Armed Forces of National Liberation of East Timor), largely untested new technology, and apparently inappropriate foodstuffs, the strategy was ill-advised.

The airdropping of food and medical aid to displaced people will inevitably prove ineffective when the decision to undertake such operations is purely a political one taken against the advice of humanitarian agencies, when conditions on the ground are unsuited, when the foodstuffs are inappropriate, and when hunger is not an immediate problem. Leafleting, radio information broadcasts, and other confidence-building measures are preferable in such situations. Airdrops should be avoided in most cases.

Humanitarianism and Managing the Transition

Having made four visits to East Timor and participated in the External Review of the Humanitarian Response to the East Timor Emergency, the author would tend to agree with the mid-2000 evaluations of the UN humanitarian operation, that the overall objective to meet basic needs was achieved across all sectors. However, it is argued that the planning for and the institutional transition of the humanitarian functions formerly coordinated by OCHA were imperfect. It appears that neither the Humanitarian nor Governance *pillars* (departments) of UNTAET assumed responsibility for the development of an overall transition plan from relief to development. Sectoral working groups, attended by INGOs, UN agencies and UNTAET, were involved in developing sector-based transition strategies. The relevant sectoral departments within UNTAET took the lead in these sectoral processes, but they were informal and coordination across sectors was largely not in place. Certainly, there were some advantages in this rather loose arrangement. For example, INGOs, most notably in the health sector, were able to stay on well beyond the CAP-defined emergency period, and in some cases worked closely with the new East Timorese health ministry, fulfilling quasi-governmental functions up until the November 2002 handover.

From March 2000 onward, the overlapping mandates, the different humanitarian tracks pursued by agencies and the lack of coordination between them, coupled with the institutional uncertainty about the transition, removed the sense that there was a body within UNTAET clearly responsible for humanitarian issues. The Special Representative's Office was certain that there would be no Second CAP for East Timor. UNTAET was keen to put across the message that the emergency phase was over by March 2000, and that the focus had shifted to building the structures for government.

For the UN agencies and NGOs, however, there remained unmet basic needs, especially shelter, vulnerable groups feeding programs and health, all of which required an emergency-type response. However, the CAP funds had been exhausted and emergency funding requests were unlikely to be met by donors. As the functions of the HAER were parcelled out to the PKF, WFP, UNHCR, UNDP and the newly-created Disaster Management Unit, concern grew that the humanitarian focus was lost too early. It is argued that the consequences of this loss of focus were felt most acutely by agencies tasked with responding to the needs of returning refugees from West Timor.

In order to avoid such transition problems, an overall coordination mechanism linking humanitarian components (and the CAP) with development strategies through a country master plan could help to map the way through the relief-to-development transition.

Humanitarianism and the CAP

The Consolidated Inter-Agency Appeal Process for East Timor was deemed to be a success in raising funds, drawing together a range of agencies into a coordination response, setting initial priorities, and ensuring a speedy response. The funding-driven timetable for the response, however, unrealistically limited the emergency/relief phase to nine months and contributed to the political unacceptability of a second CAP round to address ongoing refugee and humanitarian needs. Closer coordination, target setting, and programming between the CAP and the UNDP/World Bank Joint Assessment Mission may bridge the gap between relief and development by ensuring the availability of funding and a continuing agency commitment.

Repatriation of Refugees from West Timor

McDowell and Eastmond (2002) have written elsewhere that the general failure of mass organized refugee return programs to provide durable solutions to refugees' needs and the needs of communities that play host to them, throws into serious question the premises on which repatriation was promoted. This chapter, by focusing on repatriation in the highly complex context of UN-managed state-building and transitions from conflict to post-conflict democracy in East Timor, has shown that the problem is both political and conceptual.

As the favored solution today, the political agendas informing repatriation are largely a response to increasing numbers of refugees, relief budget constraints, and the growing antagonism of host countries. In the East Timor case, returns were symbolic showpieces. It has been argued above that the accelerated return of refugees from West Timor was significant because in one sense it permitted the UN to complete the process of "Timorization" and handover. And in another, the return of large numbers of people who were perceived as being anti-independence was proving ground for the new leadership's determination to place reconciliation before justice.

As such, the return operations demanded the swift and effective movement of large numbers of people in time for the new nation's elections. In such large-scale organized operations, standardized solutions and tight control were the key to operational success. However, these tended to overlook two of the important components of successful return, namely timing and refugees' own assessments and initiatives.

While the author acknowledges that some sort of amnesty is very often a pre-condition for return, repatriation programs should only be pursued in a context where decisions around repatriation are democratically supported and reached through consultation. Repatriation operations should operate within UN mandates, should be consistent with domestic and international law, and supported by effective monitoring and response mechanisms. In East Timor, the decision to negotiate return through the pro-Jakarta militia militated against the realization of refugees' rights. In terms of protection and durable solutions, the way in which repatriation was directed—more by political compromise than by humanitarian standards—meant that inadequate attention was paid to the needs of the refugees in the camps, and their protection needs in the repatriation process. The author would tend to conclude that in East Timor, the repatriation program was incompatible with those commitments. The return strategy, which depended on the assurance of amnesty, appeared to circumvent the UN's own legal processes, contradicting its mandate to respect refugee rights and its obligation to prosecute people accused of crimes against humanity.

From the outset, the UN's mission in East Timor was a human rights mission, described as being in response to "systematic, widespread and flagrant violations of international humanitarian law and human rights law" (UNSC Resolution 1264). Its mandate emphasized the need to bring people to justice. The same message was reinforced by four UN-initiated investigations into human rights violations. A common message coming out of these reports, all of which were accepted by the UN, was the close connection between justice and reconciliation, and of prosecutorial justice being critical for the achievement of reconciliation (Temby 2001).

UN transitional administrations, of the kind set up in East Timor, should adopt transparent and formal policies in regard to refugee repatriation, reaffirming a commitment to the investigation of human rights violations and formal justice processes. In the absence of safe access to refugee camps, UNHCR should seek to develop close operational links with international and local NGOs working in camps to generate reliable information about the needs of refugees. These links could extend to training in protection matters, and include mechanisms for consultation with refugees about conditions for repatriation. The UN should avoid entering into any negotiation process, however informally, which has the result of legitimizing the control of militias, combatant groups, or political leaders over refugees. In a situation where returnees will rely on host communities for their immediate needs, including in many cases shelter, the UN should ensure that provisions are in place to guarantee, as far as possible, livelihood security on return. This may include improved livelihood monitoring and response mechanisms. Where there is genuine concern for the protection of returnees, the UN should put in place comprehensive measures to enable both the reporting of protection problems and a response to them.

For a brief update on developments in East Timor since this chapter was completed, see the editors' postscript, page 227.

SOURCES

This chapter contains material that was previously published in the *Australian Journal of Human Rights* 8, no. 1 (article with Marita Eastmond) and I am grateful to LexisNexis for permission to reproduce that material in this volume. The chapter also draws on research conducted by the author and R. A. Ariyaratne, in East Timor in 2001. I should like to acknowledge Ari's contribution to the observations contained in this piece. Organizations and individuals consulted during field research included: United Nations Transitional Administration for East Timor (UNTAET), Dennis MacNamara, International Force for East Timor (INTERFET, Headquarters Command), Council of Ministers, World Health Organization, Oxfam/Community Aid Abroad, Save the Children (UK), Jesuit Refugee Service, World Bank, UNDP, UNHCR, and ICRC.

NOTES

1. $830 million in direct UN expenditure (i.e. trust funds, public administration support, reconstruction), the remainder either unilateral or other multilateral donor support.

2. The Sphere Humanitarian Charter and Minimum Standards in Disaster Response sets out for the first time what people affected by disasters have a right to expect from humanitarian assistance. The aim of the project is to improve the quality of assistance provided to people affected by disasters, and to enhance the accountability of the humanitarian system in disaster response.

3. The UN mission in East Timor was described as being in response to "systematic, widespread and flagrant violations of international humanitarian law and human rights law" (UNSC Resolution 1264) and its mandate emphasized the need to bring people to justice. The same message was reinforced by four further UN-initiated investigations into human rights violations: the Mary Robinson Inquiry (September 10–13, 1999), the UN Delegation of Special Rapporteurs (November 4–10, 1999), the UN International Commission of Enquiry (November 15–December 3, 1999), and the James Dunn Report (2000) (see UNHCHR website).

4. East Timor has never been under UN Trusteeship within the meaning of Chapter XII of the United Nations Charter, which was a system established after the Second World War, applicable to a small number of territories under mandate, territories detached from enemy states as a result of the Second World War, and territories voluntarily placed under the system by states responsible for their administration. The UN Transitional Administration in East Timor was established under a Security Council resolution which provided its mandate.

Chapter 8

Conclusion: Re-casting Societies in Conflict

Nicholas Van Hear

Much has changed in the global security, forced migration, post-conflict and development fields since the research for these chapters was undertaken. The forced migration complexes analyzed in the preceding chapters have unfolded against the background of substantial shifts in the humanitarian discourse and in the wider geo-political order—and indeed they have contributed to these changes. Associated with this new configuration have been new thrusts in several fields of policy and practice that relate to forced migration—including development, humanitarian action, migration management, and security. These fields are inter-related but distinct, and have different constituencies, interests and values.

Perhaps the most obvious and important shift in the geo-political order is that the challenges of the post–Cold War period have given way to a bleaker era dominated by security concerns and the "War on Terror." The events of September 11, 2001, transformed the global security scene and cast weak, fragile, failing, collapsed and war-torn states that have produced complex forced migration in a new and sinister light. The new security push is manifested in concern with these fragile and failed states as breeding grounds and bases for terrorism and crime and as sources of unwanted migrants who might spread these scourges. The recent interventions in Afghanistan and Iraq are the clearest manifestations of this new order, but other conflict societies are candidates for a similar approach (Donini et al. 2004).

Partly as a result of security concerns, but also driven by domestic political pressures in western states that are the destination for migrants, a raft
of proposals have been floated that attempt to address forced migration
in comprehensive ways: these include the UK's "New Vision" for asylum
and migration, UNHCR's Convention Plus, and initiatives from the European Union and other quarters (Ward 2004; UNHCR 2004a; Oxfam 2005).
While very mixed in their motivations, collectively these initiatives pres-
age the emergence of a new forced migration paradigm, which seeks to
contain both conflicts and forced migrants in their regions of origin. This
new configuration can be seen as part of a wider "migration management" push whose purpose is to reduce the numbers of unwanted
migrants who reach western countries, by a mix of prevention and containment (Crisp 2003).

Perhaps more positively, the debate since the 1990s over the "gap"
between humanitarian action or relief on one hand and development on
the other has seen the emergence of new mechanisms attempting to
bridge the divisions among UN agencies and in other relief and development spheres. The coordination thrust in the humanitarian sphere is
driven by the need to handle crises increasing in number and complexity,
and by the proliferation of agencies, NGOs, umbrella bodies and funding
mechanisms that have emerged to deal with such crises. A discourse on
societies in transition has emerged, refining previous perspectives on the
aspired-for continuum between relief and development (UNDG 2004).

Meanwhile, in the development arena, a new sense of purpose has been
galvanized with the setting of the Millennium Development Goals for
achievement by 2015, focusing on the eradication of poverty (UN 2002).
While there are serious concerns about the likelihood of their achievement by the deadline set, the MDGs have emerged as the policy framework for thinking and action on international development. Conflict and
forced migration were largely absent from the initial MDG framework,
but in so far as conflict and forced migration obstruct the attainment of
the MDGs, there is a growing recognition that they have to be dealt with
in development instruments associated with the MDGs, such as Poverty
Reduction and Country Strategy documents.

THE INTERPENETRATION OF POLICY FIELDS

The new concern with weak, fragile, failing and collapsed states that con-
found development, breed conflict, generate humanitarian emergencies
and forced migration, and spawn security problems like crime and terrorism has provided the impetus to bring together these diverse fields—
security, migration management, humanitarian action and development.

The upshot has been that in recent years these fields have not so much merged, as some have argued for development and security for example (Duffield 2001), but that an interpenetration of these policy fields has occurred.

In effect, each of these fields has spread into others, so we see an interpenetration of development and security, of development and humanitarianism, of development and migration management, of migration management and security, of humanitarianism and security, of humanitarianism and migration management, and so on. We have witnessed a so-called merger between the development and security fields, the aspired-for continuum between humanitarian relief and development, and the highlighting of links between development and migration management. Migration management has in turn been linked into the security field, which has also spread into the humanitarian arena, seen in the interpenetration of humanitarian assistance and military intervention, with often dangerous and sometimes fatal consequences for humanitarian workers (Donini et al. 2004).

The interpenetration of these fields is evident both in terms of vocabulary and at the level of strategy. For example, it can be seen in the popularity of the notion of "human security" in which the humanitarian, development and security fields are combined (Commission on Human Security 2003). It is evident in the term "humanitarian intervention," used to describe military involvement in humanitarian crises (Donini et al. 2004). It is seen in the notion of the "migration-asylum nexus" (UNHCR 2004a; Crisp and Dessalegne 2002), the perception that flows of migrants moving for economic purposes are mixed inextricably with those of people seeking protection or escaping conflict: here the migration management and humanitarian fields connect, as do to some extent the development and security arenas. A term for a new species of countries has been coined—Low Income Countries Under Stress, or LICUS—which include societies in conflict but also those undergoing other severe shocks, and on which the concerns of the interpenetrated fields are focused (World Bank website 2004; World Bank 2002).

Strategies that combine fields are in vogue, such as UNHCR's "Targeting Development Assistance for Refugee Solutions," developed under its Framework for Durable Solutions (UNHCR 2003). As the name suggests, the idea is the judicious use of development assistance to promote integration in the country of asylum or reintegration on return. The approach combines the development and humanitarian fields, and security in the sense of refugee protection too.

At the same time, similar strategies and vocabularies are deployed across different policy fields. One such manifestation of interpenetration at the level of policy implementation is the increasingly popular notion of "partnerships." In the development field the emphasis is on partnerships between developing and developed countries for the accomplishment of the Millennium Development Goals (UN 2002). At the same time, in the migration management field, the notion of "migration partnerships" between migrant-receiving and migrant-sending countries has come to the fore—with development assistance as a component of such partnerships (Ward 2004; Oxfam 2005).

This interpenetration of policy fields has notably found expression in the notion of societies in transition—like the cases investigated in this book—those moving from war to peace, from relief to development, from refugee flight to refugee return, and so on. For the UN, "transition refers to the period in a crisis when external assistance is most crucial in supporting or underpinning still fragile cease-fires or peace processes by helping to create the conditions for political stability, security, justice and social equity" (UNDG 2004: 6). Such societies need particular attention so that they stabilize and do not regress into a dangerous condition; but more than this they are seen as opportunities for transformation into societies with a liberal demeanor, both economic and political. The policy notion of transition, combining the humanitarian and development fields but also other policy fields, has spawned a whole series of budgets and funds earmarked to handle such circumstances (UNHCR 2004b). Above all, the interpenetration of policy fields is also seen in the expanding objectives of development assistance, which has moved well beyond economic development to include governance, democracy, human rights, the development of civil society, conflict resolution, managing conflicts, and much else besides (Bastian 2003). These new approaches to transition and the expanding ambit of development assistance raise questions about the kinds of societies that will emerge out of conflict under the tutelage of relief and development agencies.

TRANSFORMING WHOLE SOCIETIES?

The new approach is not just palliative, preventive, or fire-fighting: it is no longer simply shoring up societies in parlous straits while halting the export of terrorists, criminals and unwanted migrants from them. It goes beyond this palliation, embracing the notion of the opportunity to transform whole societies—like those examined in this book. The new approach to conflict and post-conflict societies is decidedly interventionist in character. The remainder of this concluding chapter explores how societies in or emerging from conflict have been re-cast in the interpenetrating fields and discourses outlined above. In the new perspective, conflict and displacement are seen not only as destructive, but as holding the potential for the transformation of the economy and society. This is a perspective promoted particularly by the World Bank.[1]

The destructive, anti-developmental effects of war and displacement are self-evident. Conflict, violence and displacement break down the underpinnings of the economy, undermine predictability and confidence in the future, and disrupt markets, distribution networks, and banking and credit systems (World Bank 1998). Trust in institutions is undermined and the legitimacy of states is weakened. Civil life becomes militarized and social cohesion unravels. Displacement obstructs access to previous livelihood practices, and new forms of livelihood practices are created—many of which are informal or even criminal and detrimental to liberal economic and social order. Forms of identification like gender roles and family units become altered or are broken down. Conflict resolution mechanisms—which often mediate the distribution of land and other resources—are disrupted and other social organizations adapt in unconstructive ways to the conflict situation.

However, the outlook is not unremittingly grim, because in the new thinking, conflict and post-conflict situations can be used as opportunities for the restructuring of political, social and economic systems. As an overview of the debate prepared for the Deutsche Gesellschaft für Technische Zusammenarbeit (GTZ) put it, "Post-conflict situations often provide special opportunities for political, legal, economic and administrative reforms to change past systems and structures which may have contributed to economic and social inequities and conflict" (Mehler and Ribaux 2000: 37). Such a perspective echoes the sentiments of many development aid donors, which since the mid-1990s have taken on a key role in conflict and post-conflict management and reconstruction (Doornbos 2002; Moore 2000). But it is not only post-conflict situations that create special opportunities. Conflicts themselves are now evaluated from a different vantage point: "The collapse of states in crisis need not be prevented, since a 'better state' cannot emerge until that collapse has taken place" (Mehler and Ribaux 2000: 107). While conflict was previously seen as regressive (Duffield 2001), causing a rupture in the "normal" linear development pattern of a given society, it is now presented as an opportunity for a society's social, political and economic transformation.

This realization has been clearly manifested in recent policy shifts within the World Bank concerning conflict and post-conflict societies. While it was formed after the Second World War as part of the Marshall Plan to rebuild "post-conflict" Europe, the Bank had no comprehensive operational policy for post-conflict situations in the developing world until the later 1990s. Indeed, the Bank avoided countries embroiled in armed conflict in favor of those undergoing what it regarded as more conventional development—though these countries often experienced conflict and upheaval short of civil war. This changed when the Bank set up its Post-Conflict Unit (PCU), operational by 1997, and established a Post-Conflict Fund which aimed at supporting countries in transition from conflict to sustainable peace and economic development. The *Framework for World Bank Involvement in Post-Conflict Reconstruction* (World Bank 1997) set out the Bank's thinking for intervention in the post-conflict field. The PCU—which transmuted subsequently into the Conflict Prevention and Reconstruction Unit, reflecting an expanding remit—was placed in the Social Development Department, which indicated that post-conflict operations were to be an integral part of the overall framework for social development.

The Bank's reorientation was cast both as a return to its original mandate—the reconstruction of Europe in the aftermath of the Second World War—and as an expansion beyond the rebuilding of physical infrastructure:

> Since its creation in 1944, the World Bank's role in reconstruction has moved from rebuilding infrastructure to a comprehensive approach which includes the promotion of economic recovery, evaluation of social sector needs, support for institutional capacity building, revitalization of local communities, and restoration of social capital, as well as specific efforts to support mine action, demobilize and reintegrate ex-combatants, and reintegrate displaced populations. An increased premium has, furthermore, been put on preventing the onset, exacerbation, or resurgence of violent conflict. (World Bank 2004)

The new emphasis meant that the Bank now embraced use of post-conflict situations to promote economic adjustment and recovery and to build institutional capacity. Lending operations now had post-conflict targets such as de-mining, demobilization and reintegration of ex-combatants and displaced people (World Bank 1998). The Bank cooperated with other agencies engaged in post-conflict activities in which forced migration issues were prominent, notably through the Brookings Process, a partnership between the Bank, UNHCR and UNDP initiated in 1999; this was later revived in 2002 as the "4Rs" initiative—Repatriation, Reintegration, Rehabilitation and Reconstruction—as an integrated inter-agency "relief to development" approach for countries in transition from conflict (Lippman 2004).

The new emphasis on post-conflict situations resulted in the Bank engaging much earlier in conflict countries than before. Its strategy involved a number of steps (World Bank 1998). First was the creation of a "watching brief" in countries or war areas where there was no active Bank portfolio. This was followed by preparation of a transitional support strategy, so that reconstruction could be initiated when a resolution of conflict was reached. Then came early reconstruction interventions in the form of small-scale activities—often in combination with UN agencies and NGOs—that aimed at alleviating the effects of war for vulnerable groups by creating social safety nets, restoring administration systems and so on. This was followed by post-conflict reconstruction, leading eventually to a resumption of normal operations. The World Bank now engaged earlier because: "time is of the essence in post-conflict situations. Often, there are windows of opportunities within which significant progress is possible. But these windows can quickly narrow or close" (World Bank 1998: 29). The reasoning was that if the Bank was not present in war-torn societies, the scope for action was restricted when the opportunity for intervention was possible.

Critics are wary of this new approach to conflict by the World Bank and other powerful donors. For the critics, such agencies see "the terrain of post conflict situations as ripe for implementation of their kind of state, economy and society" (Moore 2000: 14). "The wake of war leaves the 'level playing field' so beloved by . . . neo-liberal discourses" (ibid. 13). Post-conflict and even conflict conditions offer opportunities for market-friendly interventions. In this perspective, pre-conflict social and economic structures which governed property, labor and other economic factors may well have been impediments to the development of markets: if these structures have been destroyed or fatally undermined by conflict, the foundations can be laid for individual property rights and other dimensions of market-friendly "good governance" (ibid. 11). The dispensers of humanitarian relief can be enlisted to join with those implementing reconstruction and development for these market-friendly purposes. Money is on offer to humanitarian agencies through the array of transition budgets and reconstruction funds, which are increasingly attractive as other sources of humanitarian funds are on the decline.

While the critique has some substance, the degree of "neo-liberalism" attributed to the World Bank and other donors in such critiques is overstated. The "Post-Washington Consensus" (Stiglitz 1998; Maxwell 2005) is certainly still market friendly, but acknowledges the need for means to counter the harm done to people by the market and by "market imperfections." The popularity of the notion of social capital, much touted by the World Bank (Fine 2001), is in part simply recognition that relations and dimensions outside the market matter—although admittedly for the World Bank the point is that they matter for successful functioning of the market. For humanitarians, social capital and relations outside the market matter for different reasons, not least as means of welfare or social security for the poor and conflict-affected. It is thus the nature, scale and control of such social security mechanisms and social capital, and more widely the nature of "development" (among other things the form and regulation of markets) that are the real terrain of argument, rather than the desirability of the market itself. As one critic puts it, "the debate is not really about 'relief' or 'development,' but *what kind* of development in war-torn societies and indeed in the rest of the periphery" (Moore 2000: 17). This remains a salient question for the societies and communities described in this book.

RE-CASTING CONFLICT SOCIETIES: OUTCOMES AND PROSPECTS

What will be the outcome of the interpenetration of policy fields and the recasting of conflict-torn societies as described above? Will these policy changes make life better for the displaced and other people affected by conflict, as described in the chapters of this book?

In part the interpenetration of policy fields, for better or worse, is a consequence of pressure by practitioners and analysts for greater coordination and coherence in relief and development efforts. The call for better coordination is in part a response to the great proliferation of agencies in the humanitarian field, including new actors like the military who have not until recently been part of that field. Advocacy of coordination and coherence in the humanitarian field has almost become a mantra. As we have seen in some of the case studies in this book, there have indeed been improvements in the institutional architecture in respect of coordination, although more at the international level and in the capitals of conflict countries than in the field. The benefits of improved coordination are yet to make tangible impressions at the ground level among forced migrants and other war-affected people.

More widely, in this conclusion it has been argued that conflict societies involving complex forced displacement such as those reviewed in this book have been cast in the current interpenetrated humanitarian–development–security–migration management discourse as both threats and opportunities. On the one hand such societies are seen as the source of unwanted people, forces and trends—troublesome migrants, truculent fundamentalists, incorrigible criminals and intractable terrorists—which are to be contained as far as possible. On the other hand such societies, with previous economic, political and social encumbrances swept away or fatally undermined, present opportunities for remolding or wholesale transformation. The former perspective seems unremittingly bleak, and liable to promote the very forces that it seeks to contain—if indeed containment is possible, which is questionable. The latter perspective is liable to accusations of neo-imperialism or re-colonization as societies are remolded in market-friendly, western-oriented ways.

However, the two perspectives are in some ways compatible with each other, since transformation of conflict societies into stable and sustainable communities where people can live reasonable lives could remove some of the forces impelling migration, thereby helping to achieve the outcome desired by western states anxious to reduce the numbers reaching their shores. Indeed, the interpenetration of the relief, development, security and migration management fields to which we have drawn attention in this chapter signals efforts toward both such ends—although the agencies within these interpenetrated fields have very different priorities. The question is whether the policies currently being pursued will promote a positive outcome, contributing to the achievement of the Millennium Development Goals, for example, or whether they will make fragile states and societies still more insecure, and increase the likelihood of more forced migration.

The best outcome from a humanitarian perspective and for forced migrants themselves would be improvements in living conditions or human security in places that are now sources of forced migration and displacement, so that migration becomes matter of choice rather than necessity. Relief and development assistance and migration management policies should be directed to that end. Humanitarians then should not just monitor the human rights and human security dimensions of the policy thrusts we have identified, but also try to ensure that any societal transformations that unfold do so in conditions of equity and consistent with notions of global justice. This means supporting the consolidation of a social market economy, tempered by robust means of social and human security; strengthening an enabling, developmental state; fostering democracy from below; and encouraging the emergence of a vibrant civil society. Above all it means supporting the efforts of forced migrants and other war-affected people in such endeavors.

NOTE

1. The following paragraphs on the World Bank's evolving position on conflict societies draw on a background paper by Lars Buur and Helene Kyed of the Danish Institute for International Studies (DIIS) in Copenhagen.

Editors' Postscript

Nicholas Van Hear and Christopher McDowell

BURUNDI

Burundi's halting transition to peace has continued, culminating in the election of President Pierre Nkurunziza in August 2005. The newfound stability triggered a great increase in the return of refugees and IDPs. Some 285,000 Burundian refugees returned between 2001 and October 2005, around 60,000 of them in 2005 alone. The number of IDPs decreased from 145,000 living in 170 sites in 2004 to 117,000 in 160 sites in 2005. The reintegration of former combatants has also continued. Limited progress has been made in improving (local) governance in Burundi, promoting security, and addressing the needs of refugees and the internally displaced. Significant challenges however remained for Burundi's displaced citizens: many IDPs and refugees have returned to areas devastated by war, finding their homes destroyed and their land occupied, often leading to disputes. If the security situation remained favorable, UNHCR estimated that another 150,000 to 390,000 refugees could be repatriated during 2006. As of 2005, some 426,500 Burundian refugees remained in Tanzania, Rwanda and the Democratic Republic of the Congo. However, large-scale return could put great pressure on the already fragile environment in areas of return and significantly increase disputes over property, land ownership and scarce resources. The situation of female returnees described in the chapter remained largely unaddressed. General economic and social conditions remained poor in Burundi, with 68 percent of the population living below the poverty line. Displaced people and returnees continued to be dependent on basic assistance, with food, shelter, education and health largely provided through UN agencies. Shortfalls in funding for Burundian repatriation were of great concern. Overall, Burundi confronted major social, economic and security challenges that will require large-scale international assistance, particularly to support ongoing return and resettlement programs, and thereby to avoid slipping back into tension, conflict and displacement. (Source: UNHCR; USCR.)

SRI LANKA

Sri Lanka's fragile peace has become even more fraught since this volume's chapter was completed, with many fearful that the conflict would resume. The breaking away of a faction of the LTTE in the east of the country led to increased tension, assassinations and allegations that the government was covertly supporting the breakaway group. The island's difficulties were compounded by the tsunami that struck at the end of 2004, killing and displacing tens of thousands of people, many of them already displaced in the conflict areas of the north and east. After initial hopes that the disaster would draw the country's peoples together, disputes about the distribution of the huge relief donations generated worldwide exacerbated already tense relations between the government and the LTTE. Meanwhile, Sinhalese nationalists increasingly questioned the neutrality of Norwegian efforts to broker a lasting peace. With President Chandrika Kumaratunga obliged to step down after two terms in office, elections were held in November 2005 and Mahinda Rajapakse was elected president with the support of Sinhalese hardliners on the pledge of renegotiating the peace agreement. Before the tsunami struck there were some 353,000 already displaced, still awaiting a durable solution. The tsunami displaced around 570,000 people, many of whom had already been uprooted by the conflict. Most of these had constructed or had been allocated shelter of some sort by September 2005. According to UNHCR, there were some 130,000 Sri Lankan refugees living abroad at the beginning of 2005, of whom about 70,000 were housed in camps in Tamil Nadu in south India. The substantial diaspora in Europe, North America and Australia, composed partly of refugees, contributed large amounts to the tsunami relief effort. (Source: UNHCR.)

COLOMBIA

Since President Alvaro Uribe assumed power in 2002, the Colombian army has regained control over large parts of the country, and security and freedom of movement have significantly improved. The government has reorganized public services so as to allow IDPs greater access to health and education, and has dealt with some of the bureaucratic problems described in this chapter. Nevertheless, while there have been some peace negotiations with the paramilitary groups, President Uribe has opted primarily for military approaches to dealing with the armed parties, and the conflict has abated little. Its effects continue to be felt disproportionately by the rural poor, especially the Afro-Colombian and indigenous populations. To a large extent, the trends described in this chapter persist. Displacement is still endemic and refugee flows across Colombia's three borders are increasing. As of 2005, there were over 2 million IDPs in Colombia, and in the first nine months of that year alone, the authorities registered nearly 100,000 new cases of forced displacement. The government has sought international support for IDP return, but security conditions were no better than when this volume's chapter was completed. Few of the return efforts have proved sustainable and local integration programs were still wholly insufficient. However, late in 2005 the government of Colombia announced that it was committing the equivalent of USD$2.2 billion for the protection and assistance of IDPs for the period 2005–2010. In comparison, the government spent $350 million on IDPs between 2000 and 2004. If properly deployed, this funding could mean better access to work, housing and protection, including in the areas people were forced to abandon. However, given the magnitude of the problem, and the protracted nature of the conflict (more than four decades), the task of reintegrating returnees remained daunting. (Source: UNHCR; Patricia Weiss Fagen.)

AFGHANISTAN

Elections held in September 2005 were a major landmark in Afghanistan's transition from conflict, as laid out in the Bonn Agreement of 2001. Interim President Hamid Karzai was reelected, women had the vote in parliamentary elections, and completion of other elements of the political transition was anticipated by 2006. Return of refugees continued at a high rate. An estimated 500,000 refugees returned in 2005, bringing the total number of returnees from Pakistan, Iran and elsewhere to around 3 million since 2002. The rate of return and the agreements between neighboring states and international agencies to facilitate repatriation were seen as an endorsement of political, economic and security developments in the country, culminating in the first parliamentary elections in over thirty years. However, the conditions that confronted returnees and IDPs in Afghanistan were poor and progress on reintegration has been slow, particularly in the south and southeast of the country, where the level of insurgency has risen over the past two years. Successful reintegration and economic rehabilitation for refugees and the internally displaced have been hampered by a war-damaged infrastructure that impedes the delivery of basic social services, a general lack of socioeconomic development and few work opportunities. Many returnees remained landless and therefore unable to build sustainable livelihoods either on their return to their areas of origin or following local settlement. The security situation remained volatile: human rights violations were widespread and attacks on humanitarian agencies and their staff relatively frequent. The government's capacity to respond to the humanitarian challenges that remained was weak, and humanitarian funding has declined markedly since the research for this chapter was conducted. Despite these conditions, the return of refugees was expected to continue through 2006, and the UN agencies plan to end their assistance to IDPs by the end of 2006. (Source: UNHCR.)

GEORGIA

Since this volume's chapter was written, Georgia has seen profound political upheaval, but little has changed for many IDPs, refugees and others living in conflict areas. Widespread protest late in 2003 lead to the ousting of Eduard Shevardnadze, president since 1995, and elections early in 2004 brought Mikheil Saakashvili to power. Problems such as joblessness and poor living and health conditions persisted for IDPs, particularly for those who lived in collective centers. According to government data, as of October 2005 there were nearly 245,500 displaced people (including nearly 12,800 from South Ossetia) residing in Georgia proper, unable to return to their places of origin. Humanitarian assistance programs have made little headway in providing integration or security. The continued presence in the impoverished Pankisi Gorge of some 2,500 mainly Chechen refugees, of whom 80 percent are women and children, ensured that the situation remained volatile and without prospects for durable solutions. For the inhabitants of conflict zones generally, vulnerability remained high, with physical insecurity, low levels of economic development and the potential revival of violence or high crime rates. The general socioeconomic situation in both Abkhazia and South Ossetia remained poor. Despite international support for Georgia, and improved coordination, IDP and refugee programs were only partially effective and the logistics of humanitarian assistance remained difficult with security a major factor. (Source: USCR; Georgian government.)

EAST TIMOR

Since the completion of this volume's chapter, the UN and other international agencies have downgraded their involvement in Timor Leste. The remaining UN peacekeepers withdrew in May 2005 and the United Nations Office in Timor Leste (UNOTIL), a political office, was set up, with a one-year mandate to assist in the development of state institutions. The UN Secretary-General authorized the establishment of a commission of experts to review the prosecution of human rights violations. This commission has reported, but human rights organizations remained concerned about lack of progress in criminal proceedings. In general, the security situation in Timor Leste has improved, but unemployment levels remained high, and disaffection among former combatants was a potential source of instability. The UNHCR continued to seek solutions for the East Timorese refugees who remained in West Timor throughout 2003 and into 2004. Toward the end of 2005 some 16,000 refugees remained across the border not yet registered as Indonesian citizens or accepting resettlement elsewhere in Indonesia. Responsibility for the ongoing protection and reintegration of those who have returned, and for internally displaced persons uprooted by the 1999 violence, rested with the Timor Leste government. The UNHCR continued to monitor the return of refugees but without dedicated capacity to respond to specific cases. There did not appear to be specific government policies or strategies to provide assistance or support for the reintegration of returnees. Instead, the focus has shifted to Timor Leste as a country receiving asylum seekers. (Source: UNHCR.)

December 2005

Bibliography

Afghan Interim Government. "National Development Framework: Draft for Consultation." Kabul: April 2002.

AFP (Agence France-Presse). "Life for Civilians around Burundi's Capital 'Shocking': Top MP." October 9, 2000.

———. "Burundi Army Shells Northern Outskirts of Capital." October 11, 2000.

———. "Gusmão Welcomes Timorese Militia Families Home." September 14, 2001.

African Unification Front. "Communiqué of the Ninety-first Ordinary Session of the Central Organ of the Mechanism for Conflict Prevention, Management and Resolution at Ambassadorial Level." www.africanfront.com/AMIB.php. April 2, 2003.

Amnesty International. "Medical Letter Writing Action, Conditions in 'Regroupment' Camps, Burundi." AI Index: AFR 16/036/99. December 22, 1999.

———. "East Timor: UN Secretary-General Has Responsibility to Ensure Credible Investigation." ASA 21/169/99. 1999.

———. "East Timor: Building a New Country Based on Human Rights." ASA 57/05/00. 2000.

———. "Amnesty International's Comments on the Law on Human Rights Courts (Law No. 26/2001)." ASA 21/005/2001. (2001a.)

———. "East Timor: Justice Past, Present and Future." ASA 57/0001/2001. (2001b.)

———. "Afghanistan: Out of Sight, Out of Mind: The Fate of the Afghan Returnees." London: June 2003.

Anderson, B. "East Timor and Indonesia: Some Implications." In *East Timor at the Crossroads: The Forging of a Nation*, ed. P. Carey and G. C. Bentley. London: Cassell, 1995.

Archer, R. "The Catholic Church in East Timor." In *East Timor at the Crossroads: The Forging of a Nation*, ed. P. Carey and G. C. Bentley. London: Cassell, 1995.

Arusha Peace and Reconciliation Agreement for Burundi. Arusha: August 28, 2000.

Ball, D. "Silent Witness: Australian Intelligence and East Timor." *Pacific Review* 14, no. 1, 2001: 35–62.

Bastian, S. "Foreign Aid, Globalization and Conflict in Sri Lanka." In *Building Local Capacities for Peace: Rethinking Conflict and Development in Sri Lanka*, ed. M. Meyer, D. Rajasingham-Senanayake, and Y. Thangarajah. New Delhi: Macmillan, 2003.

Belo, C. "Towards Reconciliation." In *Guns and Ballot Boxes*, ed. D. Kingsbury. Clayton, Victoria, Australia: Monash Asia Institute, 2000.

———. "The Path to Independence." *Sydney Morning Herald*. August 29, 2001. (2001a.)

———. *The Road to Freedom*. Sydney: Caritas Australia, 2001. (2001b.)

Birmingham, J. "Appeasing Jakarta." *Quarterly Essay*, issue 2, 2001.

Borer, T. A. "Truth, Reconciliation and Justice." *Peace Review* 11, no. 2, 1999: 303–9.

Bouginon, C., C. McDowell, H. Da Costa, et al. "Final Report: Evaluation of the Humanitarian Response in East Timor." Dili, East Timor: United Nations Transitional Administration in East Timor (UNTAET). www.reliefweb.int/w/rwb .nsf/s/A7E2FE89349316F3852569490059044C. May 25, 2000.

British Agencies Afghanistan Group. *Return and Reconstruction: Report on a Study of Economic Coping Strategies among Farmers in Farah Province, Afghanistan*. London: July 1997.

British Refugee Council. *Afghan Refugees*. London: BRC, 1990.

Brun, C. "Finding a Place: Local Integration and Protracted Displacement in Sri Lanka." PhD diss., NTNU, Trondheim, Norway. 2003.

Burchill, S. "East Timor, Australia and Indonesia." In *Guns and Ballot Boxes*, ed. D. Kingsbury. Clayton: Monash Asia Institute, 2000.

Bush, K. "Putty to Stone: Report of a Mission Investigating Human Rights Programming Opportunities in Sri Lanka." UK Department for International Development, Sri Lanka, 2002.

Carnegie Endowment. "Georgia: A Failing State?" Meeting report. January 31, 2001.

Catholic Institute for International Relations. *East Timor: Transition to Statehood*. London: Catholic Institute for International Relations, 2001.

Cervellin, S., and F. Uribe. *Desplazados: Aproximación psicosocial y abordaje terapeutico*. Bogotá: Conferencia Episcopal de Colombia, Secretariado Nacional de Pastoral Social, Sección de Movilidad Humana, 1994. www.pastoralsocialcolom bia.org.

Chomsky, N. "East Timor, the United States and International Responsibility." In *Bitter Flowers, Sweet Flowers*, ed. R. Tanter, M. Selden, and S. R. Shalom. Sydney: Pluto Press, 2001.

Clarance, W. "Open Relief Centers: A Pragmatic Approach to Emergency Relief and Monitoring during Conflict in a Country of Origin." *International Journal of Refugee Law* 3, no. 2, 1991: 320–28.

Cohen, R., and F. Deng. *Masses in Flight*. Washington, DC: Brookings Institute, 1998.

Cohen, R., and G. Sánchez-Garzoli. *Internal Displacement in the Americas: Some Dis-*

tinctive Features. Washington, DC: Brookings-CUNY Project on Internal Displacement, An Occasional Paper, 2001.

Colombia Program. Aid Request to Congress. www.ciponline.org/colombia/04 forops.htm. 2004.

Commission for Reception, Truth, and Reconciliation in East Timor. Commonly Asked Questions. www.easttimor-reconciliation.org. 2001a.

———. Funding Proposal to USAID/OTI. www.easttimor-reconciliation.org. 2001b.

Commission on Human Security. *Human Security Now: Protecting and Empowering People.* New York: Commission on Human Security, 2003.

Conflict, Security and Development Group. "A Review of Peace Operations: A Case for Change." London: International Policy Institute, King's College, March 2003.

Consejo Nacional de Política Económica y Social (CONPES). "Documento CONPES 2804." Bogotá: Departamento Nacional de Planeación, 1995.

———. "Documento CONPES 3057. Plan de acciòn para la prevención y atención del desplazamiento forzado." Bogotá: Departamento Nacional de Planeación, November 10, 1999.

Consortium of Humanitarian Agencies (CHA). *Yearbook 1999: Consortium of Humanitarian Agencies, Sri Lanka.* Colombo: Consortium of Humanitarian Agencies, 1999.

———. *Consortium of Humanitarian Agencies Directory 2000.* Colombo: Consortium of Humanitarian Agencies, 2000.

Consultoría para los Derechos Humanos y el Desplazamiento (CODHES). CODHES Informa. www.codhes.org.co. 2000.

———. CODHES Informa. www.codhes.org.co. April 28, 2003.

Crisp, J. "Mind the Gap! UNHCR, Humanitarian Assistance and the Development Process." *International Migration Review* 35, no. 4, 2001.

———. *A New Asylum Paradigm? Globalization, Migration and the Uncertain Future of the International Refugee Regime.* New Issues in Refugee Research working paper 100. Geneva: UNHCR, 2003.

Crisp, J., and D. Dessalegne. *Refugee Protection and Migration Management: The Challenge for UNHCR.* New Issues in Refugee Research working paper 64. Geneva: UNHCR, 2002.

Dale, C. "The Dynamics and Challenges of Ethnic Cleansing: The Georgia-Abkhaz Case." UNHCR. www.unhcr.ch/refworld/country/writenet/wrigeo.htm. August 1997.

Danish Refugee Council (DRC). *Program Document 2000–2003.* Anuradhapura, Sri Lanka: Danish Refugee Council, 2000.

Deng, F. Statement delivered in Geneva to the Steering Group of the Regional Conference to Address the Problems of Refugees, Displaced Persons, and Other Forms of Involuntary Displacement and Returnees in the Countries of the Commonwealth of Independent States and Neighboring States. www.unhcr.ch/hurricane.nsf. July 13, 2000.

———. "Report of the Representative of the Secretary-General on Internally Displaced Persons, Mr. Francis Deng, submitted pursuant to Commission on Human Rights resolution 2000/53." January 2001.

Department of Foreign Affairs and Trade. *East Timor in Transition 1998–2000*. Canberra: Department of Foreign Affairs and Trade, 2001.

Department for International Development. "DFID: Transitional Country Assistance Plan: Afghanistan: 2003–2004." London: May 2003.

Devereux, A. "Accountability for Human Rights Abuses in East Timor." In *Guns and Ballot Boxes*, ed. D. Kingsbury. Clayton, Victoria, Australia: Monash Asia Institute, 2000.

Diocese of Quibdo. "Población en situación de desplazamiento albergada en 'El Coliseo' y 'Los Silos,' en Quibdó, Chocó." *RUT Informa: Boletín trimestral* 12, 2002. www.pastoralsocialcolombia.org.

Dodd, M. "Justice for All: Dili Backs International War Crimes Tribunal." *Sydney Morning Herald*. June 22, 2001.

———. "Timor Justice Shackled by 'Joke' Decree." *Sydney Morning Herald*. August 22, 2001.

———. "Murder Inquiries Swamp UN Force." *Sydney Morning Herald*. August 23, 2001.

Donini, A., L. Minear, and P. Walker. "Between Cooptation and Irrelevance: Humanitarian Action after Iraq." *Journal of Refugee Studies* 17, no. 3, 2004: 260–72.

Doornbos, M. "State Collapse and Fresh Starts: Some Critical Reflections." *Development and Change* 33, no. 5, 2002: 797–815.

Downer, A. "Keeping the United Nations Relevant: International Peace and Security, and Reform." Statement by the Hon. Alexander Downer, MP, Minister for Foreign Affairs, to the 55th Session of the General Assembly of the United Nations. September 18, 2000.

———. Speech by the Hon. Alexander Downer, MP, Minister for Foreign Affairs, to open the Donors' Meeting on East Timor. Canberra, June 14, 2001.

Duffield, M. *Global Governance and the New Wars: The Merging of Development and Security*. London and New York: Zed Books, 2001.

Dunham, D., and S. Jayasuriya. "Is All So Well with the Economy and with the Rural Poor?" *Pravada* 5, nos. 10–11, 1998: 22–27.

Dunn, J. "Crimes against Humanity in East Timor, January to October 1999." Report to UNTAET. 2000.

———. "Crimes against Humanity Demand a Proper Airing." *Sydney Morning Herald*. August 13, 2001.

East Timor National NGO Forum. "Expression of Concern at Xanana's Statement Regarding an International Tribunal." Press release. April 23, 2001.

———. "Justice and Human Rights: Briefing Paper to Donors' Meeting." 2001.

Eurasia Insight. "The War on Terrorism: Implications for the Caucasus." September 29, 2001.

Euronaid and VOICE. "Afghanistan: The Road to Recovery and the Role of NGOs: Report of the Seminar Organized by Euronaid and VOICE: Brussels, February 14, 2002." The Hague: March 2002.

European Commission. "Country Strategy Paper for Afghanistan: 2003–2006." Brussels: February 2003.

European Commission Humanitarian Aid Office (ECHO). "Commission

Approves Co-operation Actions for 250 million in Latin America." IP/04/63. Brussels: April 10, 2004.

European Union (EU). www.europa.eu.int/comm/external_relations/colombia/ intro/ip02_213.htm. February 7, 2002.

———. "EU Relations with Burundi." www.europa.eu.int. July 31, 2003.

———. "Burundi: Commission Signs Country Strategy Paper for 2003–2007." www.europa.eu.int. n.d.

Facultad de Ciencias Jurídicas, Pontificia Universidad Javeriana. *Atención a los Desplazados. Experiencias Institucionales en Colombia*. Bogotá: 2001.

Falk, R. "Criminal Accountability in Transitional Justice." *Peace Review* 12, no. 1, 2000: 81–6.

———. "The East Timor Ordeal: International Law and Its Limits." In *Bitter Flowers, Sweet Flowers*, ed. R. Tanter, M. Selden, and S. R. Shalom. Sydney: Pluto Press, 2001.

Fine, B. *Social Capital versus Social Theory: Political Economy and Social Science at the Turn of the Millennium*. London: Routledge, 2001.

Fuglerud, O. *Life on the Outside: The Tamil Diaspora and Long Distance Nationalism*. London: Pluto Press, 1999.

Government of Sri Lanka. *Framework for Relief, Rehabilitation and Reconciliation: Progress Report December 2000*. Colombo: Government of Sri Lanka, 2000.

———. *National Framework for Relief, Rehabilitation and Reconciliation*. Colombo: RRR Steering Committee, 2002.

———. "Regaining Sri Lanka: Vision and Strategy for Accelerated Development." www.peaceinsrilanka.org. May 2003.

Government of Sri Lanka/Secretariat for the Coordination of the Peace Process. Tokyo Declaration on Reconstruction and Development of Sri Lanka. www .peaceinsrilanka.org. June 10, 2003.

Greenlees, D. "UN Charges 11 with East Timorese Killings." *The Australian*. September 28, 2001.

Grupo de Apoyo a Organizaciones de Desplazados (GAD). *Report on Forced Displacement in Colombia*. Washington, DC: 1999.

———. "Informe sobre el desplazamiento forzado en Colombia, enero de 2000– mayo de 2001." Bogotá: August 2001. www.exodo.org.co.

Gusmão, X. "Reconciliation, Unity, and National Development." In *Guns and Ballot Boxes*, ed. D. Kingsbury. Clayton, Victoria, Australia: Monash Asia Institute, 2000.

Hammond, L. "Examining the Discourse of Repatriation: Towards a More Proactive Theory of Return Migration." In *The End of the Refugee Cycle? Refugee Repatriation and Reconstruction*, ed. R. Black and K. Koser. Oxford: Berghahn, 1999.

Harris, S. "Listening to the Displaced: Analysis, Accountability and Advocacy in Action." *Forced Migration Review* 8, August 2000.

Human Rights and the Future of East Timor. Report on joint UNTAET Human Rights Unit and East Timor Jurists Association workshop. Dili: August 7–8, 2000.

Human Rights Watch. *Accountability for Crimes against Humanity in East Timor*. New York: September 20, 1999.

———. *Strong Independent Commission of Inquiry Urged for East Timor*. New York: September 27, 1999.

————. *Unfinished Business: Justice for East Timor.* New York: 2000.

————. *Emptying the Hills: Regroupment in Burundi.* New York: July 2000.

————. *Human Rights Developments: Human Rights Backgrounder on Indonesia*, September 2001. New York: September 19, 2001.

————. *You'll Learn Not to Cry: Child Combatants in Colombia.* New York: September 18, 2003.

Human Rights Watch and Amnesty International. Statement of Human Rights Watch and Amnesty International at the 54th Session of the United Nations–General Assembly Special Political and Decolonization Committee. October 6, 1999.

Hunt, K. *Forced Migration: Repatriation in Georgia.* New York: Open Society Institute, 1995.

Huntley, W., and P. Hayes. "East Timor and Asian Security." In *Bitter Flowers, Sweet Flowers*, ed. R. Tanter, M. Selden, and S. R. Shalom. Sydney: Pluto Press, 2001.

International Alert. *Equal Access to Education: A Peace Imperative for Burundi.* London: 2000.

International Committee of the Red Cross (ICRC). *ICRC Newsletter, Sri Lanka.* 1999–2000.

————. "The Mandate and Role of the International Committee of the Red Cross." www.icrc.org. February 2000.

————. "ICRC in Georgia." www.icrc.org. October 2000.

————. "ICRC Special Report, Georgia." www.icrc.org. May 2001.

International Crisis Group. *Indonesia: Impunity Versus Accountability for Gross Human Rights Violations.* Jakarta/Brussels: International Crisis Group Asia Report 12, 2001.

————. *The Rwandan Tribunal: Justice Denied.* Nairobi/Arusha/Brussels: June 7, 2001.

————. *The Megawati Presidency.* Jakarta/Brussels: International Crisis Group, September 10, 2001.

————. *Colombia's Elusive Quest for Peace.* Latin America Report no. 1. Bogotá/Brussels: 2002.

————. "Afghanistan: Judicial Reform and Transitional Justice." Kabul: January 2003.

————. "Afghanistan's Flawed Constitutional Process." June 2003.

————. *Colombia's Humanitarian Crisis.* Latin America Report no. 4, July 9, 2003.

International Labor Office. Strategy paper: "The Reintegration of Ex-combatants and Ex-police into Civil Life in Sri Lanka: Immediate and Future Challenges." Draft. Geneva: International Labor Office, InFocus Program on Crisis Response and Reconstruction, 2001.

International Organization for Migration (IOM). *Diagnóstico Colombia.* July 2001.

————. "Country Profile: Georgia." www.iom.ge.

————. "Hardship Abroad or Hunger at Home." www.iom.ge. September 2001.

IRIN-CEA (Integrated Regional Information Network—Central and East Africa). Update for the Great Lakes 980. www.irinnews.org. February 8, 2000.

————. Update 1,013. September 18, 2000.

————. Weekly round-up no. 40, covering the period September 30–October 6, 2000.

Johnson, C., W. Maley, A. Their, and A. Wardak. *Afghanistan's Political and Constitutional Development*. London: Overseas Development Institute, January 2003.

JRS (Jesuit Refugee Service). Burundi Alert. October 13, 2000. (2000a.)

————. www.jesref.org/inf/alert/bilatest.htm. September 27, 2000. (2000b.)

————. *Dispatches*, no. 80, October 16, 2000. (2000c).

————. Timor Alert. www.jesref.org/inf/alert.tplatest.htm. August 6, 2001.

Justice for East Timor. Statement of international and Timorese non-government organizations. June 13, 2001.

Kingsbury, D., ed. *Guns and Ballot Boxes*. Clayton, Victoria, Australia: Monash Asia Institute, 2000.

————. "The TNI and the Militias." In *Guns and Ballot Boxes*, ed. D. Kingsbury. Clayton: Monash Asia Institute.

Kohen, A. S. "The Catholic Church and the Independence of East Timor." In *Bitter Flowers, Sweet Flowers*, ed. R. Tanter, M. Selden, and S. R. Shalom. Sydney: Pluto Press, 2001.

Lankaneson, T. *Report on the Institutional Framework for Relief, Rehabilitation and Reconciliation*. Colombo, 2000.

Lippman, B. "The 4Rs: The Way Ahead?" *Forced Migration Review* 21, September 2004.

Martin, S., P. Weiss Fagen, K. Jorgensen, A. Schoenholtz, and L. Mann-Bondat. *The Uprooted: Improving Humanitarian Responses to Forced Migration*. Lanham, MD: Lexington Books, 2005.

Maxwell, S. *The Washington Consensus Is Dead! Long Live the Meta-narrative!* Overseas Development Institute working paper 243. London: ODI, 2005.

McDowell, C. "Responding to the Crisis in East Timor: The Emergency Response." CAPSTRANS Research Paper, University of Wollongong. October 20, 1999.

————. "East Timor: Humanitarianism Displaced?" *Relief and Rehabilitation Newsletter* 16. London: Overseas Development Institute, 2000.

McDowell, C., and R. A. Ariyaratne. "Complex Forced Migration Emergencies: East Timor Case Study." Submitted to Options for the Reform of the International Humanitarian Regime Project, Refugee Studies Centre, University of Oxford, UK. 2001.

McDowell, C., and M. Eastmond. "Transitions, State-Building and the 'Residual' Refugee Problem: The East Timor and Cambodian Repatriation Experience." *Australian Journal of Human Rights* 8, no. 1, 2002: 7–27.

McLean, J. "National Response to Internal Displacement." *Global IDP Survey*. www.nrc.no/global_idp_survey/FMR98-1/McLean.htm. 1998.

Mehler, A., and C. Ribaux. *Crisis Prevention and Conflict Management in Technical Cooperation: An Overview of the National and International Debate*. Eschborn, Germany: Deutsche Gesellschaft für Technische Zusammenarbeit (GTZ), 2000.

Meyer, K. "Icebergs in the Caucasus." *World Policy Journal* 28, no. 2, 2001: 89–92.

Ministère de la Planification du Développement de la Reconstruction and UNDP. *Rapport sur le développement humain du Burundi 1999: La Pauvreté au Burundi*. Bujumbura: 1999.

Monk, P. "East Timor: Truth and Consequences." *Quadrant*, January–February 2000: 33–40.

Moore, D. "Levelling the Playing Fields and Embedding Illusions: 'Post-conflict' Discourse and Neo-liberal 'Development' in War-torn Africa." *Review of African Political Economy* 83, 2000.

New York Times. "Rebel Group in Burundi Signs Peace Accord with Government." www.nytimes.com/2003/10/08/international/africa/08BURU.html. October 8, 2003.

Norwegian Refugee Council. "Colombia IDP Crisis Worsens." By Cathy Bennetti. R/0013. www.idpproject.org. May 15, 2003.

———. "Burundi: Country Profile on Internal Displacement." June 23, 2003.

———. *Global IDP Project*. www.idpproject.org. n.d.

OCHA. Senior Inter-Agency Network on Internal Displacement Mission to Burundi, December 18–22, 2000, Findings and Recommendations. www.relief web.int/idp.

———. Follow-Up Matrix, Senior Inter-Agency Network on Internal Displacement Mission to Burundi, May 2001. www.idpproject.org.

———. "Evaluation of the OCHA and UNOCHA Response and Coordination Services during the Emergency in Afghanistan: July 2001 to July 2002." New York: 2002.

———. Update on the Internal Displacement Unit. www.reliefweb.int/idp. June 2003. (2003a.)

———. Burundi Humanitarian Update. www.reliefweb.int/idp. July 2003. (2003b.)

———. Burundi-Tanzania: "Limitations" in Refugee Camps Forcing Hundreds to Leave. www.reliefweb.int. May 15, 2003. (2003c.)

———. Consolidated Inter-Agency Appeal for Burundi 2003: Mid-Year Review. www.reliefweb.int. May 2003. (2003d.)

———. Burundi: African Force at Full Strength with Arrival of Mozambicans. www.irinnews.org. October 20, 2003. (2003e.)

———. Burundi: Mozambique, South Africa Set Condition for Full Deployment of Peacekeepers. www.reliefweb.int. September 12, 2003. (2003f.)

———. Burundi Situation Report. www.reliefweb.int. January 5–11, 2004.

Ojeda, B., and R. Murad. *Salud sexual y reproductiva en zonas marginales: Situación de las mujeres desplazadas*. Bogotá: Asociación Pro Bienestar de la Familia Colombiana (PROFAMILIA), 2001.

Organization of American States (OAS). OEA/Ser.L/V/II 102 doc 9, Inter-American Commission on Human Rights, Third Report on the Human Rights Situation in Colombia, chapter 6, "Internal Displacement." February 26, 1999.

Oxfam. *Foreign Territory: The Internationalisation of EU Asylum Policy*. Oxford: Oxfam GB, 2005.

Oxfam/Save the Children. *Listening to the Displaced and Listening to the Returned: A Community Study. Summary Report*. Colombo: Oxfam GB, Save the Children UK, 1998.

Patterson, S. "East Timor: Reconciliation and Challenges for the Future." *Human Rights Defender* 10, no. 2, 2001: 24–26.

Radio National Australia. Xanana Gusmão. Background Briefing. Sunday, November 19, 2000.
———. Xanana Gusmão. Asia Pacific. Tuesday, October 9, 2001.
Ramos-Horta, J. Diplomacy training program lecture, University of New South Wales, May 31, 2001.
Red de Solidaridad Social (RSS). Presidencia de la República (*PrensaRED*). www.red.gov.co/LaInstitucion/index.html. February 13, 2002.
———. *PrensaRED*. March 31, 2003.
Refugees International. "Burundian Regroupment Camps: A Man-made Humanitarian Emergency, an Impediment to Peace." www.refugeesinternational.org. January 20, 2000. (2000a.)
———. "Conditions in Burundian Camps Rapidly Deteriorating." March 1, 2000. (2000b.)
———. Press release. September 15, 2000. (2000c.)
RESO (Rassemblement, Échange et Solution entre Organisations Non-gouvernementales). Call for Support of Cease-fire Efforts. Bujumbura, September 18, 2000.
Reuters. "Burundi Rebel Group FNL Dismisses Peace Deal." November 4, 2003.
RFE/RL (Radio Free Europe/Radio Liberty). "Caucasus: Poor Laws Aid Groups Trafficking in Women." July 27, 2001.
———. "Caucasus Conflicts Eclipsed by World Focus on Afghanistan." October 26, 2001.
Robinson, W. C. "Rights and Risks: The Causes, Consequences and Challenges of Development-Induced Displacement." www.reliefweb.int. 2003.
Roht-Arriaxa, N., and L. Gibson. "The Developing Jurisprudence on Amnesty." *Human Rights Quarterly* 20, no. 4, 1998: 843–45.
Rotberg, R., ed. *Creating Peace in Sri Lanka: Civil War and Reconciliation*. Washington, DC: Brookings Institution Press and the World Peace Foundation, 1999.
Rubins, N. *Organizational Interaction and Conflict in Georgia*. Cambridge, MA: Conflict Management Group, 1997.
Scott-Murphy, J. *An International Criminal Tribunal for East Timor*. Sydney: Caritas Australia, 2001.
Search for Common Ground. *Common Ground Newsletter*. www.sfcg.org. Summer 2003.
Sistema de las Naciones Unidas. *Plan de Acción Humanitaria 2002–2003, Colombia*. Grupo Temático de Desplazamiento. Bogotá. www.acnur.org/paginas/index .php?id_pag=1005.
Stapleton, B. J. "A British Agencies Afghanistan Group Briefing Paper on the Development of Joint Regional Teams in Afghanistan." London: British Agencies Afghanistan Group, 2003. (2003a.)
———. "The Provincial Reconstruction Team Plan in Afghanistan: A New Direction." Center for Development Research, University of Bonn, 2003. (2003b.)
Stiglitz, J. "More Instruments and Broader Goals: Moving Towards the Post-Washington Consensus." World Institute for Development Economics Research Annual Lecture. Helsinki: United National University, January 1998.
Stockton, N. "Strategic Coordination in Afghanistan." Kabul: Afghanistan Research and Evaluation Unit, August 2002.

Strand, A. "Aid Coordination in Afghanistan." Bergen: Norwegian Ministry of Foreign Affairs, December 2002.

Strohmeyer, H. "Collapse and Reconstruction of a Judicial System: The United Nations Missions in Kosovo and East Timor." *American Journal of International Law* 95, no. 1, 2001: 46–63.

Suhrke, A., A. Strand, and K. B. Harpviken. *Strategies for Peace-building in Afghanistan*. Oslo: Chr. Michelsen Institute and University of Oslo, January 2002.

Suny, R. *Looking Toward Ararat*. Bloomington: Indiana University Press, 1993.

———. *The Making of the Georgian Nation*. Bloomington: Indiana University Press, 1994.

Tanter, R., M. Selden, and S. R. Shalom. "East Timor Faces the Future." In *Bitter Flowers, Sweet Flowers*, ed. R. Tanter, M. Selden, and S. R. Shalom. Sydney: Pluto Press, 2001.

Temby, K. " 'Wake Up My Husband and Rebuild My House': Reconciliation and Justice in East Timor." Unpublished master's thesis, Department of Anthropology, Macquarie University, Sydney. 2001.

Thubron, C. *Among the Russians*. New York: Perennial (HarperCollins), 2000.

Turton, D., and P. Marsden. *Taking Refugees for a Ride? The Politics of Refugee Return to Afghanistan*. Kabul: Afghanistan Research and Evaluation Unit, December 2002.

UK Department for International Development. *Sri Lanka Country Strategy Paper*. Colombo: DFID, September 1999.

UN. *Joint UN Framework for Programming in Relief and Rehabilitation—Sri Lanka, March/April 1999. Recommendations of Principles for Cohesive UN Programming in the Areas Most Affected by Conflict in Sri Lanka*. Colombo: UN, 1999.

———. *UN Development Assistance Framework for Sri Lanka, 2002–2006: A Common UN Response to Sri Lanka's Development Challenges*. Colombo: UN, 2000.

———. *The Millennium Development Goals and the United Nations' Role*. New York: UN Department of Public Information, 2002. www.un.org/millenniumgoals.

UNAIDS. Epidemiological Fact Sheet for Burundi, 2000. Update. www.unaids.org.

———. The 2002 Updated Epidemiological Fact Sheet for Burundi. www.unaids.org.

UNAMA. "The Internally Displaced in Afghanistan: Towards Durable Solutions." Report of the Inter-agency Mission. Kabul: May 2003.

UN Commission on Human Rights. Question of the Violation of Human Rights and Fundamental Freedoms in Any Part of the World: Situation in East Timor. E/CN.4/1999/28. March 26, 1999.

———. Report of the High Commissioner for Human Rights on the Human Rights Situation in East Timor. E/CN.4/S-4/CRP.1. September 17, 1999.

———. Situation of Human Rights in East Timor: Commission on Human Rights Resolution 1999/S-4/1. September 27, 1999.

———. Special Session of Commission on Human Rights Adopts Resolution on East Timor. HR/CN.99/70. September 27, 1999.

———. Report of the Commission on Human Rights on Its Fourth Special Session. E/CN.4 1999/167/Add.1, E/1999/23/Add.1. October 20, 1999.

————. Report of the High Commissioner for Human Rights on the Situation of Human Rights in East Timor. E/CN.4/2001/37. February 6, 2001.

UN Country Team in Burundi. United Nations System Emergency Plan for Burundi. "Without Development There Cannot Be Sustainable Peace: From Humanitarian Assistance to Development." UN: 2000.

UN Department of Public Information. "Another 300 East Timorese Refugees Return from West Timor: UN Mission." September 19, 2001.

————. "East Timor Reconciliation Committee Panel Holds First Meeting: UN Mission." September 21, 2001.

UNDG (UN Development Group). *Report of the UNDG/ECHA Working Group on Transition Issues*. New York: United Nations Development Group/Executive Committee on Humanitarian Assistance, Working Group on Transition Issues, 2004.

UN General Assembly. Situation of Human Rights in East Timor. A/54/660. December 10, 1999.

————. Identical letters dated January 31, 2000, from the Secretary-General addressed to the President of the General Assembly, the President of the Security Council, and the Chairperson of the Commission on Human Rights. A/54/26, S/2000/59. January 31, 2000.

UN-ECOSOC. Report of the Representative of the Secretary-General on internally displaced persons, Mr. Francis M. Deng, submitted in accordance with Commission resolution 1999/47, Profiles in displacement: follow-up mission to Colombia. E/CN.4/2000/83/Add. January 11, 2000.

UNHCHR. Report on the Human Rights Situation in Colombia. ECN.4/2001/15. February 8, 2001.

————. *Statement by United Nations High Commissioner for Human Rights, UN Security Council Presentation of Report of the United Nations Secretary-General on Protection of Civilians in Armed Conflict*. April 23, 2001.

————. *Guiding Principles on Internal Displacement*. n.d. www.unhchr.ch/html/menu2/7/b/principles.

UNHCR. Executive Committee Conclusion, no. 75, 1994. www.unhcr.ch. See also UNHCR and the Internally Displaced: Questions and Answers, Protecting Refugees. www.unhcr.ch.

————. *The State of the World's Refugees: A Humanitarian Agenda*. Geneva: UNHCR, 1997.

————. *UNHCR's Country Strategy for Sri Lanka*. Colombo: UNHCR, April 2000.

————. *Strategic Framework for the Voluntary Repatriation and Reintegration, Burundi*. UNHCR: July 2000. (2000a.)

————. Briefing Notes: Caucasus, Colombia, Afghanistan/Pakistan, Burundi. October 13, 2000. (2000b.)

————. *Burundi in Short: Global Appeal 2001*. www.unhcr.ch. December 1, 2000. (2000c.)

————. *Global Operations Mid-Year Progress Report 2001*. www.unhcr.ch/pubs/fdrs/my2001/globops.pdf.

————. *UNHCR Regional Strategy for Colombia Refugees, Asylum Seekers and Internally Displaced Persons*. Americas Bureau. June 2001.

———. News Stories. "Tripartite Meeting Focuses on Repatriation of Burundian Refugees." www.unhcr.ch. April 3, 2002.

———. "Real-time Evaluation of UNHCR's Response to the Afghanistan Emergency." www.unhcr.ch. May 2002.

———. *Framework for Durable Solutions for Refugees and Persons of Concern.* Geneva: UNHCR Core Group on Durable Solutions, 2003.

———. "UNHCR Assists Burundian Refugees to Leave Tanzania." www.relief web.int. September 9, 2003. (2003a.)

———. "Lubbers Discusses Burundi Returns from Tanzania." www.reliefweb.int. November 10, 2003. (2003b.)

———. *Population Statistics.* Table 13, Demographic Composition of the Population of Concern to UNHCR by Country of Asylum, End 2002. UNHCR Population Data Unit, www.unhcr.ch. August 4, 2003. (2003c.)

———. *2002 Annual Statistical Report: Burundi,* 23 July 2003, www.unhcr.ch. July 23, 2003d.

———. News Stories. "Festive Homecoming for Burundian Refugees." www.un hcr.ch. September 10, 2003. (2003e.)

———. News Stories. "Burundi: UNHCR Concerned over Voluntariness of Returns from Tanzania." www.unhcr.ch. June 3, 2003. (2003f.)

———. *Convention Plus at a Glance.* UNHCR website. Geneva: UNHCR, 2004a.

———. *Convention Plus Issues Paper on the Targeting of Development Assistance Policies.* Geneva: UNHCR. www.unhcr.ch/cgi-bin/texis/vtx/home/2004b.

UNHCR EPAU. *UNHCR's Program for Internally Displaced Persons in Sri Lanka.* Report of a joint appraisal mission by the UK Department for International Development and UNHCR. Geneva: UNHCR Evaluation and Policy Analysis Unit, 2002.

UNHCR and IOM. *Assessment Report of the Conference Process (1996–2000).* 2000.

UNHCR and OCHA. *Consulta con mujeres desplazadas sobre principios rectores del desplazamiento.* Bogotá: May 16–18, 2001.

UNICEF. *Estado mundial de la infancia* (State of the World's Children). Colombia: 2000.

———. *A Humanitarian Appeal for Children and Women.* www.unicef.org. January–December 2001.

———. Press conference, Manuel Manrique, reported by EFE. June 5, 2002.

———. *At a Glance for Burundi, 2003.* Update, www.unicef.org. 2003a.

———. *Urgent Action for Children on the Brink.* Statement by UNICEF Executive Director, Carol Bellamy. www.unicef.org/media/media_9330.html. January 14, 2003. (2003b.)

———. *The Official Summary of the State of the World's Children 2003.* www.unicef .org. 2003c.

UN IDP Working Group. *Durable Solutions Progress Report: A Weekly Bulletin of the UN IDP Working Group.* UN: Colombo, 2002.

UNOCHA (United Nations Office for the Coordination of Humanitarian Assistance). Consolidated Inter-Agency Appeal for East Timor Crisis, October 1999–June 2000. New York: 1999.

———. *Crises of Internal Displacement: Status of the International Response through the Inter-Agency Standing Committee and Their Member Agencies*. UNOCHA: Policy Development Unit, 2000.

———. "Georgia Self Reliance Fund: Seeking Proposals for Small-scale Pilot Programs." October 2000.

———. "Georgia Humanitarian Situation and Strategy 2004." Paper developed by OCHA-Georgia in November 2003.

UNOMIG (UN Observer Mission in Georgia). "Report of the Joint Assessment Mission to the Gali District." November 2000.

UNSC (United Nations Security Council). *Report of the Security Council Mission to Jakarta and Dili, 8 to 12 September 1999*. S/1999/976. September 14, 1999.

———. *Resolution 1264 (1999)*. S/RES/1264 (1999). September 15, 1999.

———. *Report of the Secretary-General on the Situation in East Timor*. S/1999/1024. October 4, 1999.

———. *Report of the International Commission of Inquiry on East Timor*. A/54/726, S/2000/59. January 31, 2000.

———. *Report of the Secretary-General on the United Nations Transitional Administration in East Timor*. S/2001/983. October 18, 2001.

———. UN Secretary-General. Children and Armed Conflict: Report to the United Nations Security Council. S/2002/1299. November 26, 2002.

———. *Report of the Secretary-General to the Security Council on the Situation in Burundi*. S/2003/1146. December 4, 2003.

UN Secretary-General. *Safety and Security of United Nations Personnel, Report to the United Nations General Assembly*. A/55/494. Fifty-fifth session. October 2000.

UN Senior Inter-Agency Network on Internal Displacement. "Mission to Colombia, August 16–24, 2001. Findings and Recommendations." 2001.

United Nations Transitional Administration in East Timor. Regulation no. 2001/10: *On the Establishment of a Commission for Reception, Truth and Reconciliation in East Timor*. 2001.

———. East Timor Consolidated Appeal Process (CAP) Review: Humanitarian Programs in East Timor from the Beneficiaries' Perspective. May 2000.

———. East Timor Consolidated Appeal Process (CAP) Review: Self-Assessment by the Humanitarian Community. May 2000.

USAID. *USAID Assistance to Colombia Fact Sheet*. www.usaid.gov/press/releases/2002/02fs_colombia.html. May 24, 2002.

———. *Burundi: Complex Emergency*. Situation Report no. 2. March 25, 2003. (2003a.)

———. *Burundi: Complex Emergency*. August 7, 2003. (2003b.)

US Department of State. "Human Rights Report for 1999." www.state.gov/www/global/humanrights/1999_hrp_report/georgia.html.

USCR (US Committee for Refugees). *World Refugee Survey*. Washington, DC: USCR, 2000.

———. *World Refugee Survey*. Washington, DC: USCR, 2001.

———. *World Refugee Survey*. Washington, DC: USCR, 2003.

van Zyl, P. "Dilemmas of Transitional Justice: The Case of South Africa's Truth and Reconciliation Commission." *Journal of International Affairs* 52, no. 2, Spring 1999: 647–67.

Walsh, P. "Towards a Just Peace." In *East Timor at the Crossroads: The Forging of a Nation*, ed. P. Carey and G. C. Bentley. London: Cassell, 1995.

―――. "Human Rights and the Duties of Citizens." *CNRT National Congress*. Dili: August 21–29, 2000.

―――. "East Timor's Political Parties and Groupings." *Development Issues* 9, 2001. Canberra: Australian Council for Overseas Aid.

Ward, K. *Navigation Guide: Regional Protection Zones and Transit Processing Centres*. London: Information Centre about Asylum and Refugees in the UK (ICAR), 2004.

WFP (World Food Program). *Review of Protracted Relief and Recovery Operation, Sri Lanka 6152*. Colombo: WFP, April 2000.

―――. "Operación prolongada de socorro y recuperación a la población desplazada por la violencia en Colombia." Project description. 2000.

―――. "Consolidated Report: Food Needs Case Study on the Displaced Population of Colombia." June 14, 2001.

―――. "Operación prolongada de recuperación y socorro, Junio 2000–Julio 2001." July 2001. (2001a.)

Women's Commission for Refugee Women and Children. *Out of Sight, Out of Mind: Conflict and Displacement in Burundi*. New York: Women's Commission for Refugee Women and Children, 2001. www.womenscommission.org.

World Bank. *A Framework for World Bank Involvement in Post-Conflict Reconstruction*. Washington, DC: World Bank, 1997.

―――. *Post-Conflict Reconstruction: The Role of the World Bank*. Washington, DC: World Bank, 1998.

―――. "Georgia: Poverty and Income Distribution." Norwegian Refugee Council. Global IDP Database. www.idpproject.org. May 27, 1999.

―――. *World Bank Group Work in Low Income Countries under Stress: A Task Force Report*. Washington, DC: World Bank, 2002.

―――. *The World Bank in Conflict and Development*. www.lnweb18.worldbank.org/ESSD/. 2004.

Index

Page references in *italics* indicate a map on the designated page.

243

neo-liberalism, 7, 67, 71, 219. *See also* free-market model; market economy

Network of Social Solidarity (RSS), 78, 84, 89–90

neutrality, of humanitarian agencies, 131–37

New Approach Support Unit, in Georgia, 157

New Approach to IDP Assistance, 10, 163, 177–79

NGO FORUT, 52

NGO Migration Sector Development Program, 166

NGOs. *See* non-governmental organizations

nocturnal displacement, 153

non-governmental organizations (NGOs), 37, 51–52, 177; competition among, 196; flexibility of, 31; human rights and, 95; IDP assistance projects and, 95; international, 52, 104–5, 112–13, 166; local, 28–29, 52, 94–95, 166, 168, 174; public perception of, 132, 137. *See also* humanitarian agencies

North-East Irrigated Agriculture Project (NEIAP), 55–56

North Ossetia, Russia, 154, 162

Norwegian Refugee Council (NRC), 153, 169

NRC. *See* Norwegian Refugee Council

OCHA Field Practice Manual, 33–34

Office of the Resident Coordinator for the United Nations in Georgia, 173

On-Site Operations Coordination Centers, 195

Open Relief Centers, 51

operational coordination, 109

organizational weaknesses, 25–29, 70

Organization for Security and Cooperation in Europe (OSCE), 144

orphans, 21

OSCE. *See* Organization for Security and Cooperation in Europe

Oxfam, 52, 56–57, 104–5, 170

PAHO. *See* Pan American Health Organization

Pakistan, 116–25, 122–25, 133–34

Panama, 81, 100

Pan American Health Organization (PAHO), 98, 104

Pankisi Valley, Georgia, 153, 167, 169

paramilitary groups, 76–77, 92–93, 110

Paris Donor Group, 53

participation, 203–4

participatory rural appraisal techniques, 129

partnerships, 216

Pastoral in the Episcopal Conference, Human Mobility section, 105

Pastrana, Andres, 84, 106

PCU. *See* Post-Conflict Unit

peace communities, 89

peace dividend, 69

peacekeeping, 5, 40

peacekeeping force (PKF), 190–92, 200

Peace Laboratories, 98, 106

peace processes, 66–67, 93, 109–10, 145

Permanent Consultation on Displacement in the Americas (CPDIA), 83

personnel. *See* aid workers

PKF. *See* peacekeeping force

Plan Colombia, 103, 106

policy fields, interpenetration of, 214–16

political economy, importance of, 71

population flight, 4

post-conflict, pre-peace conditions, 66–69

Post-Conflict Unit (PCU), 218

Post-Emergency Assistance Program for the Displaced Population and for Receiving Communities, 103–4

Post-Washington Consensus, 219

poverty, 4, 40–41

precedents, to responses, 83–84

pregnancy, 94

prevention, of displacement, 85, 98

Principled Common Programming, 127

PROFAMILIA. *See* Association for the Well-being of the Colombian Family

About the Editors
and Contributors

Patricia Weiss Fagen has held positions in UNHCR, the War-torn Societies Project in the UN Research Institute for Social Development, the Economic Development Institute of the World Bank, and the Inter-American
Development Bank. She has specialized in research and evaluation of
operational projects related to post-conflict reintegration and reconstruction. She holds a doctorate from Stanford University and has published
widely on Latin American history, human rights law and policy, political
asylum and refugee issues, and post-conflict reconstruction.

Trish Hiddleston has experience as a community nurse specializing in
child development and as a lawyer. She has worked for Human Rights
Watch, the Women's Commission for Refugee Women and Children, Refugees International, and UNICEF, on human rights, gender, and children's issues, mainly in central Africa. She is currently head of UNICEF's
child protection section in the Democratic Republic of Congo.

Amelia Fernandez Juan is Director of the Health Promotion Institute at
Javeriana University School of Medicine and Professor in the Department
of Preventive and Social Medicine, Bogotá, Colombia. She holds a master's in Community Psychology from Javeriana University and a doctorate in Economy and Health Management from the Universidad
Politécnica of Valencia, Spain.

Matthew Karanian is Research Associate with Georgetown University's
Institute for the Study of International Migration. He holds an LLM from

the Georgetown University Law Center, has practiced law as a trial attorney in the US, and is currently Associate Dean of the law program at the American University of Armenia and Director of the Legal Research Center there. His books include *The Stone Garden Guide: Armenia and Karabagh* (Stone Garden Productions, 2004) and *Edge of Time* (Stone Garden Productions, 2002).

Peter Marsden was until 2005 Coordinator of the British Agencies Afghanistan Group, which provides information to non-governmental organizations, UN agencies, donors, the media, and academics on humanitarian needs in Afghanistan and on the wider political, economic, and cultural context. His publications include *The Taliban: War, Religion and the New Order in Afghanistan* (Zed Books, 1998).

Susan Forbes Martin is Visiting Professor and Director of the Institute for the Study of International Migration in the School of Foreign Service at Georgetown University. Previously Dr. Martin served as Executive Director of the US Commission on Immigration Reform and Director of Research and Programs at the Refugee Policy Group. Her doctorate is in American Studies from the University of Pennsylvania. She is author of *Refugee Women* (Lexington Books, 2004) and co-author of *The Uprooted: Improving Humanitarian Responses to Forced Migration* (Lexington Books, 2005).

Christopher McDowell is Senior Lecturer in the School of Social Sciences, City University, London and Director of the Information Centre about Asylum and Refugees (ICAR). Dr. McDowell has conducted research on forced displacement, repatriation, and involuntary resettlement in east and southern Africa and in south and southeast Asia, and on asylum policy in the UK and Switzerland. His publications include *A Tamil Asylum Diaspora* (Berghahn Books, 1996), *Understanding Impoverishment* (Berghahn Books, 1996), and *Risks and Reconstruction* (with Michael Cernea, The World Bank, 2000).

Darini Rajasingham-Senanayake is Senior Fellow at the International Centre for Ethnic Studies in Colombo, Sri Lanka, and has held other senior fellowships in North America and Europe. Dr. Rajasingham-Senanayake co-edited *Ethnic Futures* (Sage, 1999) and *Building Local Capacities for Peace* (Macmillan, 2003).

Finn Stepputat is Senior Researcher at the Danish Institute for International Studies in Copenhagen. With a background in Geography and Cultural Sociology, Dr. Stepputat has published extensively on issues of forced migration, armed conflict, and state formation. He co-edited *States of Imagination* (Duke University Press, 2003) and *Sovereign Bodies* (Princeton University Press, 2005).

Nicholas Van Hear is Senior Researcher at the Centre on Migration, Policy and Society (COMPAS), University of Oxford, prior to which he held research positions at the Refugee Studies Centre in Oxford and at the Danish Institute for International Studies in Copenhagen. Dr. Van Hear has published widely on forced migration, conflict, development, refugee diaspora, and related issues, with research in Africa, the Middle East, and South Asia. His publications include *New Diasporas* (Routledge, 1998) and *The Migration-Development Nexus* (with Ninna Sørenson, IOM, 2003).

Roberto Vidal Lopez is Professor of History of Law, Human Rights, and Migration Law at the Pontificia Universidad Javeriana in Bogotá, Colombia. He is a researcher in legal issues on forced migration and human trafficking for the UN and NGOs.